Waking Dreams

*the text of this book is printed
on 100% recycled paper*

Waking Dreams

Mary M. Watkins

HARPER COLOPHON BOOKS
Harper & Row, Publishers
New York, Hagerstown, San Francisco, London

WAKING DREAMS. Copyright © 1976 by Gordon and Breach Science Publishers, Inc. All rights reserved. Printed in the United States of America. No part of this book may be used or reproduced in any manner whatsoever without written permission except in the case of brief quotations embodied in critical articles and reviews. For information address Gordon and Breach Science Publishers, Inc., One Park Avenue, New York, N.Y. 10016. Published simultaneously in Canada by Fitzhenry & Whiteside Limited, Toronto.

First HARPER COLOPHON edition published 1977

ISBN: 0-06-090586-7

77 78 79 80 81 10 9 8 7 6 5 4 3 2 1

Introduction

American history is basically a saga of people concerned with external voyages. At first the exploration, exploitation, and settlement of a new continent occupied their attention. This was followed by the development of industrial empires at home and the assertion of diplomatic power overseas. Then came the most distant venture of all—the probes into outer space.

In recent years, a small but growing number of Americans has placed a high priority on internal events and inner growth. Some individuals view this in terms of a spiritual quest while others consider it a voyage of self-discovery or a search for personal fulfillment.

The roads taken to attain these goals vary. Of current appeal are the quick and hazardous openings offered by LSD, the explosive encounters found in sensitivity training, the deep probes provided in Jungian psychotherapy, and the creative routes implicit in development of artistic and scientific creativity. Awareness of Eastern wisdom has helped facilitate the process of many seekers. Yoga, Zen, and the Oriental disciplines are all alternatives to consider, either in their original form or in the synthesis offered by many contemporary scholars.

A synthesis with the external world is offered by research workers in psychoenergetics, psychotronics, and parapsychology who seek to explain the relationships among consciousness, energy, and matter.

A Reformation of Consciousness may well evolve as, for the first time in its history, the entire gamut of human hopes, aspirations, and teachings are available for us to grasp and to incorporate.

Stanley Krippner

Humanistic Psychology Institute
San Francisco, California

Preface

The lives of images — imaginings — have been exiled to the domains of art, psychopathology, neurophysiology, the faculty of an imagination, and most recently to an activity of interiorized journeying. Imaginings, however, have been unable to contain themselves within a faculty, a set of pathologies or activities. They show themselves not as appendages to perception or cognition or as a mere place to which one can travel at will. Imagining is more essentially constitutive to our everyday lives than that. This book is an attempt to clear some of our approaches to imaginal experience and thereby to this appreciation as well.

We must first feel how our culture raised us to try to abandon all possible awareness of the imaginal quality of our lives — to make us distrust and belittle the imaginal until the common paths to it grew over in a bramble of both confusion and neglect (Chapter 1). Where roads to the life of the imagination of other times and cultures have been blocked by our efforts to catalogue fact and ritual, we shall hope to restore a means for some of the fantasy beneath to pass through to us, to enrich our own efforts towards honoring and participating in that realm (Chapter 2). Our private attempts to approach the imaginal, unfathered by a tradition and still bastardized from without and within, need to be nourished with suggestion and sensitivity. With alternatives in mind we may gain more inner freedom to move toward and in imaginal space (Chapters 2, 6, and 7).

Psychology has urged us to direct our attention back to the fact that the imaginal is still alive. Yet as it has discovered ways to study the life of the image, through dreams and fantasies, it frequently has used these avenues to different ends which actually lead one away from the imaginal. One passes through the imagination, but really uses that road to go elsewhere. The experience of the imaginal is lost as the eyes through which it is seen rest more on the destination in mind. In order to preserve the opportunity to see the imaginal more on its own terms, we first must learn to differentiate the signposts in our psychotherapies and self-wanderings. Throughout the text it will be the waking dream, the conscious experiencing of the imaginal, that will provide the focus for our attempts to approach. By constructing a history of waking dreams in modern psychology, it is hoped that we will see in microcosm some of the prevailing ways we have of imagining (Chapters 3, 4, and 5), and of imagining about imagining (Chapter 8).

When we are able to approach images through various kinds of imagining (Chapter 6) and to consciously dwell and move with them (Chapter 7), a phenomenology of the imaginal can arise that will be unburdened by the full weight of our present fears, misconceptions, theories, prejudices, and hesitations. This phenomenology would provide a basis for an imaginal psychology—not our usual psychologies put to the study of "an imagination," but a psychology itself derived from our experience with imaginal movements. As we learn to recognize images and to allow them to teach us their ways of imagining, we will discover that each of our actions, feelings, perceptions and thoughts can be used to approach the imaginal . . . and that, indeed, our attention to the imaginal movements of daily life can enrich and deepen our connection to that life.

M.M.W.
Zürich

Acknowledgments

The attempt to further one's sense of something so that it becomes a part of one's life happens with the help of others; others who are already more sensitive to it, who impart their understanding of it through themselves and their work, who encourage. These others often do not even know exactly how they have helped. Brief periods of sharing together expand themselves into wholly new life movements, which then find partial home and expression in efforts like this book. For this reason these others deserve a special place here within these pages: Nancy Knowles, Patricia Berry, Daniel Brown, James Hillman, Daveda Tennenbaum, Henry Reed, Stanley Krippner, and Trenton Wann.

I am appreciative to the following for permission to quote from works to which they hold the copyright: Psychosynthesis Research Foundation, Inc., for "The directed daydream" by Robert Desoille; Columbia University Press, for *The Organization and Pathology of Thought* by David Rapaport; Pantheon Books, Random House, for *Memories, Dreams, and Reflections* by C. G. Jung, recorded and edited by Aniela Jaffe, translated by Richard and Clara Winston; The New American Library, for *The Varieties of Religious Experience* by William James; Oxford University Press, for *Tibetan Yoga and Its Secret Doctrines* by Evans-Wentz; Real People Press, for *Awareness* by John Stevens; *Journal of Religion and Health,* for "The ethical relevance of a psychotherapeutic technique" by Frank Haronian; E. P. Dutton & Co., for *Inquiries Into the Human Faculty* by Francis Galton; John G. Neihardt Trust, for *Black Elk Speaks* by John G. Neihardt; William Heinemann Ltd., for *The Little Prince* by Antoine de Saint-Exupéry, translated by Katherine Woods.

I am thankful to Anne Mariella and Anne Bosch for their kind help in the preparation of the final manuscripts.

Contents

Chapter 1

Not Only the Matter of Metaphor

> The world is like the characters of our [Chinese] writing. What the symbol is to the flower, the flower itself—this one (he pointed to one of the drawings)—is to something. To go from the symbol to the thing symbolized is to explore the depth and meaning of the world, it is to seek God.
>
> André Malraux, *Man's Fate*

What happened to those imaginary playmates of ours who ate more from the family dinner table than we did? And those secret places that we found down the alleys and in the woods where we were not supposed to go? Remember the long hours spent talking to the trees and to our dolls? Of gazing in the mirror at ourselves, wondering what we would grow up to be, trying on the costumes of our fancies? There were long interminable days when we felt our future was sealed. In the morning we woke to discover that we had forgotten to punch holes in the jartop of our lightning-bug zoo and in the afternoon our brother approached us in a way from which we could only suppose that he had detected the presence of pennies where quarters had before jingled in his piggy bank. The endless trials, city jails, and certain sentencings arrested the flow of time as we waited in Purgatorial corners, full of the visions of Hell.

Other days flew by faster. We mothered our small children, speaking to their painted faces in the same tones as our Mommy did to us. Erecting grand towns, we motored ourselves as tiny trucks and tractors through the heart of our inner landscapes. The rhymes and songs and favorite tales danced between us as we jumped the rope, leered at others, and pushed the tattered book into the elder's hands. And when our parents tucked us into bed and were safely hidden in the living room, we would pop out of bed like jack-in-the-boxes and dance with the shadows or furtively bring beneath the sheets our toy

friends and fantasies. Some nights it seemed that only the bear staring
in the window or the ghost moving in the attic above could get us to be
quiet. We were quickly lost in pondering how the first got out of the
zoo (and if he knew how to open windows); or whether the latter was
waiting hungrily for us all to go to sleep so that he might sneak some
food from the family kitchen. That was the time when our sand castles
were constructed as if by the precisest of architects, who had the honor
of moving into their own creations upon completion.

Is it true that the ocean simply came and ate them up, leaving not a
trace? Did you turn to your Mother one day and feel it necessary to
explain that Laura had moved from your town, for you found it hard
to understand in any other way the absence of that imaginary friend?
Was it only the washing machine that got the better of your little black
dog as the leakage of stuffings portrayed the passage of time? Do you
remember the long afternoons of going through the toys, the collected
stones and shells, pieces of branch, pictures from young loves and
magazines, tressles from train villages, and the personal belongings of
many a doll, and packing them into cartons for the Goodwill or the
garbagemen or the younger brother? And when was that day when the
box of paints was closed and you handed them, like a philanthropic
financier (still pained, however, from the criticism of the school art
teacher), to your mother for the benefit of the local home for orphans?
Did you steal away a few friends from those cardboard graves who
seemed to be not yet totally dead—tucking them away secretly in the
attic or a place long since forgotten and now covered with the dust of
decay?

We no longer leave food for Santa Claus or set a place at the table
for our favorite doll. Though we might still talk to children and
animals we do so with complete honesty only when alone. But when we
see the child kicking that stone down the street from school with
determination that proves it surely is not just a stone, or similarly
avoiding the cracks in the pavement for fear of their harmful effects,
do we not suppress a smile that would betray our understanding? Or is
that smile lost in our notions of what foolishness is all about? No longer
do we spend hours standing at the sink whipping soap suds with
Momma's egg-beaters in order to manufacture the building material
of a snowy kingdom or an amorphous thing or two. Nor do we sit out
by the sidewalk painting pictures with our buckets of water.

In days past the sun would eat them up leaving room for more of
the visions that danced in our heads. But then the sun ate our last one,
and once more the sidewalk became simply the concrete beneath the

pedestrian's feet. The snowy villages and furry animals went down the drain for the last time and the stone lay still—though surely we have passed by it every day without noticing.

Those long debates in the dark (when our best friend would spend the night) over the pros and cons of the different proofs concerning the existence of the Easter Bunny, Hell, or the Martians have passed. One day we seemed to have finished the sorting of our experience into the bins of real and imaginary and having believed ourselves to have shipped the latter out of our houses, we thought that we had finally grown up to live in the world as it really is. We thought we had done with the unreal, the "purely and simply imaginary." But though we shone with the success of the precocious school child who has overcome the bears at his bedroom window with his new found knowledge of the animals of suburbia, the night still brought uneasiness—though we no longer knew why. The doctors conferred. The pills were prescribed.

We discarded the stuffed dogs, the fairy kingdoms, train empires, aspirations for stardom, and for early death. We turned in the secret notions that we could fly (if only given a chance), or be a tree, a Robin Hood, or a dog. The imagination is laughable. It is a lot of silliness and fairy dust and pale pastel colors which caught us like cobwebs in our eyes, blurring what is really before us in life. Having rubbed them out of our own eyes, we laugh and scorn at those who waste their time dealing with "imagination"—who lock themselves up in their rooms with their closed eyes and fancy paints, talking to themselves. We dismiss them and continue with our practical "having-come-to-terms-with-the-reality" life.

The place upon the table where the doll once stood, the paint stain on the kitchen floor, the desire for sleep and both the fear of it and of its absence betray an emptiness unfilled by our knowledge—and most likely even created by the way we have come to use it. The length of this emptiness is measured by two times. For we have used our knowledge not only to sever ourselves from conscious participation in the fantasies of our childhood past but also from the imaginal history of a collective cultural past. The rituals and practices, mythologies and religions—once so always alive with man's experience of the movement that gives birth to image and symbol—lay forgotten except in the antique shops of our scholarship. There the stories concerning the animism of the earth and heaven, no longer perceived by common man, were also sorted away. According to place, time and image they were stuffed in the drawers with the other relics and curiosities that serve now only to mark a time past. The shape of the earth and the geography of heaven and hell have been finally defined with instruments that attempt to measure out the fantasy. The movement of the stars, the oceans and the land is accounted for by the scientific community. The body is pure matter and the humors only humorous or at best curious. Fairytales belong only to the province of children. (One does not even know that that was not always so.) The symbol, once the vehicle to "explore the depth and meaning of the world" (Malraux, 1961), lies disregarded, as if asleep. No longer in our work do we make love to Mother Earth as we till in the fields, nor do we meticulously prepare the natural elements for the making of gold. We do not ask the plants and animals we eat for their permission to do so, nor do we thank coyotes for helpful widsdom given to us at nightfall. Electric lights have hidden our fear of the unknown from us, and we rest comfortably in our ignorance.

We have skilfully tried to strain the mythical from the scientific, the imaginary from the real, metaphor from matter. We have used science to tell us just what "reality" really is and we have taken our scissors of reason and accordingly trimmed into the waste basket the apparently superfluous and contradictory. We have chased the gods from the stones, the animals, and the heavens in the hope that we will be left with a clear and modern idea of matter and life. Knowledge has brandished the censors of "ridiculous," "superstitious," "unscientific," "imaginary" and "unreal" at Myth as he has disrobed her and believed himself superior. Myth leaves him standing there, coat in hand, as she hastily ducks within his closet of wraps. She has heard his censors before, at times of transition between one dominant mythic mode and a newly arising way of understanding.

Metaphor is denied its province in the material world. The experience to which it refers that has filled one shape, one particular group of metaphors, retreats before the threatening force of the prevailing doubt, fathered by Knowledge, and lies so seemingly barren. In time, however, it begins to arise to consciousness and animate a new form which does not conflict with what is known. Myth reappears, often unrecognized as such, in the dress of the day. More often than not she even ducks beneath the coat-tails of Knowledge (where he scarcely ever looks). To see her peeking out, while he smirks with the success of a victor, betrays the fact that a fundamental misunderstanding and confusion is prevalent, to which Knowledge (as well as his students, we ourselves) is usually so blind.

Our reasonable friend has confused the world of Myth, of the imaginal, with that of his own. When she has spoken he has laughed and snickered, if he has not more vehemently shut her up. He knows that there are not spirits in rocks and dragons in caves. She tries to explain herself, as well as the intimate connection, and paradoxical autonomy her world has to his. He wants nothing to do with her. Although he can make her appear foolish his actions of scandalizing and ignoring her do not make her disappear. He forgets her and proceeds in ignorance of her reality. He thinks that Myth is merely incorrectly describing the material world. When he studies aspects of phenomena in his world and draws his conclusions about them, he discards all that Myth has surrounded these same aspects with and which do not concur with his views.

He picks an argument where there is no need. Myth speaks about an imaginal reality using aspects of his material reality. Her statements are not meant to be mere literal, concrete descriptions and opinions about this world. She wants to convey her reality. When he takes some aspects away from her, she must choose others. The more he denies her expressions the more she must use his own words. Though he can discredit her means of expression and make her look foolish to his friends he cannot destroy that which she seeks to express. His inability to distinguish between the concrete level of the symbol and what the symbol refers to leaves him open to her use. It leaves her totally misunderstood. She hides in what and how he studies and her reality begins to come from his own mouth, although he does not hear her inclination.

In our confusion we, as students of Knowledge, have tried to separate the scientific from the metaphorical, matter from spirit, behavior from psyche, the real from the imaginal. They pretend to yield, and in so doing trick us. They have not separated at all, these lovers. What we find flowing down our sinks is our awareness of our participation in myth at every moment of our being in reality, of psyche in our every action. We mistake our confusion for straight-forwardness and clarity. What we have packed away in those boxes is not the imagination and the mythical but our recognition, acceptance and conscious valuing of it.

We live out the imagination in everything and yet we are against the very notion of it. In our confusion we lose something. Our actions are "nothing but." Life can be found boring, interminable and most unkind in all the harshness of its "reality." And yet it is the crushing of a dream that makes us cry; the refusing of a wish that makes us feel hopeless. Our fears send us flying into bed for far longer than our physical selves demand, or we turn to endless fidgeting with details that will never make any difference except to the time they consume and discard for us. The locking of doors and the keeping off of streets, or airplanes, or cars hardly begin to make us feel at ease. We try to get ourselves out of our fears and fantasies and back to work in the morning. And if we cannot make the continual bifurcations and dichotomies that our efforts at reason demand from us, we find or fear to find ourselves in the asylums which allow for the inability to separate and discard—but not without a most critical opinion, "crazy."

Here the images we can no longer push from our awareness rise up and frighten us. We do not recognize them from our history of dreams and wanderings, actions and feelings. Only now do their participation with "reality" seem evident. One doctor warns not to think about them. It is sickness and will go away. Another says that the images are real and have meaning, but that they should not be acted upon. And yet the doctor, having fulfilled his altruistic image of himself for the day, having confirmed his own fantasies about "reality" through his patients or his treatment of them, turns to go home to his wife, to be mothered. He dreams he falls ill and a voice says to him that he should not work so hard. He shortens his hours. His patient dreams people are chasing her and that she should turn and attack the people behind her. He interrupts her contemplations about really doing this, and confines her if she tries. The image is real, but more real some times than at others. The imaginal is experience, but experience which one must choose among, according to values of reason (that know nothing of the nature of metaphor). It is the content of vision and not the relation to content that is perceived and valued. Ambiguity and contradiction mark our efforts to deal with something we *know* nothing about.

When the last doll is tucked securely in the garbage pail, my friend, the imagination has not been overcome. We have, it is true, taken away a few more of its toys. But the imagination is a far deeper affair. It is not just a child to whom we toss toys as appeasement, to get it off our mind or nerves. It travels with us to the spaces behind closed doors to contemplate our fate and our faith. Our loneliness and our successes and failures. It sits with us at the breakfast table as we straighten our hair and head for work, and read the cries of the newspaper chroniclers. It makes us turn one way or another on streets and lanes, and having once turned down them, holds out certain items for our query, fascination, wonder, or disgust. It urges us to worry about our height and our fingernails and our ever-present symptoms. We see it in the eyes of those who love us and we argue with it at the dinner table.

It makes us have secrets and tell secrets. It is not the toys of childhood, and it cannot be outgrown by an individual or a culture. The toys are sorted away only to leave us acting out the same images using elements of our lives in their place. The imaginal is not dependent on matter, though it uses it to extend into common space. Its gods are other than physical and they dance and command without our noble permission.

When the imaginal has been pruned from the trees and exorcised from the animals, having chased the night creatures under the rocks by the light of our reasonableness—when everything is still, clean and free of the beasts of the imaginary—within the hour we feel their movement from within. One forgets a well-known name, says something unintended, cries "without reason," becomes angry at one thing and not another, loves one man and not another and does not know why. One person becomes afraid to climb stairs, another has an eye twitch. One's actions and fleeting thoughts cannot be attributed to the person one believes oneself to be. But more importantly, when we observe what we are doing, who we have become, and where we are aimed, it is often as if our lives were dreamed by another; and we are some two-bit or noble actor or actress executing a part. We are grown up, married to any number of ideas, professions, people, or ways of life. We find certain types of clothes in our closet and food in our cupboard, medicines in our chests and friends at our table. Yet can we remember the day we decided to be a mother or to go on in school, to marry, to believe in God or meditation, or the virtues or blasphemies of politics? Was it we ourselves who chose to become a femme fatale or a bustling (full of competence and confidence) young professional, a Momma's boy or a searcher of the psyche? Surely we contemplated it all before. But when it came time to sign the paper or move one's belongings, to make love or to espouse a view, did it not just happen in a dreaminess—as if indeed we were playing our parts, having memorized them well? The belief we have created that we are a continuous "I" living in certain predetermined landscapes, experiencing an outer world independent of ourselves breaks down. The science of memory, the practices of medicine, and reason fail to account. There is another force influencing our thoughts, emotions, movements, and actions. One can no longer say it is a god or a spirit and yet one has those ancient feelings of possession and movement by a force that does not answer to logic or common space and time. There is something using matter in a way that does not have to do with matter itself. Science can say just what reality is and is not, and yet something fails to be included in the inventory. Appearance hides a world that the tools of a rationalistic knowledge have no access to.

The movement can only be accounted for by positing the existence of an unknown. Psychology did just that, naming it the "unconscious" (the "unknown"). It stopped in the hallways of asylums to listen to the fantasies of many a man and woman. It noticed that when what was known, the "conscious ego," was caught off guard the life of this other world was brought into clearer focus. The early psychologists went to seances, hypnotized their patients, and went to the homes of hysterical women in an attempt to gain access to what was behind the already known. In the malady they heard other personalities speaking unheard of fantasies. Beneath the fainting, the fixed idea, and the paralysis moved a sea of images with a reality of their own. As patient lay upon the couch and allowed the unreasonable to well up, as doctor himself introspected in his study at day's end, the commonplace parted to give birth to the fantasies that had been writhing and moving within it. Action, feeling and belief were no longer such literal affairs. Beneath them flowed images which made matter and behavior concede to their unacknowleged metaphorical Mother.

Through the observations of psychology qualities were gradually attributed to what came to be seen as the two main portions of the psyche. The conscious, in its qualities of awareness and willfulness, paralleled the visible, active, and material aspects of the world. It was filled with notions of who we think we are and what we think is happening, our knowledge and our aims, our strivings. The world of the unconscious was found to be imagistic and metaphorical, rather than verbal and concrete. Its qualities of multivalency and ambiguity allow it to say what the conscious sees as opposing things without being contradictory. Its time and space are not linear but multi-dimensional. Different times can exist in a moment of conscious linear time. It does not adhere to theories of cause and effect, moved as it is by other laws of a more simultaneous and contextualizing nature. Its inhabitants, symbols and images, are always more than can be spoken of. They are not quantifiable or merely material. Though the image may use things that have a material existence one can observe that it does not concern itself with the ways of that world. The horse walks though it has three legs. A hand can be both red and green in the same space. The train is also a ship and the dream ego often man and woman.

Though the imaginal was revealed by psychology, what was then made of this discovery differed. The "unconscious," that unknown presence, became seen in a variety of ways — all to some degree dependent on how the viewer feels about a ghost in the attic. If one likes a clean house with one master, the unconscious is a threat and a nuisance. Psychotherapy becomes a means of exterminating one's soul against the blight of the unpredictable, anything unreasonable, unseemly, and ambivalent. One notes this most poignantly, though certainly not only, when the ghost seems to have taken possession of the house and the doctor intervenes to set things back into their original order, as he sees them to be. One comes upon statements, like Freud's, that a successful analysis would terminate dreaming. The ghost is rendered impotent and the invisible ceases to move.

If one finds through observation that no amount of extermination rids our psychic inventory of that ghost, then we concoct a psycho-therapy bent on "getting to know" him and of coming to some terms as long as we must be neighbors in the same house. But this is most often done a bit begrudgingly. We try to give him just enough space so that he won't raise hell—so that we can continue on our way with as little disturbance as possible. The most desirable contract for us is one where after some negotiations we can reach an agreement that can be kept for years, thereby placing the ghost in a part of the house where we can forget about him. This is often the attitude of people entering analysis who feel that a three year process of negotiation—analysis— will enable them to keep the ghost confined in the attic for the rest of their lives.

One may feel that occasional trips upstairs are necessary, but by no means is he invited to dine at our table and sleep in our beds. If one is lucky in the fulfillment of one's conscious desires, the ghost is heard rumbling upstairs only occasionally.

We light a candle and go with a put-on smile as if we loved him, and yet when we turn away again, we lock the door more surely than before, and hurry away with a look of worry but a hope of success.

There is yet another way. It lies in getting to know that ghost, but not in order to put some fast deal over on him (if we were honest about our real intentions). The ghost is invited to stay not simply because we feel we have no choice about it, but because there is something in him which we know is ours—not in the sense of our possessing him but of our being related to him in a way it is hard to explain. It is a sense of our somehow being inextricably together in this house of being alive. It is not even a matter of our always feeling that we like him; for indeed, sometimes he is the most frightening, frustrating, and dis-agreeable being that could be conjured. Still he is part of the house and after some time we not only grow accustomed to this but glad of

it — though not in a simplistic sort of way. One becomes like a couple
that may speak of divorce but who would never part. In this case the
practice of psychotherapy becomes a bit more unpredictable in its task
and goals. Extermination or extensive alteration are no longer
the objects of treatment. A contract with the ghost is seen to be
untenable, for a real relationship is a daily affair and its only terms
"commitment no matter what." Relationship implies a certain acceptance and communication (though of course that does not exclude
disagreement in the least).

A feeling of relief is experienced that he is actually around. For
though our scientific conscience no longer allows us to speak in ease
about a soul, we never the less feel our loss of it and through our sense
of despair we mourn for it. (Luckily through our mourning we often
find the means to become reconnected to it.) We have made a ghost of
the soul's movement, imagination. He has been pushed into the attic
or the cellar, the unused forgotten room. When he roams unbidden we
feel possessed. We either want to murder him or stuff him back into
some closet. We are afraid of him, of the price he asks us for living in
this house. And though we can recognize the background of angst and
fear in which we go about our houses, there is also a more subtle fear
that the ghost has died. That the demands and criticisms we have
made of soul have indeed not only disproven rationally its existence,
but have killed or made ill its being as we experience it on our sleepless
nights and long afternoons. There are those days when we are
overcome with what must be sadness, and yet no tears find their way
down our cheeks, and we set to wondering about the dryness and
brittleness of our self-chosen rationalities.

What happens to the image, the life of the imaginal, when we begin
our study of it with these different preferences and aims? In the first
case we try to kill it: to shock people out of it, to have the skillful
surgeon remove it from the brain, overpower it with drugs, convince
the patient to look elsewhere — in his work, his marriage, his penis.
One retreats to the common "reality" and learns more thoroughly how
to see only the concrete. The metaphorical is disavowed, as surely as
when children we walked out on our imaginary companions. At one
extreme a strange psychology arises which does not allow for the
postulation of an unconscious, a soul, or a psyche, nor of worthwhile
experiences of these things. The computer is consulted for models of
behavior. The thesis on imagery is rejected on terms of its religiosity.
The symbol is studied only with respect to the nuances of cognitive
paradigms; the dream only as physiological reaction.

In the second case one may go to analysis and accept the language of a particular psychotherapeutic system. The dream and fantasy images are sorted into piles of anima, superego and shadow, transference reactions and degrees and kinds of interpersonal relatedness. They are parceled out as belonging to our job, our sense of inferiority, our mothers. The individual experience is subtly exchanged for a pre-defined package process toward an end, which will remove one from the scary, disabling aspects of the imaginal. The presence of the image is acknowledged but it is then taken from its world and used to further the ego. The meaning (or what is interpreted to be the meaning) is strained from it and the image is discarded and forgotten. The image is recognized but one does not want its world. The ego relates to the imaginal on its own terms and to get from it what it wishes. The metaphor is lost though we cannot recognize it. We think we have comprehended it by saying the image is this or that aspect of yesterday or last year.

The imagination or the unconscious may become understood as a place. We then set aside time to go there in our active imaginations and introspections. We may use the Tarot or the *I Ching* or the prescriptions of one psychology or another as our new toys. But in the end we may find that what we felt enabled us to see the imagination as a place it its own right, our "respect" for it, was more likely a means to once again bifurcate our existence into two separate worlds, where we are believed to be the ones in control of the traveling between them. We relieve ourselves of the burden of metaphor and pretend that now we are rational, undreamed, and straightforward and then (in those minutes in our easy chairs) we are irrational, mythical and tortuous. At that point our ideas and feelings, work and beliefs seem self-evident and understandable. We lose sight of the imagination within them, of the "more than meets the eye" quality which disturbs us. We fidget because we cannot understand it as we are used to understanding; i.e., understanding as being able to overcome, to do away with. We acknowledge that the ghost creeps out from his quarantined quarters when we are sleeping and shows us his art and experience in our dreams. No less surely, though, does he do his work during the day—not just when we are listening to "the imagination." In the loom of our moods, beliefs, movements, arguments, loves, loneliness, in the midst of our most mundane tasks, he tosses his own threads. And though we choose to see the tapestries of our experience as our own creation, his colors and shapes make his presence known—if only we would stop to acknowledge it.

When we still the noise of our movements we can hear his — not only at night when we wake from sleep and catch him moving in our dreams, but while we are awake. We cannot catch him in the sense of stopping him. The ghost is not of this world though he moves within it. He is not made of flesh but rather of a more mercurial substance that takes a different eye to see. When we understand the secret that things are not only as they appear to common sensible perception, we find the need to nurture an uncommon kind of perception. This imaginal perception sees him moving within the metaphors of our life making them more than, different than, plain statements of fact.

At some point we may find that the ghost is not crazy or silly and that we were mistaken all those years when we laughed at his words and gestures as if they were nonsensical and absurd. We attempted to correct his broken speech and to tell him in our clear ways what it was he must be saying. But suddenly we may see that it is not the visible he has been talking about. In his gestures he has sought to make the invisible visible. He is talking about something we do not know and thereby cannot judge according to our usual standards. He does not use our language because he does not speak of the things our language was created for. He has, liked Proteus, donned the costumes of countless images, assumed the voices of many gods, to live out the drama of his experience. He has used the material from our houses and our lives, as props for his art, as before he seized our trains and pets, the heavens and waters of yesteryear. No longer can we look in a self-satisfied manner at the tip of his finger when he is pointing to the moon (Durand, 1971:99) and laugh at him for pointing to what is only darkness for us. We must grow accustomed to the twilight of his space, his images and metaphors, by dwelling there. In this way we can begin to travel within it toward that which he points to. To dwell there we must no longer assume that this ghost lives the same life as our conscious egos. We must resist our urges to flee to the concrete facts and activities, to the literalistic ways of thinking with which we try to constitute not only *our* lives, but also *his*. We are seized with fear and so we hope to reduce that which we do not understand to the realm we are in control of.

However, one cannot completely understand him. The interpretations which in the end we manufacture cannot account fully and adequately for the image's movement. If we allow ourselves this recognition (which is not at all simple, for it posits an area of knowing to which our knowledge will never be sufficient) we must go to the ghost and stay with him, hoping he will take us as pupils. We are pupils, however, who will never graduate, leave, or teach.

The medieval alchemists said that "for those who have the symbol the passage is easy." But the "passage" is not one of overcoming things, of getting linearly further. Passage is movement between endless planes, contained only by the hall of mirrors within the metaphor, the image. One begins a journey from "the symbol to the thing symbolized." Yet by the nature of the image it is always longer than we will ever know and different from what we could ever say. The image is a vehicle in that we can move in it, but its space has no terminus . . . only unending depth.

Chapter 2

The Half-dream State

The territory we shall be covering, that of the waking dream, is by no means virgin, although the extent of modern neglect of it would have us think so. The waking dream, the conscious experiencing of images, has been discovered and lost, refound and shared, countless times. Although its significance has varied in different cultures and sub-cultures, there have accrued through repetition some notions or fantasies concerning waking dreams and involvement in them.

The attempt to dream while awake, itself paradoxical, involves one in a number of paradoxical states, actions, and attitudes: the half-dream state, action through non-action, controlled abandon, uncontrolling control, disciplined dreaming. The paradoxes point to an effort and a discipline which reverse the natural flow of events. The medieval alchemists described this as a work against nature, an *opus contra naturam*. This opus creates a directionality away from the perceptual and the material, to the imaginal and the psychological.

Between sleeping and waking

The intermediary nature of metaphor is mirrored by the state of consciousness most often used to strengthen man's connection to the imaginal. The metaphor uses matter in order to convey the immaterial. In doing so it creates a third realm which lies between the other two. The state of consciousness being described uses the ego to record and to observe the non-ego. The body is relaxed until it nears sleep, and yet awareness is sustained. As the world of images appears, as if from dreams, they are recorded and remembered, and at times interacted with. This state of consciousness has been described as an intermediary state, that of the half-dream. It creates an intersection between two worlds—as the symbol itself does.

This conjunction has in many instances been regarded as sacred. The land of what we call dreams and the unconscious was understood in other times to be the world of the gods, spirits, or ancestors. In ancient Greece, for instance, it was believed that the gods came through the keyhole of the dreamer's room and stood beside his bed. The soul could leave the dreamer's physical body and travel with the gods during sleep. Similarly, the Chinese believed the source of dreams to be the dreamer's spiritual soul or *hun*. The *hun* traveled about during sleep to talk with dead spirits and souls (de Castle, 1971:4). Whether dreams came from gods, demons, or the soul, there is common to these ideas the notion that the dream and the dreamlike are connected with a force beyond the mind and body of the dreamer. The dreamlike has a quality of "otherness," of dissimilitude to the material world.

Through the waking dream a journey was made possible. Either the gods or spirits were enabled to pass into our world, or we into theirs. The conjunction was envisioned not only as a bridge from one world to another, but as a plane of co-existence of the two worlds. Through the connection of the two, the individual was able to obtain gifts of wisdom and self-knowledge from the divine benefactors. One could learn of the spirit world. The connection of the two planes — spiritual and material — through participation in the half-dream state was considered to bring health.

There have been numerous distinctions made between divine and natural dreams — those inspired by the spirits and those not, those meaningful and those nonsensical. Jamblichus of Chaldeis (1821) noted that the mystical lights and voices of religious visions occurred most often in the half-dream state. Dreams sent by God, he claimed,

take place either when sleep is leaving us, or [when] we are beginning to awake, and when we hear a certain voice which concisely tells us what is to be done; or voices are heard by us, between sleeping and waking, or when we are perfectly awake. And sometimes, indeed, an invisible and incorporeal spirit surrounds the recumbents, so as not to be perceived by the sight, but by a certain other co-sensation and intelligence.

. . . a still more perfect manner when the sight perceives, when intellect, being corroborated, follows what is performed, and this is accompanied by the motion of the spectators.

Such, therefore, and so many being the differences of the dreams, no one of them is similar to human dreams. But wakefulness, a detention of the eyes, a similar oppression of the head, a condition of the head, a condition between sleeping and waking, an instantaneous excitation, or perfect vigilance, are all of them divine indications, and are adapted to the reception of the gods, and a part of divine appearances antecedes according to things of this kind.

The Chinese, among others, also believed that their mystical dreams occurred in an unnatural daytime sleep that could not be properly regarded as sleep at all (de Becker, 1968:154).

The Romantics, as the Greeks and Islamics before them, glorified this state as if it were the most direct way to contact the muses and the creative intelligence.

To dream and altogether not to dream.
This synthesis is the operation of the genius, by which both activities are mutually reinforced.

                                                        Novalis (quoted by Béguin, 1939: 210)

The half-dream state appeared either to give one access to a realm other than that of the nightly dream, or to give one new means of approaching the imaginal phenomena of dreams that in itself changed their nature. To approach this new realm or manner of relating, one could try to become aware while dreaming or try to evoke dreaming while being aware. The former often gave rise to various meditative practices, while the latter approach was frequently incorporated in symbolic rituals of vision questing.

Waking sleep, daydreams, and hallucinations

We seem, as Gurdjieff claimed, to spend most of our lives in a form of "waking sleep." During the day we are usually neither asleep nor aware. Our usual state of consciousness is opposite of that required for waking dreams.

As our thoughts, feelings, and actions come to the edge of our conscious field, our awareness goes to meet them and merges with them. As our awareness becomes absorbed and attached to the emotion, thought, or action, we become it. There is no part of our awareness to remain outside and observe what is going on. Instead of noting that a feeling, for instance of depression, is passing through us, we *become* depressed." "I *am* depressed." That identity, created by the fusion of awareness with the emotion, causes us to lose recognition of the experience. It is only our awareness in its unattached state, that allows a part of us to remain separate, to be able to observe.

How often do we find ourselves in a daydream? What has happened to our attention in relation to the subject we are dreaming over? Do we have any idea where the daydream began and how it progressed through the linking of images? Or has our attention thoroughly merged with the subject? In most cases we are never aware of the daydreams and moods that pass in and out of us. As long as our attention is absorbed by one kind of reality, be it daydreams, mathematical computations, insecurities, or the study of the imaginal, we are not free to become aware of what is happening in our relation to these. Our gaze is fixed, glued on the center and all that moves on the periphery is missed. To begin to see, it is as if a part of us must step back and not fix itself so intently on the middle. The total absorption into the subject is lessened in an attempt to get our awareness from the mixture with which we can then discriminate what is moving. *This does not mean one steps out of the experience, becomes unrelated, and begins to analyze.* It means that our sensitivities and awareness are freed to participate independently as themselves and to bring their unique qualities into the situation. For example, if you are running you may be totally absorbed in it in a way that makes it impossible for you to hear your rhythm, your breathing, to feel your stomach and lungs, your feelings of abandonment, of triumph, of being overcome, your self-criticisms and congratulations and the images in which they come. Do you feel pursued or as if you are going towards something — or does all that, at those moments, seem superfluous to the joy of running? Has time disappeared, leaving you in the task of transversing pure space?

We are often obliged to get something accomplished and we use our awareness to get us through the motions correctly. The task is finished, but what we are left with is often just the knowledge that it is done — the groceries are bought, the baby changed, the stocks negotiated, and the paper typed. We may know we have a feeling of accomplishment, but what about all the rest that was happening in us around what we were doing?

We see the table but we seldom see ourselves seeing, experiencing, the table. We do not consciously note the geometrical elements that we recognize unconsciously in order to call it "table." Instead of seeing the sheen in the wood, the shape of the legs, the reflections from the window in the surface, we usually just see a "table" — a pattern that resides more in our minds from the past, than from the actual experience in the moment. We are unaware of how we experience our unique pasts (both historical and imaginal) in relation to the table. What is a table to us? Is it the scene of long happy meals or family arguments? Did we play on it, paint or work on its surface? Was it always too big or too small; lovely or with snagging nails that caught our shirt sleeves each time we tried to rise? Was it vacant except for our fantasies of what we wished to have happen on it, or had we always been in the situation of never even seeing its top, as it was buried long before in the debris of our daily pursuits.

We confuse aware participation in the imaginal with daydreaming, and we use the qualities of the latter to condemn the former. In daydreaming, the ego's attention becomes attached to the imaginal contents in the same way it does to our daily concerns. There is no awareness during it or memory afterward of what was going on. One could say that daydreams are a form of sleeping wakefulness, as opposed to the state of wakefulness even while sleeping that characterizes a waking dream.

The distinction between the two is fundamental and crucial and has given rise to many warnings. The medieval alchemists, for instance, warned against just such confusion between daydreams and creative imagination. *"Opus nostrum per veram imaginationem et nun phantastica."* "Our work ought to be done by true imagination [active, purposeful, creative] and not a fantastical one [nonsense, phantasm, fleeting impression]" (quoted by Jung, 1968:192). Paracelsus also cautioned against any confusion of *Imaginatio vera* (true imagination) and fantasy, the "madman's cornerstone." "Die Fantasey ist nicht *Imaginatio,* sondern ein Eckstein der Narren . . ." In the Sufi idea of creative imagination it was believed that whenever the imagination is allowed to "stray" and to be "wasted recklessly, when it ceases to fulfill its function of perceiving and producing the symbols that lead to inner intelligence," the intermediary world (that of the *mundus imaginalis* and of the soul) can be considered to have disappeared (Corbin, 1972:14).

The confusion between daydreams and waking dreams has served to discredit the latter. One condemns the imagination for its tendency to flee from difficulties, to involve one in wishfulfilling fantasies, to fill up the voids "through which grace might pass" (Weil, 1939:145). These are qualities, however, that do not arise from the imagination, but rather from our way of relating to it. In these instances one uses the imagination not in a disciplined search for the values of the imaginal, but as a relaxation from awareness. The degradation that daydreams bring to the imagination should be transferred to the "ego" and its manner of relating to images.

Similarly the phenomenon of hallucinations has been used to discredit the imaginal. Waking dreams and hallucinations, however, rely on two distinctly different psychic functions: imagination and perception. Hallucinations purport to deal with external material and perceptual reality, whereas waking dreams and dreams pertain to imaginative reality (Berry, 1974:96). Whereas visions are "non-corrigible experiences which do not admit of verification *or* falsification by reference to the perceived world" (Casey, 1974:13), hallucinations do.

In an hallucination the individual is unable to recognize image as image and external perception as perception. The two are superimposed in a way that does not permit an imaginal awareness to exist. In regard to awareness of the imaginal the hallucinator is asleep.

Disciplined dreaming

The training of the ego to surrender its usual activities and ways of using consciousness in order to maintain vigilence while dreaming has been regarded as a discipline and an art. In general, the ability to be aware must be freed from its usual tendency to attach itself to the object of awareness, thereby losing its ability to reflect on that object. Awareness cannot immediately dis-identify from its usual attachments. In some kinds of meditation a form (mantra, mudra, koan) is substituted for the usual objects of awareness. Gradually the awareness dis-identifies from daily preoccupations and daydreams and coalesces around the meditative form. Whether the object or form used has significance in and of itself varies in different systems of meditation. Similarly what one does with the awareness once it has become a separate entity depends upon the particular methods and goals of a system.[1] At this point, "reality" changes and one is faced with new phenomena.

[1] The present interest in the West concerning Eastern systems of meditation gives the Westerner another argument to add to his rationalistic disavowals of the imaginal. The fact that many Eastern systems discourage the devotee from regarding images seriously cannot be taken at face value as an indictment against the imaginal. We want to think that the "East" has realized as fully as we the ridiculousness of fantasy. To do that we ignore the fact that they have already attained a relation to the imaginal that far surpasses ours. Their texts—full of images and fantasies—lay as testament to this. "It must stir a sympathetic chord in an enlightened European when it is said in the *Hui Ming Ching* that 'shapes formed from the fire of the spirit are only empty colours and forms.' That sounds quite European and seems to meet our reason excellently. We, indeed, think we can flatter ourselves at having already reached such heights of clarity because such phantoms of gods seem to have been left far behind. But the things we have outgrown are only word-ghosts, not the psychic fact that was responsible for the birth of the gods" (Jung, 1968b:112).

In the Western tradition of contemplation, although the awareness of the ego is stressed, the ego is allowed to converse with the arising contents of consciousness and indeed to value this relation. The object is not transcendence of all content (imaginal or otherwise), as is true in many Eastern systems, but rather the attaining of a new conscious relation to content.

In the Middle Ages it was a common practice to hold conversations with the soul . . . to ask it questions and to hear answers arising from a source other than consciousness. One was aware of things outside the ego and could connect with them, but in a way that could be consciously remembered and experienced. Hugh de St. Victor began such a conversation in the following way:

I will speak in secret to my soul, and in friendly conversation I will ask her what I should like to know. No stranger shall be present, we will talk alone and openly to each other. Thus I need not be afraid to ask even the most secret things and she will not be ashamed to reply honestly.

Tell me, I ask you, O my Soul, what is it that you love above everything?

The *vita contemplativa* of the medieval Christian church used meditations to engage in what was termed "disciplined dreaming," the voluntary seeing of visions (Eliot, "Dante").

A central notion to the type of consciousness needed for disciplined dreaming is embodied in the concept of action through non-action, as taught by Meister Eckhart and Chinese Taoism (Jung, 1968b:93). In actualizing this principle our awareness is freed from its absorptions and can begin to perceive the imaginal. "Non-action prevents a man from becoming entangled in form and image (materiality). Action in non-action prevents a man from sinking into numbing emptiness and dead nothingness" (*Secret of the Golden Flower,*[1] 1962:53). The awareness refrains from identification without going to sleep. It is kept in circulation, freed from absorption into various things. It tries to remain independent.

Therefore you have only to make the light circulate: that is the deepest and most wonderful secret. The light is easy to move, but difficult to fix, If it is made to circulate long enough, then it crystallizes itself . . .

Ibid., 22

---

[1]A Chinese alchemical text concerning meditation.

Through non-action we cease doing things to the world and ourselves in order to be able to perceive in certain ways. This allows more of an opportunity for us to be moved, rather than for us to move.

As long as the heart has not attained absolute tranquillity, it cannot move itself. One moves the movement and forgets the movement; this is not movement in itself. Therefore it is said: If, when stimulated by external things, one moves, it is the impulse of the being. If, when not stimulated by external things, one moves, it is the movement of heaven. The being that is placed over against heaven can fall and come under the domination of the impulses. The impulses are based upon the fact that there are external things. They are thoughts which go on beyond one's own position. The movement leads to movement. But when no idea arises, the right ideas come. That is the true idea. When things are quiet and one is quite firm, and the release of heaven suddenly moves, is this not a movement without purpose? Action through non-action has just this meaning.

Ibid., 58

Trying to watch our psycho-mental flux without interfering in it or becoming attached to its contents (and thereby losing awareness) and yet to still be receptive to it, is one of the hardest possible things — perhaps because of the paradox of activity embodied in the principle of action through non-action. We must sacrifice what seems to us to be a sense of control on our part, but which is really not as it is the psycho-mental flux controlling us. In a sense we gain actual control through the crystallization of our awareness, and yet it is not control in the sense of authority to be exercised over anything. If we try to use it in that way, in that moment the ego reverts to its initial state, becoming absorbed in the effort of control.

When we are actually on the edge of waking and yet are fully within the landscape and action of our dream, there is sometimes a moment when we realize that we are both awake and within the images of our soul. Similarly, as we are travelling on trains or in cars, or doing some activity in which we can drift into the imaginal, there is sometimes a moment when we become aware of where we are imaginally without causing the images to immediately disappear. At these moments the imaginal and the waking worlds are known to not only co-exist, but to co-exist potentially in awareness as well.

In tenth-century Tantric Buddhism, the yogi was taught to retain his consciousness during sleep. He would hold himself between the two states of sleep and wakefulness by placing himself "between the exhaled and inhaled breaths," associated with a certain quality of energy (de Becker, 1968:153-4). It was believed that the "Lord of necessity grants [the meditator] during dreams the ends he pursues, provided that he is profoundly contemplative and places himself at the junction between waking and sleeping" (*Spandakârikâ* of Vasagupta). In Tibetan Buddhism different meditations were similarly used to allow the meditator to remain conscious while asleep in order to observe the world of visions (Evans-Wentz, 1967).

Often in attempting the achievement of consciousness while dreaming the dreamer will try to remember to do a certain activity in the dream. This may be a form of meditation or it may be simply an action like holding one's dream hands in front of one (Castaneda, 1973). Progressively the individual is able to inhabit the dream ego's body, and in some instances any of the other images in the dream. This brings consciousness into the dream in such a way that one is simultaneously dreaming and aware of dreaming. Whether or not or in what way this changes the nature of the dream is debatable. It seems more than probable, however, that "observed sleep is already trans-formed sleep and that every intervention the sleeper makes in it modifies its nature" (de Becker, 1968:156). There are different accounts of what is possible in this state of observed dreaming. The Tantric and Tibetan masters reported that they could control the dream by their conscious presence. Others despite their insistence on gaining control over dreams (however without the discipline of the yogi) have admitted their failure (*ibid.*, 156).

In the nineteenth century there was a revival of attempts to incubate dreams. These took the form, however, of trying to exert the will over the dreamworld. This was a fundamentally different approach from incubation rituals where the will is aligned with and respectful of the dream world. In these later attempts one would try to not only induce dreams on certain subjects but to induce the specific contents of the dream. Once the dream began the dreamer would try to alter the flow of images. Jean-Paul (Richter) came to the conclusion that it "was impossible to forcibly obtain or prevent the appearance of certain images and that it was impossible to know whether even induced images [would be] friendly or terrifying" (*ibid.*, 158). The most detailed of these nineteenth-century reports is that of Hervey de Saint-Denis, *Les Rêves et les moyens de les diriger* (1867). For twenty years he kept a dream diary recording his attempts to make the will intervene in sleep.

One night, while sleeping, when I felt complete knowledge of my real state and I was rather apathetically watching the passage of the whole phantasmagoria of my sleep which, incidentally, was very clear, it occurred to me to take advantage of it, to make some experiments with the power I might or might not have of evoking certain images by the use of my will alone. While seeking a subject to concentrate my thoughts upon, I recalled the monstrous apparitions which (in a previous dream) had impressed me so deeply, owing to the terror they inspired. I tried to evoke them by seeking them assiduously in my memory and wishing, as intensely as possible, to see them again. The first attempt met with no success. At this moment the pastoral scene of a countryside unfolded before me, in the midst of which I saw harvesters, and wagoners laden with corn. No suspicion of a spectre answered my summons, and the association of ideas-cum-images that formed my dream seemed to have absolutley no desire to leave the even path they had naturally taken. Then, still dreaming, I reflected as follows: a dream being a sort of reflection of real life, the events which seem to take place in them generally follow, in their very incoherence, certain laws of sucession conforming to the ordinary sequence of all real events. I mean, for example, that if I dream of having a broken arm, I shall believe that I have it in a sling or that I am using it with care; that if I dream the shutters of a room have been closed, I will have, as an immediate consequence, the idea that the light is intercepted and that there is darkness around me. Starting from this idea, I imagined that if, in a dream, I performed the action of putting my hand in front of my eyes, I should obtain a first illusion in relation to what would actually happen if I did the same thing while awake; that is to say that I would make the images of objects which seemed to be situated in front of me disappear.

Then I asked myself whether, once this interruption of pre-existing visions had taken place, my imagination would not find it easier to evoke the new objects on which I was trying to fix my thoughts. The experiment followed this reasoning closely. In my dream I saw a hand in front of my eyes, and this did indeed have as its first effect the destruction of the vision of the countryside at harvest time, that I had vainly tried to change by the force of the imagination alone. For a moment I remained without seeing anything, as would have happened in real life. Then I made another energetic call to the memory of the famous eruption of monsters and, as if by enchantment, this memory, now clearly placed in the objective of my thoughts, suddenly stood out sharp, brilliant and tumultuous, without my even noticing, before waking, the way in which the transition had taken place.

de Saint-Denis, 1867:283-6

But although de Saint-Denis achieved these types of success, he had to admit "I have never managed to follow and master all the phases of a dream" (*ibid.*, 291).

The attempts of de Saint-Denis and Jean-Paul were essentially different in method and intention from most earlier attempts to induce dreams or to control dreaming. In the Tibetan practices the yogi was not ultimately trying to subjugate the visionary to the will of the conscious personality. He was seeking to learn of the visionary in order to recognize its nature as *maya* or illusion, just as he had sought previously to be aware of the phenomenal world as *maya*. He was not interested in aggrandizing the territory under the control of the ego. . . but rather in passing beyond the ego altogether. Hippocrates had tried, as is outlined in *A Discourse on Dreams,* to introduce certain images into his patients' dreams, often while they were in the half-dream state. These were believed to be healthful images that would aid in remedying the patient's particular difficulty. The images had themselves come from the imaginal landscapes so well known to the Greeks. The attempt to induce a particular dream was aimed not at increasing the patient's power over images or at showing that this was possible, but at aligning him with certain imaginal principles in the hope that this relationship would heal the individual.

What appealed to de Saint-Denis (and later to many others, as we shall find) about the possibility of incubating dreams was quite different from the ritual uses of dream and vision incubation in Greece, Egypt, India, China, Japan, and Islam. The Age of Enlightenment had made men think that rationality and the conscious ego could be made to conquer all else and that this would prove beneficial. To make the content of the dream and the vision — that which seems most up to alien forces — yield to the will must have seemed like a most attractive endeavor. Through an example of vision incubation in ancient Greece and one of vision questing among the American Indian tribe of the Oglala Sioux, it is hoped that the practices surrounding these will alert us to a totally different possibility than the one de Saint-Denis and the early psychologists so eagerly sought for. In the following examples it is clear that the ego is used only as a humble instrument to seek for visions and to help the daily life become more attuned with (rather than triumphant over) the reality of the visionary.

Vision incubation

In times past, the elements of incubation rituals were designed to transform one's usual state of consciousness into one in which the incubant was able to receive a vision or dream from the gods. One can understand an incubation ritual as "an externalization of a psychological fact — a projection mirroring a natural inner process." It is "as if the incubant were able by aligning him or herself with the symbolic structure of the ritual, to allow a certain inner condition to arise which cannot be produced directly" (Reed, 1974). The outer symbolic actions of the ritual were able to create a state of awareness and certain inner attitudes that allowed the incubant to gradually separate himself from the usual frame of consciousness in order to be able to participate in the visionary realm with the god. By looking at it in this way one can attempt to understand the symbolic significance of some of the elements of a ritual and to ask oneself the question of how they can be incorporated in one's own attempts to incubate waking dreams.

At the Trophonios Incubatorium in Lebadela, as described by C. A. Meier (1954:649), there was an elaborate system of preparation that almost insured that those actually participating in the incubation period were committed, and in the right spirit to encounter the gods. First, the person was supposed to have a message from the god Asklepios (the god of healing) in the form of a dream advising him about the wisdom of making the trip to the sanctuary.

According to the Isis mysteries the incubant was invited by the god through a dream or vision to come and sleep in the temple. If he tried to sleep in the temple's *Adyton* ("the place not to be entered by the unbidden") without being invited, he would die. The mysteries warned further that one should not "hesitate when called, nor hasten when not commanded" (quoted in Meier, 1954:70-1). These warnings reminded him that the ego could not be the one to invite him to participate with the gods. He must passively and humbly await their invitation and permission. Similarly, when one has been called, to not accept is a defiance of the ego against the will of the gods, for which the person was punished. The action is not enough in itself. It must be performed in the right time, by the right man, in the right way. These are things that cannot be sanctioned by opinions and desires, but must be derived from inner attitudes. In the Chinese *Book of the Elixir* it is said that "When the right man (white magician) makes use of the wrong means, the wrong means work in the right way," and conversely, "if the wrong man uses the right means, the right means work in the wrong way" (quoted in *The Secret of the Golden Flower*, 1962:63).

The applicant for healing arrived in Lebadela with the conviction, the trust, that he was meant to enter the ritual, and that although he as yet did not know the content of the vision, the process would be healthful for him. The period of preparation before incubation nurtured a receptive attitude in the applicant. The incubant drew his attention away from the usual attachments to the daily world through ritual cleansings, fasting,[1] and sexual abstinence. He symbolically prepared himself for the humble acknowledgment of higher forces through the act of sacrifice. Through the ritual sacrifice he expressed

---

[1]Wine, meat, specific fish, and broad beans were thought unfavorable to the appearance of the healing vision (de Becker, 1968:165).

his smallness in relation to the gods and his high valuation of the
relation to the gods that he was seeking, i.e. that he was willing to give
up something of importance for it, in honor of and thanks to the god.

When the priest believed the incubant was ready, two thirteen-year-
old youths were sent by night to fetch him. He was taken to a river,
annointed and washed. The priest gave him the power to "forget all
that had gone before and power to remember all he would see." The
ego was thus disconnected from identification with the concerns of the
past and was used as an agent of receptivity toward the movement of
the gods in the present. The incubant was then further humbled by
being shown an "unapproachable statue of Trophonious," which no
doubt reminded him of the immensity of the force he was coming into
relationship with. Clad and bound in a white sheet, he descended by a
ladder into a cave. The patient crawled feet first into a hole as wide as
his body. When his knees were in the hole a whirlpool underneath his
feet pulled him downward. At this point the incubant was a prisoner of
the god and at his mercy. Honey cakes were always taken with the
patient in order to appease the snakes which inhabited the cave. The
patient was at the mercy of the god, and it was within this situation
that he received the healing vision.[1] The incubant remained in the
hole usually for several days (without food, of course) before he
received a vision. "At the god's will," he was ejected from the hole.

At all of the Asklepian sanctuaries the incubants were required to
pay fees, as well as to transcribe or dictate their dreams and visions
from the incubation. The experience itself was observed to produce
effects on the patient. It was not until several hundred years after the
initiation of the ritual, when the people were drifting away from the
basis of their religion, that the temple priests began to perform
interpretative tasks.

In Greece the site of the incubation was sacred and meaningful.[2]

---

[1]Similarly, we may often be more able to receive visions when we are in a state of
illness or depression. In both, one's energy is drawn away from the objects it usually
participates with. One's being is drawn inward and downward. What at first seems to
be deathly darkness, is found to be inhabited. If the creatures are given respect and
attention, "honey cakes," they may kindly approach closer so that we may see them.

[2]We can also give fantasy to whether there are imaginal sites where we would be
more likely to be able to incubate a dream or vision. This might come from a dream, a
fantasy, or an actual experience. By dwelling there imaginally we can establish a
connection to it. Different imaginal sites and benefactors (the ones who give the vision)
set up different constellations of images or archetypes. Children know quite naturally
how to find such secret magical places in which to house their treasured fantasies.
They intuitively know never to let anyone into that secret space; not even to tell
anyone, unless that person himself is *very* special.

The setting and ritual elements of the incubation enabled the incubant to change his allegiance and attention from the ego world to that of the gods. He had to learn their ways of communication. He must never in a flash of hubris lose his sense of humility.

We want the god to help us to see more clearly what is going on in us. In this sense we are *aitematikoi,* disposed to ask, and so are our dreams. But [Artemidorus] added, we should never ask the gods undue questions! And if the answer has been granted, we must not forget to sacrifice and give thanks.

Meier, 1966:313

Keeping close to the vision

Among the American Indians means were created to maintain connection with the images from visions. Visions were prepared for, actively sought, brought back to the other members of the tribe and integrated into the daily life and knowledge of the tribe. The visions, sent by the spirits, helped both young and old to find their relationship to the world—what their role in their tribe was, their relation to the spirits and sources of power, to nature, plants and animals. Black Elk, a member and a holy man of the Oglala Sioux, described how visions are quested for and understood in his tribe.[1] We will use his comments mainly to reflect on how important it was that images from the visions received were connected to daily life in a way by which the daily could bring one closer to the vision.

Black Elk speaks of a man named Crazy Horse who became the chief of the tribe because of the power he had been granted in a vision. When he was engaged in battle he would think of the world of his vision and be reassured, enabling him to "go through anything and not be hurt." He carried a stone with him in battle that he had seen in his vision. It served to relate him to the vision and to draw the strength from the vision that would aid in his protection. Even his name was taken from the name of the horse in his vision who had "danced around like a horse made only of shadow" (in Neihardt, 1961:85). Thus his identity in the daily world was integrated with the imagery from the visionary realm.

---

[1] The words of Black Elk were transcribed by John Neihardt in *Black Elk Speaks* (1932, 1961) and Joseph Epes Brown in *The Sacred Pipe* (1953, 1971). Quotes directly from Black Elk are designated simply as "in Neihardt" or "in Brown."

Black Elk's personal experience amplifies this further. He had had a vision when just a boy that he had been afraid to tell anyone about. He had become progressively undermined by it because of his attitude towards it. Finally, he told the medicine man about it, who responded,

Nephew, I know now what the trouble is! You must do what the bay horse in your vision wanted you to do. You must do your duty and perform this vision for your people upon earth. You must have the horse dance [from the vision] first for the people to see. Then the fear will leave you; but if you do not do this something very bad will happen to you.

In Neihardt, 1961:165

His vision had concerned his relation to his troubled people and Black Elk had, although not consciously, forgotten, ignored and undervalued his vision. This had left him in a disturbed state. The medicine man reminds him of the value of the vision and of the fact that it should be shared and brought into relation with the daily life of the tribe. This was done by reconstructing the vision in a pageant. Scenes and images from the vision were painted on "sacred tepees."

Black Elk was told he must not eat anything until the horse dance was over. He had to purify himself in a sweat lodge with sage. He shared the songs from his vision with a select few who then taught various members of the tribe to sing them for the re-enactment of the vision. The members of the tribe were cast as the people and animals who had appeared in the vision, and all were painted and costumed appropriately. Through this performance the vision reappeared to Black Elk as it had so many years before. "The fear that was on me so long was gone, and when thunder clouds [also images from his vision] appeared I was always glad to see them, for they came as relatives now to visit me." As long as the world of the vision was neglected, the Indian felt in disharmony. By actively valuing it, sacrificing to it, and allowing its images to come into daily life, a healing effect was produced. "Even the horses seemed to be healthier and happier after the dance" (in Neihardt, 1960:179). The power of the vision enabled Black Elk to heal members of the tribe.

Inherent in their seeking of visions is a certain attitude of respect for the power and order of the world. As had the ancient Greeks, Black Elk learned to pay homage to the forces and to prepare himself for his meeting with them through the vision. "It is necessary to go far from people when lamenting," when crying for a vision. "When going out to lament it is necessary to choose a wise old medicine man,[1] who is quiet

---

[1]Joseph Epes Brown translates *wichasha wakan* as a holy man, not medicine man as in Neihardt's transcriptions.

and generous, to help. He must fill and offer the pipe to the Six Powers and to the four-leggeds and the wings of the air, and he must go along to watch." "For if things are not done in the right way, something very bad can happen, and even a serpent could come and wrap itself around the lamenter" (in Brown, 1953:45).

When going out to "lament" Black Elk fasted for four days, drinking only water. He purified himself in a sweat lodge made with willow boughs set on the ground and bent down to make a round top.

Over this we had a bison robe. In the middle we put hot stones, and when I was in there, Few Tails [the medicine man] poured water on the stones. I sang to the spirits while I was in there being purified. Then the old man rubbed me all over with the sacred sage. He then braided my hair, and I was naked except that I had a bison robe to wrap around me while lamenting in the night.

In Neihardt, 1960:185-7

He removed his clothes to show that he was "poor to things of the world." He cried out for he was "humbling himself, remembering his nothingness in the presence of the Great Spirit" (in Brown, 1953:54).

Once when Black Elk returned to his tribe after crying for a vision, his people were so discouraged and sad that he was instructed to perform the vision he had received with *heyokas*, sacred fools "who do everything wrong or backwards to make the people laugh." It

is planned that the people shall be made to feel jolly and happy first, so that it may be easier for the power [from the vision] to come to them. You have noticed that the truth comes into this world with two faces. One is sad with suffering, and the other laughs; but it is the same face, laughing or weeping. When people are already in despair, maybe the laughing face is better for them; and when they feel too good and are too sure of being safe, maybe the weeping face is better for them to see. I think that is what the *heyoka* ceremony is for.

In Neihardt, 1961:192-3

Black Elk had never told anyone *all* of his greatest vision. He understood that to do so would dissipate its power. Similarly, if we are careless in sharing our dreams and waking dreams without a clear purpose in doing so, we seem to lose much of their benefit through not showing them respect.

This sense of relation to the vision, as we shall see, differs from much of modern psychology. For Black Elk the vision was not reduced to, or assimilated by, the daily life. The attempt was made to bring the daily life into relation with the vision. The images of the visions were the guides in this relation. They had power and through them the daily world was transformed. The lamenter must

always be careful lest distracting thoughts come to him, yet he must be alert to recognize any messenger which the Great Spirit may send to him, for these people often come in the form of an animal, even one as small and insignificant as a little ant. Perhaps a Spotted Eagle may come to him from the West, or a Black Eagle from the North, or the Bald Eagle from the East, or even the red-headed woodpecker may come to him from the South. And even though none of these may speak to him at first, they are important and should be observed. The "lamenter" should also notice if one of the little birds should come, or even perhaps a squirrel . . . All these people are important, for in their own way they are wise and they can teach us two-leggeds much if we make ourselves humble before them.

Within the vision the Indian does not remain himself, but

actually identifies himself with, or becomes, the quality or principle of the being or thing which comes to him in a vision, whether it be a beast, a bird, one of the elements, or really any aspect of creation. In order that this power may never leave him, he always carries with him some material form representing the animal or object from which he has received his "power." These objects have often been incorrectly called fetishes, whereas they actually correspond more precisely to what the Christian calls guardian angels, since for the Indian, the animals and birds and all things, are the "reflections"—in material form—of the Divine principles. The Indian is only attached to the form for the sake of the principle which is contained within the form!

Brown, 1971:58,45

Each creature is regarded as sacred because each has a *wochangi* or influence through which it is possible to gain understanding if one is attentive. Whereas modern man usually tries to understand the image with rational knowledge and the metaphor through its concrete referent, the Oglala Sioux acknowledged in their actions that it may be the material which belongs to the metaphor, to the imaginal.

Chapter 3

The Mythopoetic Function and the Early History of Psychology

The experience of waking dreams, so well integrated into the daily life of some cultures, in our own culture has been most often acknowledged only by mystics and poets, madmen and geniuses. The history of psychology relates how the elements of waking dreams, the experiential phenomena and the attending attitudes, were slowly more popularly recognized and cultivated in the context of a "psychotherapeutic" worldview. By waking dream we mean not just an experience of dreamlike character received while awake, but an experience of the imagination undertaken with a certain quality or attitude of awareness. This conscious awareness differentiates the experience of imagination (whether conveyed through auditory and visual imagery, or activities such as automatic writing or dancing, or less translatable experiences of imagination) from daydreams and hallucinations.

The way a phenomenon is viewed and/or entered into, as well as the initial choice of phenomenon, reflects the attitudes and beliefs of the experiencer. So while the history of psychology reveals the phenomena being studied, the way it reveals it, what it reveals of it, what it deduces from what it reveals, and what uses it has in mind for those deductions reflect something about the particular myths which psychology values and views from. In this history we will be concerned with both our primary topic, waking dreams and the imaginal, and the reflections cast into it by its researchers. To discriminate these is essential to an imaginal psychology—for otherwise we continue to base a psychology on our own reflections, mistaking them for the imaginal's.

The mythopoetic and creative functions of the unconscious:
Frederic Myers and Theodore Flournoy[1]

Hypnosis became a basic approach to the "unconscious" mind in the 1800's. Hypnosis (coming from the Greek word *hypnos*, meaning sleep) was considered by the mesmerists as a kind of sleep having various levels characterized by different experiences. "Under hypnosis" the subject, among other things, could have access to unconscious memories and imagery. Du Potet claimed to be able to have his subjects remain aware of and to remember the occurrences while hypnotized (Ellenberger, 1970:120). If so, his subjects probably experienced waking dreams, i.e. were aware of and remembered dreamlike symbolic phenomena. In most cases, however, the hypnotized subject was not in a conscious state of awareness. His state of induced hypnotic sleep was not unlike the self-induced trance states of mediums who often did not remember the contents of their trance experience.

The parallels between these two states were drawn in the 1850's. The psychologically-minded scientific community turned their attention to spiritism (the attempt to converse with disembodied spirits through a medium). Automatic writing, supposedly resulting from the medium's contact, while in trance, with a spirit (*ibid.*, 120-1, 399), was their primary source of data. Most often the mediums simply found themselves writing without thinking or planning what they would write. They believed themselves to be handing over the pen to a deceased person who used their hand to convey a message of importance.

The early psychologists William James (1885) and F. Myers (1885, 1886-7) came to understand such writing as a "means of access to the unconscious" (Ellenberger, 1970:121). Since psychology was becoming based on the data derived from just such an access, many of the spiritist methodologies were used as scientific procedures for investigating the "unconscious" of psychiatric patients. Du Potet, for instance, would draw a white chalk circle in the middle of a black floor and ask his patients to stare into it until they experienced visions or hallucinations. Mirror, crystal ball, and water gazing, formerly the media for the visions of diviners, now became used psychotherapeutically. Patients, as in Du Potet's method, were simply asked to

---

[1]For most of this history of Myers, Flournoy and Janet I am indebted to the scholarship of Henri Ellenberger (*The Discovery of the Unconscious*, 1970).

stare into a crystal ball or some such item and relate the visual images or dramatic play that they observed there to the doctor.

In the 1880s Myers and others of the Society for Psychical Research concluded that these methods were, as automatic writing had already been found, a "means for detecting subconscious material" (*ibid.*, 121). From his work dealing with the material arising from the "subconscious" of mediums and others, Myers postulated three functions of the "subliminal self": the inferior, superior and mythopoetic functions. He described the mythopoetic function as the unconscious tendency to weave fantasies. It is a " 'middle region' of the subliminal self where a strange fabrication of inner romances perpetually goes on" (*ibid.*, 314, 318).

Theodore Flournoy (1854-1920), a disciple of Wundt's, studied this mythmaking propensity of the unconscious in what was reputed to be the re-enactment of past lives and other experiences of mediums. He came to feel that the weaving of myths goes on continuously in the unconscious. The states of dreaming, daydreaming, "somnambulism, hypnosis, possession, medium[istic] trance, mythomania, [and] certain delusions" reveal the underlying fictions within the unconscious (*ibid.*, 318). Flournoy's observation of the mythopoetic activity of the unconscious led him also to delineate several functions of the unconscious. The "creative function" of the unconscious he saw as that which enables one to receive insights and widsom not attributable to the conscious personality. For instance, "he describes a young mother who from time to time dictated philosophical fragments that were far above the scope of her interests and knowledge" (*ibid.*, 317). Flournoy felt that the unconscious also had a protective function which would offer creatively warning and comfort. Other functions he observed in the unconscious activity of the mediums he studied were a compensatory or wish-fulfilling function and a ludic or play function (*ibid.*, 317).

The Renaissance concentration on imagination and fantasy[1] was revived in the Romantic period, partly as a reaction to the "controlled rationalism" of the eighteenth century (Singer, 1966:8-9).[2] The idea

---

[1]See Montaigne's *Essais* (1581), and Muratori's *On the Power of Human Imagination* (transl. title, 1745) for treatment of imagination and the creative unconscious in the Renaiassance.

[2]The work of Blake, Goethe, Hoffmann, Novalis, Coleridge, de Quincey, Poe, Hawthorne, Melville, Baudelaire, Mallarmé show the sensitivity of the Romantic tradition to inner fantasy. In music Schumann's song cycles, Berlioz's *Symphonie Fantastique*, and Tchaikovsky's *Symphony No. 1* ("Winter Daydreams") can be suggested to illuminate the valued creative introspection of that time (Singer, 1966:8).

of the creative nature of the unconscious revealed during each of these
early periods was a concept Flournoy, as well as Galton (1907) and
Myers, drew upon and sought to illuminate in their "psychological"
work. This simultaneous study of the creative and mythopoetic
functions of the unconscious had the possibility of revealing many
techniques and attitudes of therapeutic value. Unfortunately psychiatry's preoccupation with psychopathology shed a different, less creative
light on the unconscious. The mythmaker of the individual was often
seen as a culprit possessing the person, forcing on him delusions and
fears, superstitions and maladapted world views. Not until the work of
C. G. Jung is the creative functioning of the mythmaker-within fully
reinstated in the history of psychiatry. However, even after Jung's
theoretical statement, in the form of his analytical psychology, there
persisted a de-valuing attitude towards the unconscious psyche and its
imaginative processes — one that sees its manifestations as symptoms to
be eradicated or almost as food to be taken in, consumed and digested
by the conscious personality for its own uses.

L'abaissement du niveau mental: Pierre Janet

In the work of Pierre Janet (1859-1947), the two prevailing methods of
exploring the unconscious — hypnosis and spiritist procedures — were
notably combined. His work using these methods with patients
diagnosed as hysterical contributed to the evolving thesis that the
unconscious consists of one or more sub-personalities ("di-psychism" or
"poly-psychism"), "images" or "ideas". Through allowing the mythopoetic function[1] to become manifest the contents of the unconscious
parts were believed to be able to express themselves in symbolic terms.
  Pierre Janet sought to discover in his patients the fundamental
idea(s) or image(s) at the basis of their delirium. His term "partial
automatism" denoted a part of the person which is "split off from the
awareness of the personality and [which] follows an autonomous, subconscious development" (Ellenberger, 1970:359). These split off parts
were called "subconscious fixed ideas" and "simultaneous or successive
psychological existences." The split off parts of the personality became
separate realities, Janet observed, with which the patient interacted.

---

[1]Janet called this "mythopoetic function," "la function fabulatrice" — a term later
borrowed by Henri Bergson.

Often this interaction, resulting for instance in "hysterical fits," would interfere with the patient's adaptation to the more "common reality." Janet believed that it was not sufficient simply to make this other mythic realm of personality conscious. He felt it must be destroyed or changed by means of "dissociation" or "transformation" (*ibid.*, 373).

He developed several ways of combining spiritist practices with hypnosis to allow the autonomous personality or idea(s) to be known. In the first, he would get the hypnotized patient's conscious attention absorbed in some distraction and would then slip a pen into his hand. He would begin to write "automatically"; i.e., without conscious thought or interference, the unconscious was believed to unburden its story in the writing. He found that he could divide the content of such automatic writing into two categories: "on the one side the roles played by the subject in order to please the hypnotist; on the other side the unknown personality, which can manifest itself spontaneously, particularly as a return to childhood" (*ibid.*, 358-9).

On one such occasion Janet found that a patient, Lucie, had a second personality who seemed to be constantly reliving an episode which had happened when she was seven years old (Janet, 1888: 238-79). Such examples are not rare in his writings. In the case of Madame D. (Janet, 1892) he modified his technique to "automatic talking." A third technique, also showing the influence of the spiritists, was crystal gazing while hypnotized (Janet, 1897). Janet believed that the inner conflicts, hidden identities and scenes with which the personality was dealing were projected into the ball and experienced as images and scenes coming from the ball. Janet reports that he even had one patient whose images could at will leave the ball, and become projected onto a paper where the patient could then draw the development of his "hallucination" (Virel and Fretigny, 1968). These phenomena arose during what Janet termed an "abaissement du niveau mental," a lowering of conscious activity. This state of consciousness, where the subject is removed from his usual preoccupations with sense data and thoughts, has parallels in other cultures, as we have seen. In the other examples, however, the emerging material is valued in and of itself—for indeed, it comes not from the "unconscious" but from a world connected with no less than the gods and the spirits.

Janet appreciated the dramatic quality of the imaginal. He observed his patients being caught up in scenes where they interacted with a variety of characters in different places. He decided to simply become another character influencing the progression of dramatic action.

Marie, a patient who suffered from blindness in the left eye, claimed that the affliction had existed from birth. Janet knew differently. He had found through hypnotic age regression that the patient saw through both eyes when she was five years old. He went about uncovering the traumatic events around the period when her eyesight was lost. He found out, by putting Marie in a somnambulistic state, that when she was six years old, "in spite of her cries," she had been made to sleep with a child who had impetigo on the entire left side of the face. Since that time Janet ascertained that Marie had suffered from anaesthesia of the left side of her face and blindness in the left eye. Through fantasy

[I] put her back with the child who had so horrified her; I made her believe that the child is very nice and does not have impetigo (she is half-convinced. After two re-enactments of this scene I get the best of it); she caresses without fear the imaginary child. The sensitivity of the left eye reappears without difficulty, and when I wake her up, Marie sees clearly with the left eye.

                                                                                    Janet, 1889

Gradually through the intervention of the doctor the patient is able to befriend the image that has "blinded" her with fright, and impaired her adaptation to reality. Through the re-living of the trauma and a substitution of a different image and attitude the patient is able to transform the fantasy of the event such that it is no longer in a position of severe opposition to her conscious personality.

Another patient, Justine, had a fear of cholera and would shout repeatedly "Cholera . . . it's taking me!" after which an hysterical crisis would ensue. Janet learned to enter the drama of her crisis in a dialogue fashion. "When the patient cried, 'Cholera! He will take me!' Janet answered, 'Yes, he holds you by the right leg!' and the patient withdrew that leg. Janet then asked, 'Where is he, your cholera?' to which she would reply, 'Here! See him, he's bluish and he stinks!' " (Ellenberger, 1970:367). By entering into the fantasy with her Janet could obtain a description of her experience as well as assure himself of a position from which he, as a part of the drama, could also influence it. We see this process in other forms of psychotherapy, where the doctor enters the patient's drama and through his presence and "insight" helps to alter the patient's relation to the traumatic events which inhibit their "preferred" development. Here Janet accomplished this through having the patient relate the event on an imaginative level where the doctor could enter into the myth and help the patient change the basic structure of the experience. This was accomplished through the media of fantasy, not interpretation. He tried to break down, to dissolve, the fantasy through substitution: "suggestions of a gradual transformation of the hallucinatory picture." "The naked corpse [which Justine visualized next to her] was provided with clothes and identified with a Chinese general whom Justine had been greatly impressed to see at the Universal Exposition" (*ibid.*, 367-8). Janet was gradually able, through suggestions, to make the general comical rather than frightening. The whole treatment, more complicated than presented here, lasted a year.

From these examples it can be noted that the patients Janet worked with, primarily diagnosed as hysterical, experienced inward dramas, similar to dreams, that, through a lowering of conscious attention, could be elicited and shared with the doctor. The resulting fantasies expressed the other than "worldly" personalities, situations and ideas (believed to be contained in the unconscious) that the patient lived with. They were primarily understood as results of actual traumatic events and were believed to express the condition of infirmity needing to be dealt with. In a variety of ingenious ways the doctor could enter into the expressed fantasy with the patient and slowly alter the nature of the symbolic situation into which so much of the patient's energy and attention was contained. This transforming and alteration of the images in the fantasy is an important precursor of later French and German schools of the therapeutic use of directed daydreams (to be discussed in the next chapter). The fact remains, which Freud later took up, that the drama the patient was involved in was not just a rehearsal of a memory. It had an independent nature to it. The doctor intervened in this imaginal setting and started re-directing characters, firing some, introducing new parts and feeling tones, even throwing away the script and using his own. The imaginal structure of action and image were radically disrupted according to the wishes of an "outsider." It is important to think about what is lost here and what is gained.

Free association: Sigmund Freud

Breuer had evidenced the cathartic value of hypnagogic imagery in the famous case of Anna O. In Freud's and Breuer's *Studies on Hysteria* (1895), they note that in catharses where old memories are re-lived, the imagery is primarily visual, "often nearly hallucinatory in intensity." Through the use of hypnosis Freud would encourage his patients to have such visual images in order to facilitate the re-living of what he supposed were repressed traumatic events in their early life.

In 1892 Freud dispensed with hypnotism for the first time and used a "concentration" technique. Bernheim had stressed that things recovered during hypnosis were only *apparently* forgotten afterwards and that, with the forceful suggestion of the physician, the patient could regain them in his regular state of consciousness. Freud hypothesized that this should be equally true for the forgotten memories of hysteria (Jones, 1961:154). In the case of Frl. Elizabeth von R., who was not susceptible to hypnotism, Freud had the patient lie down with eyes closed; he then asked her to concentrate her attention on a particular symptom and any memories that might surround it, and to form an image relevant to the time when the symptom first appeared. When progress was not forthcoming Freud would press her forehead with his hand. He assured the patient that when he lifted his hand a memory or thought would form — perhaps as a visual image — and that all the details of the image and the associated emotions should be reported (Horowitz, 1970:259-60). Sometimes it would take four presses before success, but Freud reported that images and emotions did not fail to appear. This led him to acknowledge that

. . . it is possible for thought-processes to become conscious through a reversion to visual residues [and] in many people, this seems to be a favorite method . . . . Thinking in pictures . . . approximates more closely to unconscious processes than does thinking in words and it is unquestionably older than the latter both ontogenetically and phylogenetically.

Were, however, these thoughts in the form of pictures really just the same as thoughts? Did they arise from the same place and express the same things only in a different form?

One day Frl. Elisabeth "reproved him for interrupting her flow of thought by his questions" (Jones, 1961:154). Freud succumbed to her reproof and allowed her to report her stream of thought without his interference. "The more confidence he acquired in the belief that relaxing conscious censoring would inevitably lead to the important memories, the less need had he to urge, press, or direct the patients' memories" (*ibid.*, 155). The early work with imagery was de-emphasized as Freud changed altogether from the use of hypnosis to "free association." He did this not only because of the unhypnotizability of certain patients but because he came to see that the state of hypnosis concealed what he felt were the most essential elements of the psychotherapeutic process—the transference and the resistances. This shift from trying to evoke imagery to free-association may have been ill-advised, as Jerome Singer points out (1971a). Subsequent research (Reyher and Smeltzer, 1968) has shown that more "primary process material" and associated affect, more direct drive expression and less defensiveness, can be correlated with experiences of visual imagery than from their verbal associates. This suggests that indeed visual imagery in not simply "thinking but in the form of pictures" but has different qualities than verbal cognition.

The idea, however, that analysis was completed when free-association was spontaneous makes it clear that Freud valued the ability to allow a free stream of images—whether they be verbal or visual. The patient was told that the success of the psychoanalysis depended upon his noticing and telling everything that passed through his mind. He was told not to suppress a single idea because it seemed unimportant, irrelevant or nonsensical (Freud, 1965:192).[1] Ideally, one learns to allow the contents of the unconscious to arise without pre-judgment. Such communication, whether implicit or explicit, has the effect of encouraging and training patients to allow and to be aware of whatever arises in one's stream of consciousness. The setting of the psychoanalytic session—the position of the analyst out of the patient's view, the quiet darkened room, the reclining patient—all maximized the opportunity for imagination imagery and their associated affects to

---

[1]Ernest Jones (1963:156-6), Freud's major biographer, hypothesizes that Freud's "obscure intuition" that free association was connected not only to the undoing of the phenomenon of repression but also to the meaning of the content of the repression had an interesting source, which Freud himself never remembered. Freud related that the first author he was ever absorbed in was Ludwig Borne, whose collected works he had received as a present when he was fourteen. Among these was an essay entitled "The art of becoming an original writer in three days" (1923). It concluded the following:

Here follows the practical prescription that I promised. Take a few sheets of paper and for three days in sucession write down, without any falsification of hypocrisy, everything that comes into your head. Write what you think of yourself, of your women, of the Turkish war, of Goethe, of the Fonk criminal case, of the Last Judgment, of those senior to you in authority—and when the three days are over you will be amazed at what novel and startling thoughts have welled up in you. That is the art of becoming an original writer in three days.

This example points to not only a commonality in the source of art and analysis but of a rudimentary methodology—in terms of training oneself to gain access to the "unconscious" or the "imagination"—as well.

arise.[1] With the emphasis on verbal free association, however, much of the information which might have been gleaned about the role of the visual image in psychoanalytic treatment has been lost. As Singer points out (1971a:167) the implicitness rather than the explicitness of the analyst's approval for visual imaging (through, for example, the reporting of dreams which often entails a visual re-living of the dream) has produced rather unsystematic ways of training the patient in the use of his image making faculty.

Such failure to be explicit may have been due to an ambiguous attitude towards what others had termed the creative and mythopoetic functions of the individual. For though Freud was respectful of creativity, as shown in his statement "before the problem of the creative artist analysis must, alas, lay down its arms" (1952), he was also "suspicious of fantasy processes and tended to emphasize their defensive nature" (Jerome Singer, 1971:169). Because Freud regarded the unconscious as a repository for forgotten and repressed experiences, the contents (images) were reducible to infantile tendencies, repressed because of their incompatible character with the prevailing moral influences in the child's environment (Jung, 1953:127). The "image was but a symptom of something else, which again reduced the imaginal to a way of being alien to its nature and structure" (Durand, 1971:90). Freud made the common mistake of advancing a proposition and then adopting a methodology that by its nature produces results which concur with the proposition. If we envision the "unconscious" to be filled with a certain kind of concern and yet it does not express that concern, then our claiming that it is hiding what it is really concerned about (our hypothesis) under what we observe it to be expressing (manifest content), covers over the fact that we are actually studying our own hypotheses and beliefs thinking they are the dream's. The dream and its images are lost. The image was not seen as who it appeared to be but rather who we felt it was, even though we did not think we knew anything about it. One can say that by nature the image is sneaky and deceitful, but once that is our hypothesis we can find the "true nature" of the image to be anything we further attribute it to be. We can then argue that whatever else is seen to be "given" by the image is merely meaningless camouflage, supplied by the image itself in order to guard its reality (our attributions, that is).

---

[1]Subsequent research has confirmed that subjects lying down report more vivid imagery (Segal and Glickman, 1967) and earlier and more frequent memories (Berdach and Bakan, 1967) than subjects sitting up.

Freud's method of investigating the unconscious (free association), however, greatly contributed to the life of the image and the fantasy behind it. By teaching the individual to allow his inner life to emerge without conscious censorship, the image and the image maker could not fail to have an increasingly receptive audience. Freud was able to draw parallels between the unconscious material that arose and myths of other times. Though he did not seek to evoke material directly from the imagination as Jung came to do, he had a sensitivity for recognizing the myths present in the actions, "memories," and thoughts of his patients as well as in their dreams. He discovered that the "memories" of sexual mishandling by parents, reported by so many of his patients, were not memories of actual events at all. They were wishes and fantasies. This meant that the childhood that analysis came to deal with was not so much the one that dwells in the actual events of a historical childhood of traumatic events, but the one that lives amid the fantasies and wishes that constellate around the actual, and in addition to the actual. So although Freud's technique did not specifically seek to evoke the imaginal, it was part of the substance of his work and a primary means through which his understanding was advanced.

Two early Freudians, Warren and Silberer, became interested in the half-dream state from their own experiences. The following were their first accounts of waking dream phenomena.

In a dark room with eyes closed a definite scene will appear before me in apparently as bright an illumination as daylight. I seem to be looking through my closed eyelids. The scene is apparently as real, as vivid, as detailed as an actual landscape. The phenomenon lasts not more than a minute. I have never been able to hold it long enough to notice any change or movement. It is a scene — not a happening. The two most vivid cases occurred quite automatically, either as I was dosing off and for some reason came back to consciousness, or immediately on waking during the night.

Once the scene was a tropical landscape, with palm trees and a body of water. It was clear and detailed and appeared so real that I was suprised to find it unchanged by winking.

Warren, 1921

The origin of my observations can be briefly told. One afternoon (after lunch) I was lying on my couch. Though extremely sleepy, I forced myself to think through a problem of philosophy, which was to compare the views of Kant and Schopenhauer concerning time. In my drowsiness I was unable to sustain their ideas side by side. After several unsuccessful attempts, I once more fixed Kant's argument in my mind as firmly as I could and turned my attention to Schopenhauer's. But when I tried to reach back to Kant, his argument was gone again, and beyond recovery. The futile effort to find the Kant record which was somehow misplaced in my mind suddenly represented itself to me—as I was lying there with my eyes closed, as in a dream—as a perceptual symbol. I am asking a morose secretary for some information; he is leaning over his desk and disregards me entirely; he straightens up for a moment to give me an unfriendly and rejecting look.

The vividness of the unexpected phenomenon surprised, indeed almost frightened me. I was impressed by the appropriateness of this unconsciously selected symbol. I sensed what might be the conditions for the occurrence of such phenomena, and decided to be on the lookout for them and even to attempt to elicit them.

                                                                    Silberer, 1951:195-6

The sense of discovery these men share shows how alien such inner experiences of visual imagery had become to their culture and yet how a new movement, psychology, with its freedom for introspection and free association, allowed for observation that revealed this human capacity. Herbert Silberer indeed followed his conviction to "be on the lookout" for such "autosymbolic phenomenon." Through such self-experiments he came to understand the hypnogogic image as relating an important symbolic representation of the state of the dreamer (1912).

Active imagination: C. G. Jung

It was primarily through his own experience of the unconscious that Jung came to formulate his ideas concerning active imagination and the imaginal realm. After his split with Freud, Jung decided he would try to adopt an open attitude towards the unconscious, unencumbered by pre-thought theory, in an attempt to discover more about it. Jung pledged, "Since I know nothing at all I shall do whatever occurs to me" (1961:133). From 1912-1917 he acknowledged his promise by allowing the unconscious to reveal itself, working earnestly to record all that had happened.[1] He found himself engaged in spontaneous activities— building sand castles, hewing stone, painting mandalas and pictures, seeing visual images and holding dialogues with unconscious figures. These activities offered him a "rite d'entrée" to the unconscious, as had automatic writing and crystal ball gazing to mediums and to Janet's patients. He found, as had Flournoy, that the unconscious is always in a sense dreaming, mythmaking. Because our attention is

---

[1] I refer the reader to Jung's own excellent account of his experiences during this period, "Confrontations with the unconscious," in *Memories, Dreams and Reflections* (1961).

outwardly directed we fail to notice the mythic dreams being constantly spun.

In order for the imaginal world to come into our awareness, Jung found that we must look for and at its images in a particular way.

> . . . *looking*, psychologically, brings about the activation of the object; it is as if something is emanating from one's spiritual eye that evokes or activates the object of one's vision. The English verb, to look at, does not convey this meaning, but the German *betrachten*, which is an equivalent, means also to make pregnant, but it is used only for animals. . . . So to look or concentrate upon a thing, *betrachten*, gives the quality of being pregnant to the object. And if it is pregnant, then something is due to come out of it; it is alive, it produces, it multiplies. That is the case with any fantasy image; one concentrates upon it, and then finds that one has great difficulty keeping the thing quiet, it gets restless, it shifts, something is added, or it multiplies itself; one fills it with living power and it becomes pregnant.
>
> Jung, 1967:100-1

This way of "looking," Jung showed in his researches, has an ancient and rich history.[1]

> In antiquity when a man had to direct a prayer to the statue of the god, he stepped upon a stone that was erected at its side to enable people to shout their prayer into the ear, so that the god would hear them; and then he stared at the image until the god nodded his head or opened or shut his eyes or answered in some way. You see this was an abbreviated method of active imagination, concentrating upon the image until it moved; and in that moment the god gave a hint, his assent or his denial or any other indication, and that is the *numinosum*.[2]
>
> Jung, 1937:2

Interpretations of the images that attempted to resolve them into memory complexes, referring back to actual events and people, and underlying instinctual components (Freud's objective method of dream interpretation) no longer seemed to fit. Jung heard another life going on within, which had heretofore been disregarded by Freud. It could be heard only if the unconscious was approached with the possibility that it was purposive, not only repressive; only if the form of questioning about it preceded in the form of "what is it trying?", not "what is it hiding?" (Progoff, 1963:71). Rather than being just a "reactive mirror reflection" (Jung, 1953:185) of conscious activities the unconscious seemed to have an objective existence of its own, with its

---

[1]See especially Jung's writings on alchemy.

[2]For further research into this phenomenon see Jaynes, *The Origin of Consciousness and the Breakdown of the Bicameral Mind* (tbp).

own values and ways of knowing — no less significant than the conscious personality. The image was able to express that "as yet unknown" by the conscious personality. Jung observed, as had Flournoy, that the unconscious performed some extraordinary tasks. It seemed at times to serve in a compensatory fashion to ego-consciousness — as if it sought to maintain a dynamic psychic equilibrium by concerning itself (in dreams and fantasies) with those underdeveloped and missing parts of the conscious personality. It anticipated "in its symbols future conscious processes," recognized consciously overlooked personal motives and meanings in daily situations, drew undrawn conclusions, admitted unadmitted criticisms and affects (*ibid.*, 177-8).

In Jung's subjective method of analysis one seeks to see the symbolic contents not as references solely to memory and real things in the external world but to different elements or parts of the person himself. The images or people in an active imagination or dream are understood as possibly referring to a real person or object in the outside world (the objective level of interpretation); but more importantly the image is believed to appear because it represents an unrecognized or undervalued part or attitude of the person dreaming or imagining. For instance if one experienced the image of a critical woman who seeks to undervalue what the person is doing, this might indeed be related to the subject's mother or another woman in his life. But, Jung claimed, the critical voice has become a part of the person himself. Once this happens it gets into one's life situations as well as one's dreams and fantasies. The myth seeks to express itself. Realizing that the mother embodies this attitude is good, but one must now (in the present) deal with that attitude within (and without, when projected). The external referent may disappear, the mother may die, but the introjected attitude remains with the person as before. The image moves one not only back into the conscious world but draws one into its land — the "archetypal," the "collective unconscious." The attitude that the image may represent belongs also to an archetypal dimension, which is more than the individual situation. It cannot be reduced to the subjective or objective. It amplifies itself, when given the opportunity, allowing one access to the world of the image. The symbol can never be grasped in terms of what we already know. The very nature of it is to take us beyond.

Jung found that patients "spontaneously reported dreams and fantasies. [He] would merely ask 'What occurs to you in connection with that?' or 'How do you mean that, where does that come from, what do you think about it?' The interpretations seemed to follow of their own accord from the patient's replies and associations." Soon he "realized that it is right to take the dreams in this way as the basis of interpretation, for that is how dreams are intended. They are the facts from which we must proceed" (Jung, 1961:170-1). Unlike Freud who saw the latent content of the dream as the meaningful portion, Jung gave attention to the manifest content—to the images in and of themselves. This connection between the image and the meaning was central to Jung's psychology.

. . . interpretation must guard against making use of any other viewpoints than those manifestly given by the content itself. If someone dreams of a lion, the correct interpretation can lie only in the direction of the lion; in other words, it will be essentially an *amplification* of this image. Anything else would be an inadequate and incorrect interpretation, since the image "lion" is a quite unmistakable and sufficiently positive presentation.

Jung, 1954:par. 162

Once the image relates to the conscious mind of the individual its meaning, the unconscious position towards something, the individual must do something about its "moral" connotation. That is, one must not just seek out the other side, one must bring it into a relation with his living. Jung understood this as "a moral necessity." It is not easy to give up parts of our life, the way it is now, in order to accommodate other aspects of our being. In fact the difficulty of this is too often minimized. Even if one is unconscious of something, however, that something still lives in the person and through him in the world. Jung envisioned the process of growing into consciousness, as a progression towards becoming responsible for one's self, for what comes to be through one's living. Jung's notions of the purposive and creative aspects of the unconscious (not unlike those of the Romantics) as well as its objective status, required a different attitude toward and way of working with the unconscious than previously had been created by modern psychology. An attitude was needed through which the unconscious and conscious could work together; an attitude that was a "combined function of conscious and unconscious elements, or, as in mathematics, a common function of real and imaginary quantities" (Jung, 1971: par. 184).

I have called this process in its totality the *transcendent function*, "function" being here understood not as a basic function but as a complex function made up of other functions, and "transcendent" not as denoting a metaphysical quality but merely the fact that this function facilitates a transition from one attitude to another. The raw material shaped by thesis and antithesis, and in the shaping of which the opposites are united, is the living symbol. Its profundity of meaning is inherent in the raw material itself, the very stuff of the psyche, transcending time and dissolution; and its configuration by the opposites ensures its sovereign power over all the psychic functions.

Ibid., par. 828

Through his own experiences Jung found that he was able to wilfully withdraw his awareness from distractions and enter into the world that the mythopoetic spins. These experiences differed from nightly dreams, however, and in so doing they provided an exciting alternative method of establishing contact with the imaginal. This was of immense importance to Jung. He had found that using dreams as the only "road to the unconscious" was unsatisfactory in several ways. He felt that he himself could not adequately interpret his own dreams . . . nor his patients theirs. The dream, originating in the state of sleep,

bears all the characteristics of an "abaissement du niveau mental" (Janet) or of low energy-tension: logical discontinuity, fragmentary character, analogy formation, superficial associations of the verbal, clang or visual type, condensations, irrational expressions, confusion, etc. With an increase in energy-tension [as in the half-dream or waking states] the dreams acquire a more ordered character; they become dramatically composed and reveal clear sense connections and the valency of association increases.

Jung, 1960:77

The dream does not provide for direct dialogue between the conscious and the unconscious. It is the acts of recalling, recording and associating to the dream that provide the points of meeting. In these activities, however, there is a discontinuity even in terms of time. There is a lack of balance and simultaneous interpenetration. When one is dreaming the unconscious and its attitudes have the upper hand. When one is recalling and interpreting the dream, most often the conscious ego is inflicting its attitudes on the dream. The confrontation with the unconscious through dreams is not often a direct experience, full of affect, but a remembering often distorted by the translation from symbolic visual terms to words, from their own terms into the ego's. The dreamer has limited control over his dreams (except by learning to recall them and in some cases to influence and to incubate them).[1] They happen to him. If he has no other direct active way of getting in touch with the unconscious, he must simply

---

[1]Henry Reed (1974), Richard Carroll (1973), and Carl Meier (Jung Institute, Zurich) have done some fascinating and encouraging work in the area of incubating dreams.

wait for a dream. Some maintain it is hopeless to wait for a dream if one has drifted toward a wrong attitude — for wrong attitudes can in some instances keep "the releasing dream" away (Hannah, 1967:21).

There needed to be a more active means of approaching the experience of mutual penetration of the unconscious and conscious worlds. Jung felt this need particularly for his patients in the latter part of or after the termination of their formal analysis. He found that the ability he had observed in himself to allow the unconscious and conscious to speak together while awake could also be helped to develop naturally in the second half of his patients' analyses. This ability of actively imagining also would emerge at critical times in analysis when the polarities of the psyche sought some image of integration.

He had found that the acts of allowing the images to arise while conscious and aware, and of participating with them, invested "the bare fantasy with an element of reality, which lends it greater weight and greater driving power" (Jung, 1954b:par 106). Through the use of awareness and participation the daydream, "passive fantasy," was transformed, as was the conscious personality. The images became psychically real.

The piece that is being played does not want merely to be watched impartially, it wants to compel [the imaginer's] participation. If [the imaginer] understands that his own drama is being performed on this inner stage, he cannot remain indifferent to the plot and its dénouement.

If you recognize your own involvement, you yourself must enter into the process with your personal reactions, just as if you were one of the fantasy figures, or rather, as if the drama being enacted before your eyes were real. It is a psychic fact that this fantasy is happening and it is as real as you — as a psychic entity — are real.

Jung, 1954b:par. 706,753

Active imagination was not a part of the therapeutic hour. Jung would often let it arise naturally from the patient's own work with his dream material. Othertimes he would make more direct suggestions.

The point is that you start with any image, for instance, just with that yellow mass in your dream. Contemplate it and carefully observe how the picture begins to unfold or to change. Don't try to make it into something, just do nothing but observe what its spontaneous changes are. Any mental picture you contemplate in this way will sooner or later change through a spontaneous association that causes a slight alteration of the picture. You must carefully avoid impatient jumping from one subject to another. Hold fast to the one image you have chosen and wait until it changes by itself. Note all these changes and eventually step into the picture yourself, and if it is a speaking figure at all then say what you have to say to that figure and listen to what he or she has to say.

Thus you can analyse your unconscious but also give your unconscious a chance to analyse yourself, and therewith you gradually create the unity of conscious and unconscious without which there is no individuation at all. It you apply this method, then I can come in as an occasional adviser, but if you don't apply it, then my existence is of no use for you.

Jung, A letter to Mr. O., 1973:459-60

It is in the creation of fantasies that we find the unitive function we are seeking. All the elements engaged by the active tendencies flow into the imagination. The imagination has, it is true, a poor reputation among psychologists. . . . Imagination holds in itself an irreducible value, for it is the psychic function whose roots ramify at the same time in the contents of the conscious mind and of the unconscious, in the collective as in the individual.

Jung, 1953:286

Jung came to believe that turning willfully to the unconscious while awake, "purposive introversion," was the "basic condition for the act of creation" (1959a:180) and the integration of the personality.

This purposive introversion, the meditative attitude discussed in Chapter 2, is the means by which one can initiate active or creative imagination. Although the contents of this process are "expressed in the same picture-language as the dream, they are, nevertheless, nearer to consciousness, and as such more readily interpreted. Furthermore, active imagination, in which consciousness [through awareness] and the unconscious have collaborated, does not call for the same degree of criticism as does the dream, but primarily for understanding; and in this respect is a considerable advance on dream analysis as a means of arriving at a working partnership between consciousness and the unconscious" (Peterson, 1971:162).[1]

This does not mean that Jungian analysis always leads to active imagination. Often the goal of the person in analysis is different from the process that Jung described as the individuation, and for which active imagination was considered to be so important. At a lecture in Zurich (Spring, 1951; see Hannah, 1967:13) Jung gave six reasons for introducing active imagination to the patient.

---

[1] The question of whether or not to interpret active imaginations, and if so how, is a controversial and crucial one to which we will continue to return. In contrast to Peterson, however, Humbert (1971:105) says "the analyst does not participate and, particularly, does not interpret. It would be wrong to treat the reports presented by active imagination as if they were dreams, for in dreams consciousness does not at all play the same part."

1) When it is obvious that the unconscious is overflowing with fantasies
2) To reduce the number of dreams when there are too many
3) When there are not enough dreams remembered
4) When someone feels or seems to be under indefinable influences, under a sort of spell
5) When the adaptation to life has been injured
6) When someone falls into the same hole again and again

Active imagination was felt to enable an individual to take responsibility for himself by providing him with a means of coming to terms with his own unconscious material. In attempting active imagination and the subsequent processes of seeing the relation of the material to one's life the patient is given the "inestimable advantage of assisting the analyst with his own resources and of breaking a dependence which is often felt as humiliating. It is a way of attaining liberation by one's own efforts and of finding courage to be oneself" (Jung, 1960:91). This has a profound effect on the phenomenon of transference. Jung understood the transference not as a projection of infantile erotic fantasies, but rather as "a metaphorical expression of the not consciously realized need for help in a crisis" (*ibid.*, 74). Jung asked himself what kind of mental and moral attitude the patient must have in order to receive the help he needs from within. Once again "the answer consists in getting rid of the separation between the conscious and unconscious" by recognizing the significance of contents of the unconscious in compensating the one-sidedness of consciousness. Analytical treatment can be described in these terms "as a readjustment of psychological attitude achieved with the help of the doctor" (*ibid.*, 72-3). Through analysis the patient is often able to acquire the psychological attitude necessary for active imagination. Through this he comes to learn to use his own directive principles and sources of inner guidance. In the beginning of analysis the analyst often takes on the role of the guide for the analysand. The myths within the patient and the doctor are projected into their relationship together—transference and countertransference. As the analysis progresses, however, the analysand becomes increasingly able to feel his portion of the drama and strength coming from within himself.

In analytical psychology the ability to actively imagine is seen as a sign that one has developed the "capacity to be alone, in a positive and creative sense, without isolation and without retreat from the outer world or absorption in a world of fantasy, or without otherwise being

cut off from outer relatedness" (Fordham, 1958:73). Jung believed it to
be the "touchstone by which one can tell whether someone is genuinely
aiming at psychological independence and individuation or whether
they are content to become a satellite, i.e., to push the responsibility
of their lives onto someone else" (Hannah, 1953:4-6).

In later stages of analysis, the objectification of images replaces the dreams. The
images anticipate the dreams, and so the dream-material begins to peter out. The
unconscious becomes deflated in so far as the conscious mind relates to it. Then you
get all the material in a creative form and this has advantages over dream-material. It
quickens the process of maturation, for analysis is a process of quickened maturation.

                                                                        Jung, 1968a:194

As Janet and Flournoy before him, Jung recognized the positive
expressive and communicative value of the inner myths and fantasies
of mediums and psychotics. The "successive psychological existences"
that Janet found living in the lives of his hysterical patients, Jung was
able to identify within himself. He became aware through his own self-
experiments that in fact the psyche itself—not just a part(s) of it that
may become exaggeratedly split off in hysterical or psychotic-like
crises—has an objective autonomous existence. The unconscious he
observed operated independently from the person we think of ourselves
as. Psychological integration in Jung's terms depended on the recognition of this independent objective psyche and the taking of active
steps to become aware of its values and qualities, its reactions and
needs. Instead of attempting to eradicate the subpersonalities or
independent ideas and images which arise, Jung believed that one
must come into closer relation to them. "Image is psyche." It must not
be abused. The allowing of oneself to participate with the images of the
unconscious through wilfully creating an *abaissement du niveau
mental* with sustained awareness and the recognition of the need to
live in a connection with the meaning of these movements and images,
was Jung's contribution to helping modern man have a way to become
at home once again with his soul and its imagination. The processes
of such dialogues and of allowing oneself to be moved, as we have seen,
were not in themselves new. But modern man needed a way to
recognize the need for this again, a method for beginning, and a
conceptual framework (a schema of the psyche) that could begin to
chart the way for him, encouraging him to travel in the imaginal. To
these needs Jung's work adeptly spoke.

Conclusion

As had others before them, the early psychologists discovered ways to elicit images through the cultivation of a half-dream state. They too viewed these waking dreams as coming from a source outside of who the person knows himself to be. For the psychologist, however, this source was not divine. It was the "subconscious"—an unknown region of the person lying *below,* not above. The people they observed having these visions were not honoured shamans or holy men, but mediums and hysterics. The contents of the visions were not guarded as being sacred knowledge through which healing and guidance were given, but were more often taken as the proof that something had gone wrong, was off the track (into superstition and delusion). Instead of wilfully attempting to establish the vision within the day world in order to bring one's activities into relation to it, the young psychology more often sought to elicit waking dreams in order to impose the seemingly more important day world on them.

Flournoy, however, was impressed by some of the activities of the "unconscious." It knew how to play, to create wonderful stories, to warn and comfort, and even to think often better than feeble conscious attempts. This sounded a bit more godlike. As Janet's work proved, this world of fantasy was surely present and, if one took a bit of patience and care, it would express just what it was experiencing and was up to. Janet and Jung both valued the ability of the unconscious to express itself dramatically in waking dreams. Jung, however, did not try to transform and destroy what arose as had Janet, but rather to bring the reality of the unconscious into the conscious' view.

In other times the world of visions was considered to be autonomous and was at least as, if not more, important than the material daily world. One went to it, prepared for it, and sacrificed to it. When a vision was brought into the day world, it was done so on the vision's own terms. It was brought into the activities of the day world not to abolish or to belittle the realm from which it came, but to allow the day world to pay tribute to it and to grow closer to it. Although there was a tendency with some of the early psychologists to see value in the world of images, one feels that it generally was not equal to the importance attributed to the non-dream world. There was a current created which drew the dream and the half-dream worlds into the conscious in an effort by the ego (of doctor and patient) to kill it, transform it, or use it for the more efficient functioning of the conscious personality.

Chapter 4

Waking Dreams in European Psychotherapy

The influence of the Romantics, Gaston Bachelard (in France), Flournoy, Janet and Jung was able to favorably prejudice European psychologists (especially clinicians) toward recognizing the value of the imagination in general and of mental imagery in specific as a means of its expression. This acceptance was relatively unperturbed by the growing self-consciousness of an increasingly behavioristic psychology toward its subject matter, operations, and intervening variables. It gave them the freedom to experiment with techniques using the patient's capacity to visually imagine and to be able to accept more easily their subsequent observations (Singer, 1971a:169). The mythopoetic and creative functions of the unconscious became working assumptions, taken as fact, freeing the psychotherapist to ask **not** *if* these functions or qualities of the "unconscious" could be used in effecting a cure, but *how* they could be used. Whereas Jung thought of active imagination as an activity to be primarily carried out while alone and usually only towards the end of and after termination of analysis, clinicians in France and Germany[1] explored the uses of fantasy as a *method* of *doing* therapy. A proliferation of techniques as well as theory concerning waking dreams has grown out of the accumulation of data from the therapeutic session.

Many arguments were advanced to express the advantages of using waking dreams as the central experience of the psychotherapeutic encounter. Most of these centered around four objections to traditional therapy: the limitations of verbal discourse, analytical interpretation

---

[1] I am indebted to Andre Virel and Roger Frétigny (1968) for much of this French and German history. Their work *L'Imagerie Mentale* shows clearly the unfortunate gap in communication between European and American psychotherapists, to which this chapter is particularly addressed.

and emphasis on the past, the high valuation of transference phe-nomena, and its consequent length of treatment. By dealing on a symbolic, non-verbal level the contents of the unconscious were believed to be more directly and adequately expressed. The image can reveal that which is being experienced but which often cannot yet be grasped or translated into words. The experience of waking dreams was considered useful both to patients who are not particularly analytical about their lives, who are not as amenable to orthodox analysis, and also to patients so analytically well-defended that a verbal rational method fails to be of aid. In both cases one does not have to depend on the patient's understanding of and ability to relay the unconscious situation, but rather the unconscious situation can be allowed to emerge itself through the imagery. While relating to the therapist his waking dream as it occurs, the patient is most often not attempting to analyze or interpret his experience. Such attempts, one soon finds, usually hinder, distort or stop the flow of images. Freedom from interpretations allows the patient to be relieved of the embarrass-ment and anxiety that would often occur simultaneously on a verbal level, thereby making communication more threatening.

The emphasis is not on interpreting the material, but on the experience of the imagination itself. Interpretation is believed to be of use to those who wish to make a study of the interconnections between their daily lives and the images of the unconscious. It is not believed to be sufficient, nor usually necessary, for a "cure." The cure depends on getting in touch with the fantasies and myths occurring within and to learn how on that symbolic level to move more freely. Although one can see and analyze the similarities between daily life and the imaginal, the connection between the two is assumed from the beginning. Free movement on one level affects the way one moves on the other. Since both, supposedly, arise from the unconscious, dealing with one's movement on that level is felt to be a more direct way of influencing one's being-in-the-world. Resistances—those impediments to movement lying between the patient and his full participation in life (signified by his ability to participate fully in the waking dream)—take a symbolic form which can be worked through on that level. There is an emphasis, foreshadowed by Janet's work, on learning new symbolic responses to the affect-producing situations and images in the waking dream so that the patient can gradually substitute what is considered to be "healthy response tendencies for the previously neurotic [move-ment impeding] responses of anxiety and avoidance" (Gerard, 1967b: 21).

Exactly how the myths that determine one's behavior evolved from the personal past is not considered as important as experiencing where one is in the present. Instead of immersion into the past, there is an active experience in the present — the past being dealt with by its influence in shaping the prevailing myths the individual is dealing with in the present. It is hoped that by training the patient to experience his fantasies from within, progress will not need to rest on his projections (and their subsequent withdrawal) into the therapeutic situation. The transference is often seen as an unnecessary dependence on the therapist that prolongs therapy and promotes a more passive, irresponsible attitude to one's unconscious contents.

Before the experiencing of unconscious visual and auditory images could be used as an effective therapeutic technique, many things had to be discovered: how to train the patient to relax, to separate his consciousness from its usual contents, to turn his awareness towards the movements of the imaginal; how to help him learn to enter into his imaginary body, to insert himself in the imaginary scene, to move within it, to encounter threatening images and to allow affect to arise; how to recognize and work with resistances; how or whether to interpret and analyze the waking dream; how to see the patient's experience in the imaginal realm in relation to the other aspects of his existence. Many individuals contributed to the recognition and partial solving of the technical and theoretical problems arising in the psychotherapeutic use of fantasy. The ways in which they envisioned the problems to begin with as well as their contributions to the "solutions" convey their attitudes toward the imagination, toward the relation between the conscious and the unconscious, and the desired goals of psychotherapeutic practice and technique. It seems in retrospect that although imagination and two of her many children, the visual and auditory image, were invited into the consulting room, the invitation was not all in her favor. She was often put to work to serve the will and whim, belief and interest, of the doctor and his patient.

Early contributions to the psychotherapeutic use of fantasy: Binet, Happich, Kretschmer, Schultz and Luthe, Frank, Guillerey, Caslant, Clark

In Germany it was Alfred Binet's "method of *provoked introspection*" that stimulated the Würzburg group first to consider the subject of imagery. Binet had his patients, through a *"dialogue method,"* talk to the visual images in their provoked introspection. He and Janet, both early proponents of dipsychism, believed that images arising from this introspection expressed the various unconscious sub-personalities of the patient. Carl Happich elaborated on Binet's early work by encouraging *"emergent images"* through the use of muscular relaxation, passivity of respiration, and meditation. He postulated that between the conscious and unconscious lies a zone, the *"meditative zone,"* in which "creations ripened in the unconscious appear to the mind's eye" (*geistiges Auge*). Happich (1932), in contrast to Freud's change in emphasis from imagery to free association, argued that the experience of imagery from the "meditative zone," not verbal abstraction, was necessary for personality changes. Happich attempted to stimulate such imagery by suggesting various landscapes for the patient to visit in his imagination (prairie, mountain, chapel, sitting by a fountain listening to the water).[1]

These landscapes were much later explored by Kretschmer for their symbolic significance and integrated into his idea of *"meditative techniques for psychotherapy."* He would introduce an initial image to serve as a point of departure and crystallization for other symbols related to that particular psychic realm.[2] Unlike many religious meditations centered on images or concepts, the suggestion of surroundings was not as well-defined, and personal as well as more universal archetypal imagery was encouraged to arise, leading one away from the initial image. For Kretschmer the important necessity was to bring the symbols which "expose internal psychic problems" into a higher (conscious or supraconscious) level of awareness. He felt that the "art of psychotherapy" depends on the stimulation of the "deeper levels of the unconscious" and can really only be described by the "unscientific term 'exorcism'" (Kretschmer, 1969:228). It is not clear what Kretschmer means by exorcism, but there is the indication that the contents of the imagination are brought up into the ego-world in an effort to separate them from their source.

Another group of researchers arrived at similar uses of waking dreams, not through the practice of introspection that was popular in psychology at that time, but through a bio-physical approach to consciousness. J. H. Schultz (Berlin), stimulated by Oskar Vogt's work

---

[1]Nachmansonn (1951) was doing similar work called *"experimental dreaming."*

[2]Kretschmer (1922) called the process of inner visualization *Bilderstreifendenken*, "thinking in the form of a movie".

on "autohypnotic" exercises, began in 1905 to study how hypnotherapy could be used without developing a passivity in the patient and a subsequent detrimental dependence on the therapist. Schultz noted in his hypnotic work that his patients experienced feelings of relaxation and heaviness in the extremities and then agreeable sensations of warmth. Instead of the therapist inducing a hypnotic state of consciousness that gave such physiological results, he had the patients suggest to themselves, to imagine that they were having, the physiological feelings which he had found would in turn produce the desired state of consciousness and physiological condition. Schultz and Luthe (1969) developed *"meditative exercises"* to be done in this *"autogenic state"* of relaxation. These involved *"progressive visualizations"* from "static uniform colors, to dynamic polymorph colors, to polychromatic patterns and simple forms, to objects, to transformation of objects and progressive differentiation of images, to film-strips, to multichromatic cinerama," or what might be similar to a waking dream. Through this training in relaxation and visualization the patient could gradually learn how to sustain complex imagery on his own and to use this for physical and psychological disturbances.

Ludwig Frank (1910) was, as Schultz and Luthe, discovering the importance of deep relaxation for the spontaneous occurrence of hypnagogic visions.[1] An outgrowth of Breuer's work with Anna O., Frank called his work the *"cathartic method."* The relation between relaxation and catharsis became important also to Schultz and Luthe. They believed that relaxation encouraged catharses and that these catharses, called "autogenic discharges" (the bodily components being emphasized), were results of the "self-normalizing activity of unknown brain mechanisms which select, co-ordinate, adapt, and terminate the release of a variety of neuronal impulses which are related to accumulated brain-disturbing material" (Schultz and Luthe, 1969:6). The brain-disturbing material of the unconscious was related to the body through physiological reactions. Marc Guillerey (Swiss) in his experiments on *"directed revery"* also worked on the relation of psychological conflicts to "motor tendencies." He understood the conflicting images of the directed revery as proceeding from the neuromuscular tendencies, and that the solving of conflicts on an image level produces a "psycho-physiological harmonization" that

---

[1]Frederking (1948) also had a system of therapy called *"deep relaxation and symbolism"* which attempted to combine these insights. For further work on relaxation see E. Jacobson (1938).

promotes a cure (Fretigny and Virel, 1968). Guillerey believed that in *"lived dreams,"* where awareness could be directed to imaginary kinaesthetic tactile sensations, many complexes dissolve without the necessity of stopping to analyze them.

These ideas connected the imagination to the body. On the one hand, the body's state of relaxation (attained through imagination) helps one to receive the emerging images. Through relaxation one approaches the physiological state of sleep, in which dreaming, of course, occurs. On the other hand, the emotions belonging to the contents of the unconscious affect the physiological functioning and condition of the body (the basic premise of psychosomatic medicine). This realization has enabled the imagination to be selectively used for somatic control, especially of the autonomic responses (Chappell and Stevenson, 1936). The physiological state desired can be attained through different qualities of imaginative experience.

The psychoanalytic movement had several members in this early period who were interested in various forms of imaginal experience (Groddeck; Varendonck, 1921; Silberer, 1951). Pierce Clark (1926) attempted to integrate the viewpoints of psychoanalysis with the experience of induced revery. He had his patients use visual imagery, *"phantasms,"* to return to their inner childhood. The reclining patient was asked to imagine with closed eyes the sensations, attitudes, and behaviour of his childhood (Virel and Fretigny, 1968).

Subjects were reported to have often believed that the contents of their revery were only actual memories. As Freud had discovered, however, many of these "memories" were indeed really fantasies which revealed, as he saw it, the fixations and problems of the patient. Clark would try with the patient to discover the diversions from fact contained in the phantasms. He noted that progress depended not on intellectual understanding based on the terminology of psychoanalysis, but on gaining a closer relation to the imagery. This was encouraged through a process of *"secondary introspection"* in which the patient would complete a report on his imagery "seance." As in the reporting of dreams in analysis, omissions and refusals to do the reports were noted as resistances.

Clark also felt that the childlike state of defenselessness involved by the technique should be sustained until a catharsis was achieved. This waiting until the affect is brought out into consciousness supposedly avoided the probability of the contents of the imagery simply returning to their former plane in the unconscious, re-creating the same situation for the patient (Fretigny and Virel, 1968). Clark used a method entailing the free association of imagery,[1] one of Freud's early methods (Singer, 1971a:170). The patient would describe the flow of images occurring to him rather than associate from word to word.

Unlike Clark's work that combined memory and imagination imagery, Eugene Caslant (French) encouraged his subject to allow imaginary images to emerge, rather than reminiscences (1921). This allowed the emphasis to be on travel within imaginary space. Charles Henry, Caslant's teacher, had explored in *The Chromatic Circle* (1888) the associations created by directional movement in imaginary space. Henry found that movement was provoked in the imagination when one suggested to the subject that he move upwards from left to right, or downwards from right to left; whereas, up and down associated with the inverse left and right directions proved inhibitory.[2] Caslant used his teacher's observations to form a therapy based on ascensional and descensional movement in the imagination.

Caslant, in his darkened consulting room, taught his patients to ascend and descend from one imaginary level to another in order to obtain different affects and varying degrees of vividness of images. The therapist evoked the image of a ladder, a staircase, or a flying chariot and asked his subject to place himself on it and to begin venturing into interior imaginary space. Caslant noted that ascension not only brought about an inner feeling of elevation but also markedly affected the nature of the vision. The patient, by willfully being in control of what level he was on, could explore at his own discretion and return to a more pleasant level when he desired. Higher levels were *usually* associated with more pleasant affect than lower ones. Caslant claimed that the heights which a subject could explore were correlated with his stage of development. Through this type of self-controlled movement the patient could find his own speed of inner exploration (Caslant, 1939). Threatening affects and imagery too powerful for the present

---

[1]This method also proved useful to Kubie (1943) in the removal of amnesic blocks as well as to Reyher (1963) in his research on imagery (Singer, 1971a:170).

[2]The importance of directional movement to the imagination can be recognized in many rituals and myths, See: Eliade (1952); Jung (1961:81); Gaston Bachelard's work on poetics and ascensional dynamics; Roheim's (1952) discussion of descension into and in the hypnagogic dream and sleep in terms of uterine regression; Durand; Godel.

ego to withstand, in Caslant's judgment, could be balanced by returning to levels associated with pleasurable or supportively meaningful imagery and affect.

Le rêve éveillé dirigé:[1] *Robert Desoille*

Desoille, Caslant's student, continued work on the psychological effects of imaginary ascents and descents and eventually made them the principal technique of his "waking dreams." The waking dream for Desoille was primarily a means by which the patient could achieve a meeting with the "collective unconscious."[2] This meeting enabled him to experience the collective background of his personal conflicts, to see his individual problems within the larger contexts of man's inherent problems (Kretschmer, 1969:229). Desoille, however, was not content to rest with the symbols that arose spontaneously in his patients' reveries. He believed that psychological disturbances were the result of habitual vicious circles that make varied movement impossible. By introducing new symbols and symbolic modes of movement into the patient's waking dream the therapist could offer "new lines of force," alternatives to the patient's habitual modes. Desoille attempted to teach the patient not only how to participate with the various "archetypes" that arise but how "to control," "to be free from them and thereby to lose his fear of them" (Kretschmer, 1969:229). Treatment thereby consisted of three phases: first, Desoille attempted to observe the patient's patterns of movement; secondly, he sought to decondition the "maladaptive" ones; thirdly, he tried to establish "new and appropriate dynamic patterns" of movement (Desoille, 1966:30).

Desoille had the patient repeatedly insert himself into six archetypal imaginary situations (for example, descent into the ocean or a cave, meeting with a dragon) until the anxiety provoking images which appeared were drained of their painful affective charge. Each of these

---

[1]Translated, "The Directed Daydream." "Le rêve éveillé," waking dream, was a term first used by L. Daudet.

[2]His schema of the personality shows clearly the influence of Jung, though his resulting techniques and emphases are quite different. After his book *Exploration de l'Affectivité Subconsciente par la Methode du Rêve Éveillé* (1938) and *Le Rêve Éveillé en Psychotherapie* (1945) Desoille came to understand his therapeutic process in Pavlovian terms. His ideas of cerebral mechanisms are now outmoded by recent advances in neuro-physiology.

situations (as well as descension and ascension) were attempts to couch in symbolic terms specific questions (i.e. what is the patient's relation to the parents, the unconscious personality, to the society). The contents of the waking dream were considered to answer symbolically the specific question. For example, the revery resulting from an imaginary descent was seen to deal with the question, "what is going on in the depths of your personality; what painful feelings are capable of upsetting you?" Moving downward patients experienced anxiety, fear, rapid breathing, coldness and shivering, darkness, faster pulse, and threatening images. Desoille associated this with the personal unconscious. In order to explore the psychodynamic level he would suggest to a relaxed patient (in a quiet, darkened room) that he begin to imagine himself falling and to report any sensation and imagery as they occurred. Ascension, often associated more with the spiritual levels of the psyche, produced warmth, slower respiration and heart-beat, sensations of light and euphoria, and more "positive" imagery.[1] Movement from left to right he believed was associated with the future, whereas movement from right to left led the patient to experience images from his past. Movement of the imaginary right arm (in right-handed people) was seen as indicating optimism, struggle, and altruism, whereas the bringing of the arm closer to the body was associated to feelings of fear, avoidance and the wish to retreat into oneself (Desoille, 1966:18-19).[2] Desoille attempted to borrow from myth and fairytale not only the images he suggested but ways of moving among the images. For example, to help make the patient secure when faced with threatening imagery Desoille would sometimes suggest that he see a hand reaching to help, that he have a magic wand that can produce desired metamorphoses of the images, that he could make an ascension to a level with more pleasant imagery.

Desoille's techniques arising from his theoretical notions can end, I think, by often imposing on patients' inner worlds a structure and set of values not necessarily their own. The possible beneficial results of

---

[1]For symbolism of ascension see the following: Egyptian funerary texts; literature on Orphic and Mithraic initiations; Tartar or Siberian shamanistic practices; Vedic sacrifices; Louis Beirnaert (1951); and the familiar tale of "Jack and the Beanstalk" (Eliade, 1952:48-50).

[2]It is important to understand that the associations with these directions are not always the same for each patient. There are theories about the significance of directions, but individual experiences (for instance, the association of movement upward with heaven and death) may reverse the meanings for some individuals (Fretigny and Virel, 1968).

having a person establish contact with his imagery and learn to move in that realm is compromised by a detailed schedule of places to get to and things to be accomplished that the therapist thought were important. For instance, in his sixth theme in which the male patient supposedly tries to come to terms with his Oedipal situation through the story of Sleeping Beauty, Desoille asks the patient to:

evoke the memory of an experience he actually had with his mother, whether it was agreeable or unpleasant. I then have him ask his mother to lead him into a forest where they will look for the castle of Sleeping Beauty. When they find it, they enter and the man leaves his mother in one of the reception halls. He then goes upstairs by himself, finds Sleeping Beauty's bedroom, and awakens her. If all goes well, more often than not the subject will spontaneously feel that in emulating the prince of the fable, he is achieving adult maturity. I then ask him to offer his sword to Sleeping Beauty as a token of his esteem, to tour the castle with her, and to make an ascension in her company. I next have him imagine coming back down to the castle with Sleeping Beauty and introducing her to his mother; whereupon Sleeping Beauty welcomes her future mother-in-law to her home and leads her to a wing which has been reserved especially for her. In this symbolic way the mother permits her son to take a wife. Although completely imaginary, this theme can give rise to extremely dramatic scenes, even with men who have had many sexual affairs without being able to choose a wife.

Desoille, 1966:7-8

Desoille emphasized that the use of suggested archetypal situations and ways of movement allowed for short-term treatment because time was not wasted waiting for the important scenes to arise from within the patient. Those familiar with waking dreams know, however, that by the end of a sequence like the above the individual will have had many incidents occur which did not fit into the scene. If the suggested scene becomes more important than what is actually emerging from the patient's unconscious the values behind the scene, which are the doctor's, must be made explicit. Is it indeed sufficient to claim that the scenes are archetypal and are thereby the patient's as much as the therapist's? Desoille believed that his directiveness was justified because he understood the patient to be in need of alternatives for movement. However there is a harm, I believe, in not being willing to wait for the client to generate his own symbolic situations and modes of being. The therapist assumes a set of ways of being and teaches them to his patients. This is done in good faith—it is sharing one's own way with the patient; but it is not helping the patient to find his particular way. These two kinds of "therapy" should be differentiated.

Those in favor of directivity and suggestion by the therapist argue that it is indispensable with "severely disturbed" individuals. Controlled situations are deemed desirable so that the patient does not feel overwhelmed or that he has too much material to deal with, so that he has enough "positive" experiences to offset the "negative" ones. It is also argued that directed visualizations encourage creativity. Friedrich Mauz (1948) in his work with "psychotic" patients used an extremely directed mode of visualization in which, as Kretschmer describes it (1969:226), "the unconscious is most carefully tackled and channeled into productive performance." It is almost "a monologue in which the therapist depicts to the patient in plastic and sympathy-evoking representative pictures from childhood: the experience of a procession, Christmas celebration in the family, or children's song, etc." They are meant "to unlock and enliven the suppressed emotions of the psychotic so that later a real conversation can develop" between the therapist and the patient (Kretschmer, 1969:226). Rather than letting the scene take its own shape Mauz impregnates it with symbols which he hopes will produce positive affect and meaning. He believes that through these feelings the patient becomes able to experience a connectedness with the world, and that through the energy behind these feelings and symbols the personality is helped to heal (Kretschmer, 1969:226).

There exists the conviction that people in difficult periods of their lives often find it to their advantage not to encourage an open passivity to the forces they and the doctor are afraid of. The doctor then falls into the role of suggesting positive images—whether they be in the form of "hope," valued activities, or Christmas celebrations.

Does this attitude recognize any value in the "negative" imagery it hurries one away from? Such non-recognition may, in fact, constitute the primary dilemma. In imagination therapy, as in many other psychotherapeutic schools, fear and trembling first and avoidance and "caution" as fast seconds are too often experienced by both psychotherapist and patient when "negative" imagery arises. There is a rush to "securify" the patient, and thereby the doctor. Perhaps this is necessary. But it may also proceed from an assumption about how we would like the psyche to be. When it deviates more than a certain degree from this course, we feel fear, discomfort, and disagreement and begin to desert—fleeing back to the past, hopes, pastimes, and the ego. One loses the desire to stick by the psyche and her experience. One must ask "Why?" Does one distrust the patient's unconscious more than one's own? When one wishes to suggest where and how to move in the imagination, rather than allowing the other person to move as his or her imagination chooses, where is this helpfulness coming from and leading to? Does one not fall into the trap of peddling but one variety of soul, and with a feeling of self-righteousness? If the psychotherapist tries to "protect" the patient through an increased directivity (encouraging positive images, attitudes and meanings) he must ask himself if that directivity does not conceal a basic lack of trust in, a devaluation of, the unconscious processes in relation to the conscious.

Desoille felt that the introduction of new symbols to the person's unconscious liberated him from "vicious circles." These "vicious circles" may, however, be that person's means of getting in touch with his psyche. It is true that they may stand in the way of certain lines of growth, but are these preferred lines the choice of the therapist or of the patient? In my opinion, directivity should not seek certain ends which are not the patient's. It seems that the value system of the therapist (and often of the patient's own conscious position) must be put aside in deference to the evolving myths and codes that are arising from the person who has come in search of assistance. One must question an attitude or action that accepts some parts of the unconscious and not others. There is always the possibility that what the unconscious presents in its imagery is truly its experience and that one is not aided in the long run by turning one's back. What are our fears and values? And what goals do they feed and protect?

Guided affective imagery: Hanscarl Leuner

Hanscarl Leuner's "guided affective imagery" (GAI) or "symbol-drama" provides a systematic synthesis of previous work with imagery (especially that of Schultz, Happich, Desoille). Through the use of "catathymic imagery" (*experimentelles Katathymes Bilderleben*), "inner visions which occur in accordance with and are related to affect and emotion," Leuner is able to: (1) train patients who because of naivete or over-intellectualization cannot release their imaginations; (2) diagnose patients (GAI is called in this instance *"initiated symbol projection"*—ISP); (3) do free association through imagery; (4) check on progress of the therapy; (5) do "intensive" psychotherapy with patients suffering from "neuroses, psychosomatic disturbances, and borderline states" (not with "full-blown psychotics or with addicts"); (6) do short-term therapy (Leuner, 1969); (7) use when resistance occurs in the therapeutic dialogue (Horowitz, 1971:303-4).

The first aim of training patients to recognize their faculty of imagination is accomplished by the introduction of three scenes which do not *usually* provoke negative emotions (meadow, mountain, brook). Through repetition of the scenes the patient becomes accustomed in an unthreatening way to the technique of travelling in imaginary space and relating what occurs to the therapist.

Virel and Fretigny (1968) have summarized Leuner's ten suggested themes which can be used for psychodiagnostic purposes as well as therapy and have suggested various meanings as follows: (1) a prairie (symbolic expression of present psychic harmony); (2) the ascent from a prairie to a mountain (excursion in one's field of existence); (3) the descent of a river's course (exploration of one's field of being); (4) a house visited from top to bottom (the house being one's personality); (5) a Christian name, then the personage of the same sex that it represents (the ideal personality); (6) a person in the subject's circle of acquaintances; (7) for a woman, a meeting with an automobilist on a lonely road (symbol of a heterosexual situation); (8) a walk in a swamp or cave (landscape propitious to the appearance of archetypal images); (9) images drawn from nocturnal dreams; (10) a succession of all these various images, a sort of summary. Each theme is left general so that the patient can project his own fantasies into it. When used for diagnostic methods, rather than for developing intense feelings, the therapist "guides the patient quickly through a variety of imaginary situations" in order to get a "wealth of imaginative content." ISP (initiated symbol projection), usually taking from one to three sessions, proceeds by checking the following points:

a) "The qualities of the different themes such as the meadow, the mountain, the rosebush, the house." [For instance, are there green grass and children in the meadow, or is it full of dead trees with little sign of regenerative potentiality? Is the mountain impossible to climb—perhaps indicating a feeling of hopelessness and impotence to reach desired goals?]

b) "The factors that inhibit progress on the given tasks such as following the brook or climbing the mountain." [Is it always the mother, or a mile high wall, or fatigue, etc.?]

c) "Registering incompatible situations, for instance, in the land-scape two seasons may occur at the same time, or the refrigerator in the house may contain no food."

d) "The nature of the emerging symbolic figures and their behaviour. The latter can be tested by having the patient approach the figures and describe his feelings." [Is the patient's inner world essentially threatening at the present or is it supportive?] (Leuner, 1969).

The therapist looks for hints of positive images that might later help the patient. A small patch of green grass in a barren meadow signifies an area of growth that can be encouraged. Perhaps amongst the threatening animals and people there is one that appears to be a friend. He might prove helpful in supporting the patient and leading him, for instance, into a cave or tunnel, where frightening psychodynamic material might appear. Leuner believes one can note the gradual progress in therapy by the frequency of positive images, the increased ability to face threatening ones, a decrease in resistances which curtail the flow of imagery. He checks on the development of transference periodically by leaving the room for a few minutes and noting the change in the patient's imagery. If transference or dependency is present the individual's imagery may suddenly become frightening or abruptly stop. As in the case of Desoille we must recognize that this view separates images into positive and negative ones according to certain values of the therapist and patient. Therapy then becomes a means to get from the negative to the positive. One attempts to get away from parts of the person and feels successful if this is possible.

Leuner believes the therapist should primarily remain passive. After the initial suggestion, he tries to leave the patient relatively free to follow what develops in his imagery. He does however use "six specific techniques for guiding and managing the course of the on-going symbol dramatic events:"

A) *Inner Psychic Pacemaker*. This pacemaker corresponds to the idea of a directive, purposive psyche. When given a chance, by the therapist's refraining from taking over the direction and velocity of the treatment, the psyche seems to help govern and protect the patient. Often a figure will arise from within the person (an animal, a mother-image, a good fairy, the wind, a god-image, a wise old man or beautiful maiden) and take on the responsibility of guiding him through those areas he needs to know about and confront in order to grow. The therapist helps the patient know how to recognize and talk with these figures.

B) *Confrontation*. This is a strategy for situations in which images arise that threaten the person's safety (a snake, a bear, a frightening person, etc.). The patient is encouraged neither to escape nor to struggle. Instead he is instructed to stay put and watch, for example, the animal. He should notice and describe every detail. By staring at the animal the patient's feelings not only become neutralized but there is an opportunity created by which to "discover the message or meaning which the creature's existence conveys". "The frightening animal may become weaker and smaller, and it may sooner or later be transformed into another creature"—a less frightening and often even a benign one.

"Psychoanalytically speaking, the end result of successful confrontation is a strengthening of the ego" (Leuner, 1969:16-20). The ego confronts the imagination and in a variety of ways is taught to overcome it. The ego becomes stronger. One must sadly (or so it seems to me) assume that the imagination becomes weaker—less of "a threat," so they say. Learning to take a position toward the figures of the imagination so that they do not dominate us entirely does not mean necessarily that we must come to dominate them altogether either. It could as easily mean that we allow them a place . . . that we stand for them. Images tend to dominate us more completely when we try to lock them out, when we treat them as if they have no value. When the threatening image changes as we take time to be with it, we can realize the degree to which we infuse elements of ourselves with power (that then frightens us) by turning away altogether or by seeing them as things to be overcome.

C) *Feeding*. Feeding is deemed appropriate when confrontation seems impossible because of the enormity and viciousness of the giant, fish, etc. The patient is urged to feed the image until it is overfed. This overfeeding makes, for instance, the giant drowsy and he usually lies down and goes to sleep. Often the giant will refuse the food, but patience and coaxing are reported usually to work. "In this symbolic fashion, the patient learns subconsciously that he can face frightening aspects of his own psyche, he can give them their due recognition and he can work out a *modus vivendi* with them. Subsequent confrontation may lead to transformations of the frightening giant into a milder, more benign symbol" (Leuner, 1969:18).

D) *Reconciliation*. Reconciliation can be combined with the latter two. Its purpose is to make friends with the threatening image—to show tenderness towards it. It seeks to use energy positively that might otherwise turn into more fear.

E) *Exhaustion and Killing*. Leuner says this should be used only by experienced therapists who know the patient well enough to sense the wiseness of such an attempt. Since the image is an introject, the patient may himself experience the pain he inflicts on, for instance, the monster. Leuner warns to be cautious because the patient may not have the "ego-strength" to win. He does not take up the more difficult problem of how one tells if it is part of the person's myth to kill the image or not.

F) *Magic Fluids.* Magic fluids (spring water, cow's milk, mother's milk, spittle and urine) are used for the "relief of bodily aches and pains."

In relation to the last technique Leuner warns that it "must always be done carefully because the reactions can be ambivalent. Much depends on whether a patient feels comfortable subjectively with what we are trying to accomplish in a given instance. In other words the patient must understand and accept the purpose and goal of treatment" (Leuner, 1969:16-20). Here I believe Leuner states the case quite correctly. The therapist must himself understand the purpose and goal of treatment and what the assumptions and values beneath them are. Then the patient can see if his goals mesh with the therapist's. Leuner appears to ascribe to the hero's way of relating to the underworld. One goes down, experiences and observes, confronts and kills, and returns victorious, stronger than before. The treasures are stolen, i.e., brought up to the ego-world, separated triumphantly from their home. In this view of the conscious relation to the unconscious all that tends to keep the person in the unconscious, that refuses to be brought up, becomes threatening, "monstrous" indeed.[1]

Oneirodrama:[2] *André Virel and Roger Frétigny*

André Virel and Roger Frétigny (1968) have been the most successful in the attempt to consolidate and differentiate the European work done in the psychotherapeutic uses of imagery, called by them *oneirotherapies.* Their own resulting therapy—oneirodrama—they characterize as follows:

1) A thorough and scientifically conducted relaxation.

---

[1]Leuner (1970) uses symboldrama in short-term therapy of children and adolescents. He particularly recommends it for adolescents who, because of age, have outgrown play therapy and are not yet ready for adult methods of psychotherapy.

[2]From *oneiros* (Greek) meaning dream; oneiric means dreamlike.

2) Some training so that the subject can translate his images into words.

3) The mental imagery, initially obtained by induction or suggestion, must become absolutely spontaneous. Only under this condition can it have a liberating function.

4) The use of precisely-determined standardized triggering-images is precluded because of its effects on the spontaneity of imagery.

5) The subject does not only conceive of a scene, but he participates in it.

6) The subject participates "bodily" — in what is called the Imaginary Corporal Ego.

7) The oneirodramas involve dramatization and are dynamic; they evolve constantly and build up to a breaking point.

8) All the categories of sensitivity, including the kinaesthetic ones are used. Cold and hot represent anxiety and securifying, respectively; on another level, light and dark represent revelation and uneasiness.

9) The operator should strive to bring the subject to attempt "second-degree imagination".

10) The oneirodrama may reslove itself in an abreaction, which should be the end result of a progressively structured imaginary dramatic situation (the immediate, or premature, abreaction, in fact, has traumatic rather than liberating consequences), necessitating a de-dramatization at the end of the seance session of oneirodrama (Frétigny and Virel, 1968).

The treatment consists of three phases: (1) anamnesis, dialogue, analytical interpretation; (2) oneiric phase (engaging in the oneiro-drama or waking dream); (3) maturational phase (between sessions the patient records his oneirodrama, tries to test and use his insights in his life, and works on any "homework" the therapist may give).

Virel (1968) believes the "fundamental imagery pattern of the individual" is "partially idiosyncratic in the sense of its relationship to family experience, partially shared with others of the same sex by virtue of constitution, and partially collective in the sense of commonality of culture and the emergent expression of man's primal development" (Singer, 1971a:171). Exploring the particular pattern for each individual is the focus of the therapy. In general, the sessions are less directive than Desoille's though initial images are provided. Virel recommends, especially for "non-visualizers" (people who have difficulty in seeing visual images), a ten to thirty microgram dosage of LSD to facilitate the oneirodrama.

In addition to their excellent summary work of the various existing "oneirotherapies," Virel and Frétigny have established a clearing-house for mental imagery techniques and a journal for the communication of findings in this field.[1] Virel, Frétigny and others in Europe[2] today are working to integrate the therapeutic insights already gained in oneirotherapy as well as to carry out organized research concerning the oneirodrama, its physiological parameters,[3] and the uses of imagery in psycholytic therapy.[4]

And once we know the dragon is hungry?

This history shows a gradual systematization of the use of mental imagery into a viable therapeutic process. The shared theoretical basis for the use of waking dreams in therapy is threefold: (1) visual images and inner drama express the situation of the patient, revealing his attitudes, strengths and conflicts; (2) the unconscious expresses itself in a creative way, often offering guidance, new needed attitudes, and support; (3) the conscious experiencing of and participating in the evolving myths of the unconscious as expressed in the images and actions of the waking dream is in and of itself liberating. The waking dream is now used for: (1) treating traditionally labelled neurotic and psychotic disorders; (2) group therapy (Rigo, 1970); (3) child and adolescent therapy (Rigo-Uberta, 1970); (4) aiding other forms of therapy; (5) psycholytic therapy; (6) therapy helping the individual to

---

[1]Société internationale des techniques d'Imagerie Mentale. The Journal is *L'Arbre Vert*, 12 Rue St. Julien-Le-Pauvre, Paris V, France.

[2]Mario Berta, Gabrielle Charbonnier, Gilbert Durand, Asvedo Fernandes, Jeem Granier, A. Jellinek, Emil Nobi, Leopoldo Rigo, Jacques de la Rocheterie.

[3]To Desoille's observations of lowered rectal temperature and rate of respiration, Virel adds that the subject exhibits abundant alpha-rhythms, little reactivity, absence of reactivity to external sounds or all other stimuli *except* the oneirotherapist's voice, no forward diffusion of the alpha-rhythm, no slowing of the tracing to a sub-alpha rhythm. See also Costello and McGregor ("The relationship between some aspects of visual imagery and the alpha rhythm," 1957) and Antrobus, Antrobus and Singer (1964).

[4]For other European work in the combined use of psychoactive drugs and waking dreams see Exher, Kraepelin, Daudet (1927), Munsterberg, Meyer-Gross, Delmus-Marsalet, Dupouy, Horsley, Rouhier, Jongh, Delay (1958). Gerhard Grünholz (1971), however, uses five sessions of guided imagery to help his patient replace the use of hallucinogenic drugs.

improve his contact and ways of working with and appreciating the unconscious for his general development.

Much conflict arose over the necessary degree of *directedness* needed for successful therapy. It was seen to vary according to the disturbance of the patient, his degree of security as regards his capacity for imagination, as well as the therapists' different views toward the value of spontaneous imagery, which appear to arise from more fundamental views concerning the desired relation of the ego to the unconscious. In general, it seems that a less directive mode than Desoille's has been adopted, though with some caution to provide a structure and a "meaningful" scene in which the patient initially projects himself.

"Fantasy-life symbolism really seems *there* for most of the European therapists; it is not merely a reflection of conflicts but a fundamental part of the personality that may require treatment and modification" (Singer, 1971a : 174). The psychotherapists mentioned have a respect for it. They seem to have recognized it as more expressive and important than what the ego might say. And yet there is the notion of "treating" the unconscious or the imagination from the position of the ego, with some goal in mind. It leaves one with the feeling of trying to take the best from both worlds—which is usually accepted as an honorable and justifiable thing to do.

But I wonder. We know so little about the imagination that it seems presumptuous to doctor it. Might we not doctor out, or "exorcise," some things of value? Are we so sure that "negative" imagery is in fact negative and not the way we look at it? This brings to mind questions which should surround every psychotherapeutic technique or practice. What are we trying to nurture? What are we trying to destroy? Or what are we doing anyway and why? Which element of "we" is doing what to "whom," to which other elements of ourselves or the other?

First of all the European oneirotherapies sought to have individuals regain their ability to observe their imagination. Secondly, they encouraged the individual to enter into the fantasies. This allowed for dialogue between the ego and the arising images. Thirdly, the therapist sought to make suggestions as to how the patient could more effectively enter the scene and learn from the images.

Once the unconscious situation presents itself and the patient becomes aware of alternatives, his exercising any suggestion (either his or that made by the doctor) expresses a value, both as to *what* should be done—and *why* (though that is generally less apparent). The mythology of psychology sets up two lines of force—the unconscious and the conscious. The imagination is envisioned as lying in the unconscious, though the conscious experience of it requires the receptivity of the conscious ego. Through the waking dream one has an experience in which both the conscious and the unconscious are actively present. The attitude the conscious takes can vary though — that is the fact we have control of.

The imagination presents the perennial dragon and the dragon is hungry. Now what are you going to do? Watch it? (If it will let you . . .). Feed it? (If you can . . .). Tie it up? (If it only would succumb . . .). Try to kill it? (If you are a hero or aiming to become one). Protect yourself with magic potions? And when you put the imagination back in its sack and decide that it is time to go home (which is a temptation when you understand the imagination as a place one can get away from rather than, for instance, a quality inherent in all experience), do you see the dragon as the dragon, or your mother, or your courage, your instinct or your archetype? Is the situation to be accepted? Meditated upon? Overcome? Is it to be appreciated? Assimilated? Transformed? Or destroyed? Each expresses an attitude of the conscious toward the unconscious and the relation between the two that is being sought by and reflected in the ego.

There is a strange admixture of these in the oneirotherapies. There is first of all the belief that participation in the fantasy is beneficial in and of itself and secondly that interpretation is not necessary, necessarily that is. These express a real valuing of the waking dream experience and an attempt to take it on its own terms. Not to kill it or convert it or assimilate it. One wonders though how the "anamnesis" is used, and the "homework;" what is meant by integrating the insights from the session into daily life; and how, in fact, by what means and methods of translation, were the insights derived. The person who travels in the oneirodrama is equated with the person whose oneiro-drama it is, or who observes it — even though the imaginary body (or dream ego) and its reactions are often different from the habitual ego. There is an identification made which simplifies, or at least makes simple, translations from the waking dream to "real" life. It is possible that such translations are facile because the two worlds and the two travelers may not be the same at all. Is my imagination mine or is it itself? Or is it both me and itself?

What is the end point of therapy, the desired goal? Leuner looks for positive images, naturalistic congruent sequences, the ability to confront the frightening and not let it "get the better of us". Things in the imagination are returned to what the ego considers their rightful

place. The food gets put in the icebox where it belongs; the tiger out of
the living-room and into the jungle or cage. One seems to wait until
the dragon is slain or turned into a helpful dwarf. In doing so it
appears that we try to create the imagination in the image of the
ego-world.

What makes it so difficult for us to leave the pie in the sky or the
cannibals with their hunger? Do we really distrust the imagination? If
so, let us admit it. Is it because we know what we want (or think we do)
and we realize that psyche has her own and different claims?

I mean only to have us become clear about the terms we have been
setting as regards our relation to the imagination—just what we look
for, what we turn away from, what we do and do not hear, what and at
which points do we try to change things, at what junction do we pull out.
And let us be certain that seldom have we asked the imagination when,
where, and how she prefers to meet us. It is possible that her idea of a
"therapy" (or even a more informal meeting between the two of us)
based on the experience of imagination is quite different from the
ego's or the therapist's.

I can suggest only that each of us who is so inclined, ask our
imagination about this some day soon. And if you are a therapist and a
theoretician (as most all I know are) ask her (or him if you insist) just
how she prefers to come into the consulting room. Does her dragon
want to be slain, or understood as your boss, or your mommy, or your
ambition? I simply do not know but I do think that by all rules of
etiquette (not to speak of those of science or understanding) we might
at least ask. We have been assuming things a long time about that
dragon and her Mother — without really knowing what they are. Good
reason that they have to be breathing fire at us!

Chapter 5

Imagery and Imagination in American Psychology

Our normal waking consciousness is but one special type of
consciousness. Whilst all about it, parted from it by the flimsiest of
screens, there lie potential forms of consciousness entirely different.
We may go through life without suspecting their existence; but
apply the requisite stimulus and at a touch they are there in all
their completeness; definite types of mentality which probably have
their field of applicability and adaptation. No account of the
universe in its totality can be final which leaves these other forms of
consciousness quite disregarded. How to regard them is the
question for they are so discontinuous with ordinary consciousness.
They may determine attitudes, though they cannot furnish formulas; and open a region though they fail to give a map. At any rate,
they forbid our premature closing of accounts with reality.

William James, 1953

What man chooses to study and how he chooses or is able[1] to go about
studying are intimately related. Often the desire to study a certain
subject selects and/or generates methodologies seemingly appropriate
to the subject matter. Such selection, however, is made narrow by the
historical situation of the discipline the researcher belongs to. The
methodology chosen reveals certain aspects of the subject and conceals
others. If one does not know much about the subject to begin with,
methodologies may be chosen which are appropriate only to the
aspects of the subject already known, and those as yet unseen may
remain sadly unrevealed. Often we act as if the unrevealed aspects do
not exist, could not exist, rather than acknowledging the excluding

---

[1]There are, of course, certain natural restrictions on how he can study. For
instance, how a man studied the stars before the telescope was invented was a matter
of choice, but one limited by the available resources.

side, as well as the including side (the concealing as well as revealing nature) of methodology in general. More often than not, auxiliary hypotheses are glibly propagated to account for inconsistent data — forestalling the replacement of one set of theories and methodologies with another more adequate one.

Subject matter and methodology can be seen to trade off the leading role in the history and development of a science. In the early history of experimental psychology the chosen subject matter — the contents of mind and, especially, the primary elements of thinking — generated the methodology of introspection. When it became doubtful whether introspection was that useful or reliable, a new methodology — one consistent with the natural scientific approach — was invented. But with this change in approach a corresponding change in subject matter resulted. The behavioral approach dictated the subjects appropriate to itself. For a great many years it neglected others. Lately many of the exiled subjects have reared their heads in the corners of neighboring sciences, and within psychology itself. This has prompted a further modification of methodology which enables the science to encompass in its study a wider range of experience. Imagery and fantasy — whose fates reveal much about this dialogue between subject matter and method — were part of the banished areas of American psychology. Through their reappearance they join a crisis of modern psychology as a whole: whether psychology will continue to apply the methodologies of the natural sciences to issues of human existence or whether psychology will derive approaches that are more adequate and appropriate to their particular domain of study.

As yet a more phenomenological approach to researches concerning imaginal experience is still to be inaugurated. We are left, therefore, with studies that do not clarify their own philosophical positions concerning imagery and imagination and which, for the most part, sever and segregate images from the daily human life of meaning they seem to us to be a part of.

The death of introspectionism and the fall of the image

Through the introspective observation of their own "stream of thought," early psychologists noted — often quite surprisedly and excitedly — the appearance of visual imagery. As early as 1860 there was an attempt by Fechner to classify the kinds of imagery that had emerged up to then. For Titchener and his students it was of utmost importance that the psychologist be able to analyze the various complex states of mind into their most elementary units. The attempt to do this through introspection led to a later re-statement (Titchener, 1915:73-79) of Fechner's list of imagery (Holt, 1964:256).

The problems inherent in such research in imagery were signalled by Sir Francis Galton's work, as well as by the Würzberg group. Galton (1889) surveyed through questionnaires, scientists and artists, school-boys and statesmen, about their ability to see images. In this interesting work he found that most scientists (except for some mathematicians) did not see images, whereas the ability to visually imagize was common among the artists. Even more important, however, was his finding that each group had assumed for years that others thought and experienced as they did. When they were informed otherwise the artists thought the scientists strange, and vice versa.

> To my astonishment I found that *the great majority of the men of science to whom I first applied protested that mental imagery was unknown to them,* and they looked on me as fanciful and fantastic in supposing that the words "mental imagery" really expressed what I believed everyone supposed them to mean. They had no more notion of its truth than a color-blind man, who has not discerned his defect, has of the nature of color. They had a mental deficiency of which they were unaware, and naturally enough supposed that those who affirmed they possessed it were romancing. To illustrate their mental attitude it will be sufficient to quote a few lines from a letter of one of my correspondents, who writes:
>
> "These questions presuppose assent to some sort of a proposition regarding the 'mind's eye,' and the 'images' which it sees . . . This points to some initial fallacy . . . It is only by a figure of speech that I can describe my recollection of a scene as a 'mental image' which I can 'see' with my 'mind's eye.' . . . I do not see it . . . any more than a man sees the thousand lines of Sophocles which under due pressure he is ready to repeat. The memory possesses it."
>
>   Galton, 1880

From Galton's findings it seemed probable that people could exclude imagery from their scientific pursuits by virtue of their own lack of relation to it. Moreover, this exclusion either would not be recognised or if acknowledged not mourned over. When certain kinds of experiences are not had, or if had not recognized focally and valued, one wastes no time studying them and does not bemoan or often even realize the fact.

The Würzberg school of psychology, through their studies which gave the subjects a task and asked them to report what went on in their minds while trying to solve it, threw doubt upon the method of introspection and the importance of the subject matter which it yielded, including imagery. They claimed that the subject's introspective reports were insufficient to account for the operations, the actual problem-solving, of the mind (Holt, 1964:256). This latter was their interest. Introspection could seemingly reveal the conscious activities of the mind, but these, it was being found, were simply inadequate for a "full explanation of mind and its accomplishments" (*ibid.*). A new methodology based on other than the exploration of conscious contents was needed. Both psychoanalysis and behaviorism answered this call. Holt points out, however, that it was the polemics of behaviorism that granted it the popular accord needed for full instatement into the mainstream of psychological research.

The study of behavior with objective operational methods banished the subject matter of states of consciousness, "thought, imagery, volition, attention and other such seditious notions" (Hebb, 1960:736). They were "anathematized as 'mentalistic' and cast into outer darkness" (Holt, 1964:257). In the 1920s "mental imagery began to fade as a serious subject for investigation and completely disappeared as a theoretical construct" (Richardson, 1969:ix). Psychology was no longer James' "science of mental life" in which imagery and daydreams had played such an important role (Singer, 1966:xiv). The "subjective" studies which had revealed imagery and fantasy became confined to analytical circles — out of the mainstream of psychological thought and research. Even there, however, a prejudice often abounded against imagery and fantasy, which failed to recognize any positive aspects to them.

Unlike many European psychologists[1] who were culturally influenced to accept the creative aspects of an "unconscious," Americans did not on the whole have a similarly kind view towards so-called "unconscious products and faculties." "In America such phenomena as daydreaming and vivid imagery have too often been regarded as symptoms of neurotic dispositions [whereas] the intrinsic value of one's image has been widely accepted in Europe" (Singer, 1971a:169). If and when imagery was dealt with there was an associated bias against it (connected with the notion of mental illness) and a wish for its extinction rather than its cultivation. For instance, up until World War I clinical interest in imagery rested primarily in hallucinations. It dealt overwhelmingly with the "pathological" aspects of the types of imagery occurring in hysteria, psychoses and organic diseases (Holt, 1964:255).

---

[1]See Chapter 4.

Introspectionalism's methodological impasse was a justifiable excuse to many for pursuing the more "visible measurable behavioral pole of what a person experiences" (Jourard, 1968:102). Psychology devoted itself to primarily studying "1) individual differences following Galton, 2) the role that various aspects of mental life play in the efficient functioning of the organism, 3) the psychology of animals." All three neglected what had been subsumed under the heading of "inner experience" and focused instead on behavioral variables (Klinger, 1971:10-12). From 1920 to 1960, Klinger notes, there was a "moratorium" on inner experience in the United States of America. There was not one book published in the United States that devoted itself to a systematic examination of fantasy until 1966[1] (*ibid.*). Psychology, in its attempt to become scientific, disowned its other historical origins: philosophy (except for the philosophy of science) and psychoanalysis (Jourard, 1968:103). It tried to fit itself within the framework of the natural sciences—participating as much as possible in its approach, methods, concepts, and frames of reference (Giorgi, 1970:55). Psychology became concerned not with modifying scientific methods and techniques to the study of the person, but with studying those aspects of behavior which could be quantified and dealt with by the pre-existing so-called "objective" methods.

In order for the study of "inner experience" to be once again included in the structure of psychology as a "science," a frame of reference had to be created for it which would enable it to be seen as a valuable and necessary subject to study; approaches would then have to be created with which to explore it.

Beginning the "return of the ostracized imagery"[2]

By examining the relation of the subject matter of imagery to psychology during the period 1920-1965, it would appear that the resurgence of interest in imagination and imagery occurred at first almost in spite of experimental psychologists. Slowly implications of certain experiments and clinical practice, as well as philosophical and

---

[1] *Daydreaming*, by Jerome Singer.
[2] See Robert Holt's excellent history, "The return of the ostracized—imagery." 1964.

cultural changes, encouraged the reacceptance of the study of "inner experience"—that category under which imagination was generally understood. In general, however, the approaches of behaviorism and physiological psychology could comment on the occurrence of imagery but were inadequate to take up the issue of the lived significance of such imagery. Thus imagery became re-introduced as a subject matter for psychologists, but its re-introduction was at the same time a reduction of the phenomena of imagery to the grounds available to the experimental psychologist—grounds, as we shall see, that are wholly inadequate.

During the interim mentioned, imagery was not studied for its own sake but rather to avoid certain practical problems, and to accomplish certain tasks with greater utility. Researchers, in other words, did not begin with imagery as a subject of concern, but rather found it occurring, as it were, between themselves and the solutions that they sought. While they studied other things, imagery emerged as a reality to be coped with, controlled, and overcome. Its comeback, Holt (1964:257-265) notes, seems to have been brought about largely by developments outside theoretical, experimental or clinical psychology: from engineering psychology, sensory and perceptual deprivation studies, biochemistry, neurophysiological research, studies of cognition and memory, of sleep and creativity. All revealed imagery and held it up to psychologists' views as an honorable subject matter coming from "hard" science rather than metaphysics. But although it was becoming respectable to study imagery, it was still not becoming laudable to have experiences of imagery. Psychology was still approaching such experiences as "being in the way of" average everydayness.

Engineering psychology was forced to face imagery as a practical problem. Radar operators, long distance truck drivers, jet-pilots and operators of polar snow-cats were all subject to the "emergence into consciousness of vivid imagery, largely visual but often kinaesthetic or auditory, which they may take momentarily as reality" (Holt, 1964: 257). Subsequently their perception of reality, which was necessary for their safety was impaired. Similarly scientists (Paloszi-Horvath, 1959) puzzled over the "cinema" of prisoners, the pseudo-hallucinatory "imagery"reported by prisoners in concentration camps when subjected to prolonged isolation, sleep deprivation, and multiple regressive procedures (Holt, 1964:257). In sensory deprivation and perceptual isolation, subjects observed hypnagogic imagery and hallucinations. In all these studies "normal" people reported experiences of imagery usually felt in America to be pathological.

Neurology has turned its interest toward imagery in the last twenty-five years because of the findings from 1) electroencephalography, 2) direct stimulation of the brain, and 3) the work of Magoun on the reticular activating system of the brain (Holt, 1964:258). In the first, Short (1953) discovered that people with different behavior of alpha waves have different types of thought imagery. He claimed those with persistent alpha are verbal imagers; those with "normal" alpha have the usual predominance of visual imagery; whereas those who lack alpha waves experience vivid visualization. In the second set of findings it was discovered that photic stimulators,[1] used for their influence on EEG patterns, produced experiences of "illusory colors" and "subjective" visual phenomena (*ibid.*, 258). In the third set of findings, dealing with the brain's reticular activating system, it was proposed that the reticular substance of the brain stem is responsible for degrees of behavioral and subjective alertness (Moruzzi and Magoun) as well as for a critical role in the production of hallucinations because of the connection of the efferent fibers from the reticular formation with the retina (Polyak, Cajal). Such work re-introduced the notion of states of consciousness (Holt, 1964:258) and their corresponding physiological correlates.

Penfield and his colleagues, through their work on temporal-lobe epilepsy, "developed a technique of opening the skull under local anaesthesia and then directly stimulating the exposed cortex by electrodes" (*ibid.*, 259). They often found that the patient would experience an "hallucination" — defined as a perception without an object.

The hallucination thus produced may be auditory or visual or both, but is neither a single sound, nor a frozen picture . . . such hallucinations, or memories, or dreams continue to unfold slowly while the electrode is held in place. They are terminated suddenly when the electrode is withdrawn. This is a startling discovery. It brings psychical phenomena into the field of physiology.

Penfield and Jaspers, 1954:242ff

Penfield, Robert, and Jaspers' work show that stimulation of the exposed temporal cortex often produces visual imagery. Although not always, this imagery is related to memory — a link now pursued by psychologists. The phenomenon of photographic memories, and the visual images experienced in hypnotic regression also are used to

---

[1]Delivers a series of regular light flashes to the eye.

support the case that imagery is a vehicle of memory (Holt, 1964: 262).[1]

Dement and Kleitman's (1957) discovery that everyone dreams several times each night and that such periods of dreaming can be recognized by rapid eye movements, and thereby studied in the laboratory, opened up the whole field of dreaming to the objective methodologies of the new scientific psychology. Dreams were everyone's. Images were becoming seen as simply part of the mental processes of thinking and memory. The mystery of the image as a product of only mad men or artists was being dispelled by scientific investigation. In making the image scientifically respectable, the *numina* that others had seen within it was scrubbed away. One was caught up in asking, "When and what fiber, with which electrode?" "After how many flashes of the photic stimulator?" "With which dosage of drugs?" "In which type of sensory deprivation environment?" It was the matter behind the image they concentrated on. The metaphorical and significatory nature of the image were not bothered with. Technology at times did not aid the study of the image, but overwhelmed it.

Experimental psychology, in splitting man into various systems (such as perception, cognition, memory, sensation) has failed to approach imagery in a structural fashion—giving attention to the situation in which it arises spontaneously. By studying imagery through various methods of stimulation the experimental psychologist removes the subject from meaningful everyday experience. By reducing the understanding of imagery to a situation in which one is laying on a table with one's brain exposed, one creates man in the image of animal behavior as well as physical studies in general. Merleau-Ponty in *The Structure of Behavior* has criticized this manner of researching on the grounds that it gives us access not to the true living of an organism but to the pathological.

This critique, however, is not meant to underestimate the difficulty of understanding imagery in either a non-physiological way or through a situated approach. Experimental psychology studied instances of imagery in situations where the individual was removed from his

---

[1]Julian Jaynes in his history of "bicameral consciousness" has pointed out the similarity between the reports of Penfield's patients who heard voices upon the incidence of brain stimulation and the voices heard by the early Greeks which they attributed to the gods. In both cases the auditory image has an "otherness" to it causing the experiencer to conceptualize it as outside of himself. This is, of course, also the case in hallucinations.

everyday surroundings and was made to suffer marked minimization of sensory experience. These situations do parallel the more common situation of pre-sleep withdrawal from external stimulation, in which hypnagogic imagery occurs. But how is one to understand the significance of imagery in these situations? Imagery poses a difficult problem of understanding because unlike most behavior that can be at least partially elucidated through the behavioral context, people who are experiencing imagery are participating in a context that deviates from the shared and the behaviorally observable. In not having anything obvious to do with the shared context, it is easy for the experimenter to ignore the image itself and the person's experience of it. One does not ask why the subject hears his aunt speaking to him about the next door neighbors rather than see a man with a sharp instrument or feel oneself covered with bugs of a particular variety.

To delve into the significance of the image one must not remain as the external observer of manifesting behavior. The context of the subject is no longer simply externally observable and merely physiologically measurable. The imagery itself provides a new context for the subject and at first this context is not public but private. Behaviorism fails here. Its approach cannot reach the full situation of the subject. One is left with gross observations of brain waves, eye movements, and the simple appearance or disappearance of imagery.

Before the mid-1960's fantasy and imagery were neglected in American psychotherapy, except in those areas where it could scarcely be avoided. People dealing with child psychology encountered it daily in their work and derived a technique dependent on it—play therapy. Some continued to try to unravel and understand "fantastic" imagery and ideation in their studies of psychotic language and hallucinations (Klinger, 1971:13). One of the most interesting integrations of fantasy with personality theory and psychodiagnostics was the formulation and sophistication of two major "projective" tests: the Rorschach Inkblot Test and the Thematic Apperception Test. In the latter projective technique, the subject is asked to tell a story about various pictures of situations. The personality, through the story making, through fantasy, is externalized, is "projected." The ease with which many people are able to produce such stories and the findings of studies using free or induced imagination in children's play showed how intimate, how revealing and expressive a part, the imaginary is to human being. It became evident to these workers that a "mere fantasy" has the ability to express the situation of the person often more aptly than the one's verbal attempts.

Imagery also found its use in behavior modification and in psychosomatic control. In the former the image is not used for its own intrinsic sake, but for its pragmatic use in symptom control. Its power is recognized but not its own purpose. The techniques of using adversive imagery and of positive image substitution enable the patient to discourage or encourage internal response patterns. The emphasis is not on allowing the imagery or waking dream to occur naturally, and for the patient to grow according to its development. Rather the patient and the therapist have an endpoint of development in mind and the image is used to facilitate the achievement of this desired state. Similarly in the use of imagery for psychosomatic control the image is used to aid in the attainment of a predetermined desirable state. In one study, for instance, Chappell and Stevenson had the patient imagine a pleasant experience each time anxiety was experienced. This enabled the patient to wilfully reduce his anxiety, and his formerly resultant ulcer symptomatology.

In the psychoanalytic movement the usual concern with the latent aspects of a dream were increasingly balanced by a study of the dream's manifest content (French and Fromm, Erikson, Fisher, Saul and Sheppard). This helped to turn more attention to imagery, because in studying the manifest content of the dream the observation of the imagery in and of itself is all important. One begins to trust that the story the image is telling is its own autobiography, not a mere farce covering up for the latent content. The seemingly malevolent aspects of imagery that had formed common prejudices were slowly being dispelled and supplanted with the notion that people able to introvert and to daydream were in fact less prone to mental disturbance. Introverted children were shown to be, in contrast to former speculation, the least likely to be labeled later as "schizophrenic" (Silvan and Tompkins). It was also shown that people diagnosed as adult schizophrenics had more often been hyperactive and antisocial children rather than the usually indicted shy and introverted type, to whom a more active fantasy life was attributed. Research began to show also that people who reported hallucinations showed less ability to daydream than non-hallucinators (Singer, 1966:xii). Cross-cultural studies showed that hallucinations in and of themselves are no particular indicator or negator of psychic health. Rather it depends on the culture in which the hallucinator is living. In Erik Erikson's terms, "when an individual potentiality (such as the capacity for intense imagery of some kind) meshes with a social modality and thus becomes an intelligible and useful part of a shared reality, it will readily appear in behavior and not necessarily have any pathological significance" (Holt, 1964:262). Contrary to former prejudices, the ability to experience dreamlike hypnagogic imagery was correlated by Foulkes (Spear and Symonds, 1966) with greater psychological health, social poise, less rigid conformism, more self-acceptance and greater creative achievement. The non-hypnagogic imagers as measured by the Thematic Apperception Test and the California Personality Inventory were shown to have a "typical authoritarian syndrome and emerged as rigid, conventional, intolerant, and anti-introspective."

It appears, then, that the hypnagogic dream might profitably be viewed as an ego-controlled excursion into inner thoughts and feelings followed by the ego's voluntary decathexis of sensory input from the external world. Subjects with rigid defenses against impulse life tend to resist any encroachment of such regressive mental content upon wakeful levels of ego-functioning, and thus experience little dream-like content at sleep onset. The nocturnal dream, on the other hand, may be viewed as the ego's involuntary response to unconscious impulses and anxieties which become active during REM sleep. Subjects with egos lacking adequate defenses against impulse life tend to be overwhelmed by it during REM sleep, hence experience especially vivid REM dreams.

Foulkes, *et al.*, 1966

In the 1950's some attention was given to the problem-solving and creative aspects of imagery. Kris (1950) observed fantasy-like thought during the inspirational stage of creative problem solving. Creativity, he felt, was characterized by controlled ego regression from which imagery emerges. *The Creative Process* (1959) edited by Ghiselin, also emphasized the role that spontaneous and vivid imagery have in the illumination phase (after the preparation and incubation phase of the creative process) in symbolically representing the solution sought (Richardson, 1969:125). Philosophers and scientists (Descartes, Kekule), as well as artists and poets (Blake, Rilke) had acknowleged this. Studies showed that individuals differ markedly in their ability to focus on subliminal stimuli (Holt, 1964:260). This ability was demonstrated to be an important factor in creativity—for it is often on the edges of our consciousness where creativity flourishes. In 1953 insights from the study of the creative process were introduced to business in A. F. Osborne's *Applied Imagination: Principles and Procedures of Creative Thinking,* and later in J. J. Gordon's *Synectics* (1961). This work meant the introduction of a pragmatic attitude toward imagery to a previously ignoring, if not hostile, population. Osborne recommended that one pour out ideas and images without evaluation while the "brainstorming" was in process. He had found that criticism reduces the rate of ideas coming from the individual's "preconscious." Synectics (meaning the joining together of different and apparently irrelevant elements) aimed at stimulating the "rate and complexity of combinations [of ideas] through use of metaphor, symbol, and fantasy" (Barron, 1958:144). The image was becoming "popular"— with all the good and evil that such a development usually implies.

The *"second phase"* of the return[1]

As we have seen the elements of waking dreams were encountered by scientists of all descriptions. Though their attitudes varied from neutral surprise to annoyance and hostility, they none the less recorded their findings. Meanwhile the "methodological approach of psychology had been slowly changing so that it became easier to conceptualize subjective phenomena as part of the inner workings of a theoretical model" (Holt, 1964:263). This change ushered in what D. O. Hebb called the "second phase of the American revolution in psychology": whereby the objective operational methods, developed and refined by behaviorism could now be brought to bear on "discarded topics necessary to the understanding of man" (Hebb, 1960).

The subjective world of images and the like had progressed from being at first the total subject matter of psychology, then a marshy realm of uninteresting epiphenomena, and now a legitimate output of a theoretically constructed psychic apparatus.

                                                                   Holt, 1964:263

The types of experiments that were performed were no longer of the variety concerned with learning how to eliminate imagery, but rather in inquiring what produced it, how it could be stimulated, what is observed once it is evoked, and how it is correlated to personality factors. Imagery was studied in a variety of laboratory situations—for instance, pre-sleep, perceptual isolation, inducement by drugs, photic stimulation, sensory deprivation. Subjects' observations would range from perception of darkness, to dots, lines, geometrical patterns,

---

[1]D. O. Hebb termed the period from 1960 onwards in American experimental psychology as the second phase of the behavioristic revolution.

"wallpaper" patterns, isolated objects without background, to integrated scenes (Hebb, 1954). The thing that became obvious in these experiments is that "most people remain unaware of their imagery, even of their after-imagery, because they have been trained to ignore it. It is a distraction if it is noticed for it [seemingly] has no positive value in most of the practical activities of life" (Richardson, 1969: 122-3). The ability to imagize varies amazingly among people, for instance, hypnagogic imagery occurs more frequently among children than adolescents or adults (Partridge). Subjects who have images in one modality are more likely to experience images in other modes (Zuckerman *et al.*, 1962), indicating perhaps that a general attitude of openness is involved. Because we have been socialized out of attending to imagery, when it does occur we are more likely to feel anxious. When imagery is stimulated in a person unfamiliar with his internal stimulus environment he will either report weak imagery or be sadly unable to distinguish between percepts and images (Seitz, 1947; Griffiths, 1924; Thale, 1950; Richardson, 1969). The images will be seen as autonomous and appear as hallucinations.

Richardson (1969:128-9) reported that 66% of the adult population in the U.S. claims to be unaware of ever having had a spontaneous hypnagogic image. Mr. B's lack of introspective awareness is prevalent. In Bertini's (*et al.*, 1969) dream lab

Mr. B, who was extremely sleepy, dozed and dreamed (so labelled by him) briefly that "this experiment was over and . . . I was on a basement step with Mr. F (the assistant) and he was saying 'Don't be discouraged . . .' It is interesting that during this brief dream the EEG showed a fully waking record.

Another subject reported "If you want me to fall asleep again, I'll get another image." It did not occur to these subjects that they could be awake and still experience dreamlike imagery.

Studies had shown imagery to be little of an ogre, and even a bit helpful — but the life of the image was still restricted in the experiments being done by (among other things) the subjects' unfamiliarity with their own inner space and by experimenters who themselves had little idea of the full range of imagery experience. People were not accustomed to being aware of their imagery. It was "nonsense" or "crazy" or "non-existent." When imagery is seen as a mere physiological response, to a stimulus where dots and geometrical patterns are given the same import as imaginal images, there is little reason to learn how to observe it. Under these conditions one learns more about the state of ignorance concerning the topic than about the topic itself. The subjects' reports of imagery revealed in the end more about the

complex and interactive function of at least the following variables: the degree to which the experimenter is aware of, and looks for, the full spectrum of images; the range of phenomena the different subjects are *capable* of experiencing; their prior familiarity with these subjective phenomena; the expectations set up in them by the specific experimental instructions, by their general reading, rumor and other sources of notions about what to anticipate, and by the attitude towards imagery that prevails in their particular subculture.

Holt, 1964:261

If we measure what we know, in the end we know what we already knew a bit better. At best we observe what we now see to exist. What happens to the other aspects of a phenomenon though? What happens to modes of perceiving, experiencing and understanding that our culture has forgotten? What enables us to learn of these aspects and ways of perceiving using the instruments of our modern science?

As in psychology, American philosophy had experienced a corresponding turn away from "metaphysics" and its subject matter towards a logical positivism and the pragmatism of Peirce and Dewey. Suzanne Langer's work shows, however, the development of a trend back to old subjects also, but in a new way—"without being metaphysical" (Langer, 1942). She argues that by studying man's magical and ritual practices, art and dreaming—all dependent she claims on processes of symbolic transformation—it becomes evident that we must "reconsider the inventory of human needs." If, as in other animals, "preservation and increase of life" were the only things important to man, the impractical and ineffectual processes of dreaming, ritual and art would surely be abandoned. As this is not the case, Langer argues that we can still conceive of the mind as an organ of primary needs but that

instead of assuming that the human mind tries to do the same things as a cat's mind, but by the use of a special talent which miscarries four times out of five, I shall assume that the human mind is trying to do something else; and that the cat does not act humanly because he does not need to. This difference in fundamental needs, I believe, determines the difference of functions which sets man so far apart from all his zoological brethren; and the recognition of it is the key to those paradoxes in the philosophy of mind which our too consistently zoological model of human intelligence has engendered.

Langer, 1942:43-4.

This "something else" would appear, she argues, to be a primary need, but a characteristically human one. It is the need of symbolization, which she describes as "the fundamental process of the mind and goes on all the time." Sometimes we are aware of it, sometimes we merely find its results (*ibid.*, 45). Langer says, "the brain is following its own laws; it is actively translating experiences into symbols, in fulfilling a basic need to do so" (*ibid.*, 46). One might say not that one is translating, but that experience for humans is already symbolic.

Langer tries to make it clear that one need not be metaphysical to study something that is a basic part of man. But what one does need is a science that can be careful that the description of the nature of the phenomenon to be studied is not solely a function of the systems of measurement used. If man is measured just as the lower animals, then his characteristically human traits will be ignored.

People who had sensitivities towards the excluded or poorly included subject matters of psychology were able to gain energy for their critiques of psychology from the growing philosophy of science. The critiques, which began to arise in the early 1960's (Koch, 1964; Zangwill, 1956), had an impact on our rather extraverted, self-consciously scientific psychology. The attacks on the "objective" nature of science produced a warning to the researcher that he must become self-conscious. It is he who decides what is to be studied and how. In this decision making an image of man is first projected and then sustained through the subsequent findings. Sigmund Koch lamented in 1964 "that modern psychology has projected an image of man which is as demeaning as it is simplistic, few intelligent and sensitive non-psychologists would deny." He claimed there "is a mass de-humanization process which characterizes our time — the simplification of sensibility, the homogenization of taste, attenuation of the capacity for experience — continues apace. In all fields in the community of scholarship it should be psychology which combats this trend. Instead, we have played no small role in augmenting and supporting it." This was achieved partially because it is so simple to reduce people "to the forms of evidence about them we find it easiest to collect" (Hudson, 1972:155). This certainly seems to be the case in the study of imagery.

When one approaches an experimenter and inquires into his topic of study, one often gets an answer that leaves one with the feeling that the other is dealing with an aspect, a particular, of a larger subject. One's curiosity is wetted and you try to understand who the father is, where the magic is that gets someone involved in trying to find out about something. Frequently, the other knows what he is doing (in quite a convincing way), but the why is lost. There is no larger scheme with which his work communicates, except that of the tradition itself.

It is bad not to see the wood for the trees, but worse not even to get to see a real tree because you're lost in the bushes, the undergrowth of insignificant detail and so-called replications, the trivial, the transient, the papers that haven't any idea anywhere about them. This, one must find his way through also. There is a useful maxim that I owe to my colleague Reg Bromiley: What's not worth doing is not worth doing well. The journals are full of papers that are very well done and will not be heard of again.

D. O. Hebb, 1974:71

One remembers the story of the three blind men and the elephant — each of whom are convinced that they know the elephant and that the other is wrong. Each do in fact know an aspect of him. Their flaw lies in the fact that they take characteristics of the part they know to be those of the whole elephant. No one would dispute that the elephant is his trunk and legs and rear end and that through studying these things one learns about the elephant. But if one forgets or does not recognize that he is working with an elephant, he learns nothing about *the elephant*. He also is unable to learn from his colleagues' studies. He becomes embroiled in fights — thinking others are wrong and are dealing with something other than he is.

In respect to the study of the image, this situation produces several ramifications. The immensity of the topic and the subtlety of all of its parts is lost. In this loss is a reduction of "the image" to whatever particular image one is involved in. Imagery becomes what is happening in the retina or the result of an electrode stimulation. It becomes after-images or hallucinations or psychedelic paraphernalia. The imaginal image is subsumed by other topics and one disproves or limits it by guilt of association or lack of discrimination.

The appearance of third forces

The general cultural attitude in the United States has been changing to recognize experientially fantasy and imagery. Within psychology this has been particularly enhanced by the advent of a "Third Force," which has emphasized the recognition of and breaking out of habits that have given us limited access to experience and its possibilities. The interest and participation in various states of consciousness has in recent years provided the experimenter with subjects who are more familiar and respectful of their imagery and thereby who are more likely to be able to report a wider span of experience. Little attention has been given so far to the effects of pretraining subjects (as part of the methodology) to be aware of their own inner space and imagery.

Presumably investigators fear that they may be unwarrantably influencing their subjects, but some study of the advantages and disadvantages of using experienced subjects should be undertaken. Failure to see what is there may be due to inexperience with what to look for. This problem was noted when discussing the observation of after-images. Failure to report what is seen or heard may be due also to a fear of seeming to be abnormal or odd.

Richardson, 1969:108

At Princeton University a series of experiments were begun in 1971 in the dream laboratory under the direction of Henry Reed (1973). Subjects were trained in a variety of ways to attend to their inner space: through recalling and recording dreams, learning to observe hypna-gogic imagery and to engage actively in fantasy, relaxing by means of autogenic training, meditating, and incubating dreams. In these ways a group of people were helped to increase their facility to observe what is considered as pre-conscious or pre-reflective phenomena. This aided the experimenters in finding more than the usual range of experiences, as well as enabling the experimental paradigm to be beneficial as a learning process for the subjects or co-participants. In my portion of the research I trained subjects to engage in waking dreams by first of all helping them to understand that this was even a possibility. Such an introduction helped the subject to recognize and value the experience of waking dreams which they were able to have after simple training in relaxation, awareness, and fantasy induction had been shared. In several sessions the subjects were able to learn how to observe their visual and auditory imagery at will and to enter into and move within imaginal space. With ten individuals this was accomplished solely in a group setting. Emphasis was placed on providing an experimental environment where imagination images could emerge in whatever form(s) was most natural to that person — movement, drawing, visual fantasy, auditory imagery, etc.

There is much individual difference in the kinds of imagery people have. Experiments with imagery need to leave the ends open on the ways that such fantasy can express itself; or they must be aware that they do not do so. A variety of media should be made available for the subject's use: room to move in, art materials, writing materials, tape recorder. The causal influence of expectations on the events being studied should always be noted. The range of freedom the subject has should be noted in detail so that the experiment is clearly the "occurrence of imagery in a certain population under these conditions." In this way the notion that "this is imagery" can be avoided. Oversimplification and reduction of the possible phenomena can be guarded against, even if it is not able to be totally avoided. Research should be continued that further reveals the correlation between the type or quality of imagery an individual has and his general personality. There is a wide source of variance because of personality, as well as cultural and experimental biases. Hermann Witkin's studies (1965) of field dependency/independency reveal that there are different perceptual types that relate also to inner perception. The field dependent personality is less likely to produce imagery or to be aware of ongoing inner processes. Whereas the field independent person has a freedom from the stimulation of the environment and is more able to look inward (Singer, 1971b:85). It might be that "field dependent" individuals have imagery that is not conveyed visually or auditorily. Once these differences in perceptual style and their effect on the types and quality of imagery in particular and the way a person relates to his "inner life" in general are more fully explored, the effects of training in imagery on one's outer and inner modes of perception can be assessed more fully. It might be a useful paradigm for conceptualizing part of the therapeutic effect of imagery work.

"The interpenetration of observer and observed will then be seen not as an accident, peripheral to the social and behavioral sciences, but as a medium through which they work." This statement of Liam Hudson's (1972:137) can pertain to the interpenetration of the experimenter and the subject, as well as to the subject and his observed imagery. Through the careful delineations of these interpenetrations, imagery can be more revealed in all its intricate and various aspects. In these experiments scientific rigor must be, as Amedeo Giorgi defines it, "a coincidence between the intention of research and the method chosen," not a method applied regardless of the phenomenon under study. This allows for, in fact demands, the creation of new methodologies more adequate to the subject of fantasy and imagery. As well as studying what "is," psychology can improvise methodologies that allow for what might be (Tyler, 1973). In order to understand imagination imagery, and how limited our view of it is, it will be useful to study how other cultures have used it and to develop an attitude which will enable us to experience that for which we perhaps have little conceptual understanding. New methodologies are being created and worked with.[1] Controversy flies between camps (as between those blind men) concerning the validity of both old and new. It is possible that in this exchange the various aspects of a phenomenon which all the methodologies reveal will become well-heard and, with a bit of grace, we might find we are talking about the same thing in our different ways. None are singly sufficient to appreciate our subject, but each is useful if always seen in relation to the whole (as far as we can know it at any one moment, from the sums of our experience of it). This takes a lot of work. Most of all it requires a weeding out of what does not belong to the image itself—that which has fallen beside it, from our pockets, as we have been bent on seeing it from our particular stances.

Although fantasy and imagination had been utilized in analytical psychology, psychoanalysis, hypnotherapy, behavior therapy, and child psychology, it was not until the mid-1960's that the European work being done in the therapeutic uses of fantasy began to be popularly introduced in the United States—mostly through three psychological schools, themselves rooted in Europe: psychosynthesis, existential psychology, and psychodrama.

Psychosynthesis, developed by Roberto Assagioli of Florence, Italy, endeavors to make the goal of growth the creative synthesis of man's many psychic parts and functions. Imagery and visualization are two of the many techniques that psychosynthesis uses to assist the individual in the development and recognition of his "functions," his "will," and the "higher self." The Psychosynthesis Research Foundation in New York City has made available translations of much of the European work done on imagery as well as contributions of Americans and Canadians who have used imagery for the various goals of psychosynthesis.[2] The following table, created from an article by Robert Gerard (1964), is a classification of ways to use visual imagery in psychosynthesis. "Controlled symbolic visualization" and "symbolic visualization for spiritual psychosynthesis" can be likened to systems of

---

[1]"What happens to the philosophical foundations of scientific methodology if exploration of certain phenomena requires substituting a symbolic ritual for a technical method? What becomes of our traditional reliance on the ideal of the unbiased, controlled replicability of scientific knowlege if participating in such an experimental ritual further presupposes surrendering as if in faith to the operation of factors necessarily beyond our individual control?" (Reed, 1974).

[2]See Gerard, Crampton, Haronian, Swartley, Krojanker. Swartley introduced Leuner's work in the United States, stressing its diagnostic use—"Initiated Symbol Projection." Krojanker introduced its therapeutic aspect, "Guided Affective Imagery."

meditation where a static image is used to train concentration, as well as often to evoke certain qualities. "Controlled visualization of symbolic scenes" were used by Mauz, Desoille, the behavior therapists and others (see Chapters 3 and 4). "Spontaneous symbolic visualization" is most akin to what has been discussed here as a waking dream. In psychotherapy it has been used, for instance, in Jung's active imagination, Leuner's guided affective imagery, Virel and Frétigny's oneirotherapy (see Chapters 3 and 4). Only in spontaneous symbolic visualization is the "mythopoetic" allowed to express itself freely. Although images are used in controlled visualization they are introduced from the "conscious" with a particular aim in mind.

TABLE I   *Symbolic Visualization: A Technique of Psychosynthesis*

A. Controlled Symbolic Visualization
   "Although some of the details may be spontaneous, the basic pictorial content is specified in advance. A preparatory state consists of sitting in a comfortable chair, closing the eyes and achieving as relaxed a state as possible."

   I.   Controlled Visualization of Dynamic Symbols
        a. The *"self attempts to maintain the image in a pre-determined form*. This experience gradually brings to the patient a dramatic realization of his ineffective control. Unwanted thoughts and feelings intrude to disturb his concentration. The image itself tends to change or fade." "This experience helps the patient to distinguish between the self or 'I' that wills to concentrate on a certain image, and the changing contents of consciousness." With practice one "acquires control over imaginative processes and his sense of self-identity as a directing agent of his inner and outer life becomes strengthened."[1]
           1. *Symbols of synthesis*, of integration and balance around an inner core, such as a sunflower. Mandalas, basic geometric forms.
           2. *Symbols of harmonious human relations*, such as two hands clasping each other.
           3. *Symbols of masculinity* (sword) *and of femininity* (a receptacle, such as a cup or vase).
           4. *Symbols of affective states.* Subjective color vision.

        b. The *"self attempts to change the image in a previously predetermined direction."*
           1. *Symbols of transformation* (transformation of a worm to a chrysalis to a butterfly).
           2. *Symbols of growth* (a rose opening, a seed growing into a tree).

---

[1]In one sense "control" is necessary to be able to actively imagine rather than to daydream. This "control" is one of awareness, however, and not necessarily of the ego over the imagination. Gerard seems to be implying both.

TABLE I (*continued*)

II. Controlled Visualization of Symbolic Scenes
Symbolic scenes may be suggested by the therapist, depending upon the needs of the patient.
  a. *Controlled visualization of desired personality characteristics.*
  b. *Symbolic representations of the process of reconstruction of the personality* (building a home or temple, restoring a garden and watching its growth).
  c. *Symbolic sequences portraying the discovery and identification with a unifying center around which personality conflicts can be resolved.* Perhaps reaching the safety of a lighthouse after a dangerous swim, climbing to the top and surveying the scene "with the awareness that this sequence may represent the ability to stand firm in the midst of emotional turmoil, and to survey one's conflicts with the attitude of the observer identified with the self, the ' I,' the center of one's consciousness."
  d. *Symbolic representations of inter-individual psychosynthesis.* A couple helping each other along a path, etc.

B. Spontaneous Symbolic Visualization
No attempt is made to "predetermine the form or sequence of symbolic representations, although a starting image may be given to induce the process. The spontaneity of symbolic formation is facilitated by relaxation on the couch."[1]

I. Symbolic Visualization of Somatic States.
II. Symbolic Visualization of Emotional States.
  a. *Technique of the door.*
  b. *Technique of the heart.*
III. Symbolic Visualizations Derived from Projective Techniques.
The patient is asked to enter the scenes pictured in his projective drawings or Rorschach blots, etc.
IV. Symbolic Visualizations Derived from Dreams and Daydreams
V. Symbolic Visualization of Thought Contents.
"The patient is asked to associate a perceptual picture with certain thoughts, ideas and concepts. Metaphorical language lends itself particularly well to this substitution of verbal by non-verbal material."
  a. Technique of the Reflected Self-Image.
  b. Visualization of Abstract Ideas.

C. Symbolic Visualization for Spiritual Psychosynthesis
"Inasmuch as symbols can express not only infantile, but also unrealized potentialities for growth, symbolic visualization may serve to evoke inner wisdom and inspiration as well as ethical humanitarian and altruistic values."

I. Guided Daydream Technique.
II. Technique of Light.
III. Technique of Inner Dialogue.

---

[1]Gerard warns here that whereas controlled symbolic visualization may be performed by an individual on his own, "spontaneous visualization is best done in the presence of a trained psychotherapist" — a professional who has been trained in the technique and gone through it himself. This is in distinct opposition to Jung who felt active imagination should be done while alone.

Some existential therapists, to whom "psychotherapy is essentially a free-making, a humanizing of the person who lost his freedom in some sector of his existence" (van Kaam, 1968:14), have also adopted the directed daydream.[1] In existential therapy "the therapist invites his patient to face his world here and now, not to excuse himself but to return to his world in a new mode of being and to accept in a new way the tasks with which he is confronted in this world" (*ibid.*, 16). Van Kaam notes that there are several requirements that must be fulfilled by a technique in order to be viable for existential therapy (*ibid.*, 14).

1) "In order to make the patient free we have to place him in real life situations where he reacts with his whole human existence spontaneously and pre-reflexively."
"The person is only knowable in his world, in the situation, in his concrete relation to people and things" not through conceptualization and introspection.
2) The "real life situation has to be induced during the therapeutic sessions."
3) The "basic responses of the patient to the crucial aspects of everyday life" must be revealed — showing "how and when and to what degree anxiety is aroused in the patient."
4) One must be able to gain insight out of these artificially induced concrete situations — not necessarily conceptual insight.
5) "The therapeutic model has to enable the clinician to start the reconditioning of the behavior of the patient to his new freely chosen evaluation of people and things."

The imagination is believed to present the situation of the patient as well as his mode of responding to it. The directed daydream enables therapy to deal with a "consciousness that is involved" (Merleau-Ponty), a "being in a situation" (Gabriel Marcel), as well as providing an opportunity to move in new ways.

J. L. Moreno had found by spending time in the parks of Vienna that children would spontaneously play out their conflicts in a dramatic and imaginative form. He used this dramatic quality of the image (noted also by Jung and Janet) to create what he called psychodramas. Instead of experiencing imaginal images within, Moreno had the individual begin to be the image, to act the image.

---

[1] Van den Berg (1953) was the first to integrate the guided daydream into an existential frame of reference.

The person could allow other people in a psychodrama group to play different images from his imaginal scene among which he, as one of them, could interact. One could begin with a life situation, a memory, a fantasy, or a dream and through the acting, becoming the image, the myth of that image was played out. Moreno emphasized spontaneity, liberating the fantasies and memories of the person, as well as the cathartic value of the dramas.

Psycholytic therapy (therapy done with the aid of psychoactive drugs), now relatively banned in the United States, also contributed to the growing body of technique concerning the psychotherapeutic uses of imaginal images. The psychoactive drugs were observed to help individuals bypass many of the resistances that usually keep people from observing imagery. These induced waking dreams have been used with alcoholics (Hoffer & Osmond, 1967), terminal cancer patients (Pahnke, 1969), drug addicts, psychiatric patients and others. The effects are often dramatic and appear to enable some who are "locked in self-impairing behavior patterns," to get outside of these inhibitors and find new meanings, and ways of self-acceptance and expression (Horowitz, 1972:299). The types of imagery that arise have begun to be sorted and related to different imaginal processes and themes (Grof).

Many who were involved in such work, among them Dan Brown, Jean Houston, Walter Clark, and Helen Bonny, have taken the insights derived about the mythmaking capacity in people and applied it to non-drug research and therapy. Jean Houston and Walter Clark (1972, 1973) speak of man's *imaginal-symbolic processes*. They have found that these processes are activated when one is released from the inhibitors of time and space. In order to accomplish this release they use certain mechanical devices ("witches cradle," subtle sensory overload devices, etc.) and sophisticated trance inductions. The resulting imagistic thinking is found not to be inhibited by the mechanisms that do inhibit verbal thought. This enables many tasks to be performed much more quickly with the use of images. For example, people who have used such imagistically accelerated mental processes can practice some task and in a few hours attain the results of a much longer time span. Helen Bonny, who did music therapy with psychedelic subjects at the Maryland Psychiatric Research Center, has developed a form of therapy using a combination of music and imagery without the facilitation of drugs. The music is chosen to provoke imagery, often of a particular quality, intensity or theme.

Eugene Gendlin has developed a method called *experiential focusing*. He has a client

sit quietly while attending to bodily sensations and permitting an upsurge of feeling. This method is different from others in that it minimizes verbal report and encourages genuine passive introspection. The patient usually becomes aware of the sharp intensification of a generalized emotion; gradually there follows a flow of images, associated memories, or fantasies, which seem to supplant the intense "pure" feeling. Here the effort is to help the patient become aware of the deep reservoir of emotion which is so often suppressed or denied.

Singer, 1971a:174

Gendlin notes that the feeling and the image usually remain the same until the subject comes to know the feeling. Then a "release" occurs, the image changes, and words may arise (Gendlin & Olsen, 1970). This sounds similar to the changes that occur in a frightening image when one steadily watches it. Weitzmann (1967) has also speculated that just staying with the anxious feeling or image helps it to subside and gives one a sense of greater competence for dealing with it in the future (Singer, 1971a:174).

A number of new therapies have developed in recent years, designed particularly for what is envisioned as the expansion of man's use of his potentials. Many of them are based on or use fantasy. The group aspect of such therapies has enabled the ideas behind such uses of fantasy to be opened to a wide number of people. Ira Progoff, the founder of Dialogue House Associates in New York City, through his writings and workshops has been sucessful in introducing to thousands, techniques using the ability to fantasize, particularly in the form of dialoguing with interior parts of oneself through the use of an "intensive journal." Fritz Perls and his gestalt therapy co-workers used fantasy often in a psychodramatic type of way. The individual takes the role of the various parts and characters of his dreams, life situations, memories, fantasies. Through acting them himself he is supposed to see that they are truly parts of himself and that their energy, formerly often inhibiting growth, can be re-integrated into the conscious personality (Perls, 1969; Perls et al, 1951). Group leaders of all descriptions have integrated fantasy into their work in often unique and valuable ways. A proliferation of techniques and exercises abounds.[1]

---

[1] See Assagioli (1965), Masters & Houston (1972), Huxley (1963), Stevens (1971).

On the closing of accounts

Hopefully such exposure to fantasy will enable us to understand more of its world and our possible relations to it. Now, as so often happens when a realm is enthusiastically uncovered, the imagination when viewed in the light of its accomplishments (that others claim for it) would seem to be on the order of a general panacea—for phobias, impotence, recovery of memories, creativity, psychic integration, playing, working, praying, controlling moods, getting in touch with moods, relaxing, improving planfulness, getting away from plans, maintaining alertness, for getting it together with the personal unconscious or the superconscious, or the polarities of the psyche, for regression or progression, or being-here-now. There has been little work done on why and how certain "fantasy techniques" work; what about them is valuable and what is superfluous; and what their functioning indicates about the structure of the imagination, or what we mean by "imagination" to begin with.

We know that if a person is relaxed and sees a tree growing toward the sky in his "mind's eye" that he is affected. It is not simply a picture of a tree. Physiologically his brain waves, temperature, galvanic skin response, respiration and heart beat may change. He may experience an affect of awe, curiousity or fright. Depending on what frame of reference he is participating in he will be able to verbalize any experience of meaning in different ways. In general, however, psychology seems to be *using* the vision, converting it into something "useful" and "helpful"—to tell us about ourselves or to literally help us go about creating ourselves in various desirable images.

Too infrequently when we are participating in the psychotherapeutic process do we take the image and ask not what it shows us about our life, but what it shows us about the imagination. When we assume we know about the imagination and how it can be used, we set about using it. The black box remains so. Our "positive" assumptions on the one hand encourage people to enter into the experience, but on the other hand they make it increasingly difficult (the surer we become) to have the experience without viewing it in a pre-determined way, and taking it from its unique context into another.

Through reports of imagery in experimental situations the subject matter has been reacknowledged within experimental psychology. There has been little attempt, however, to separate observations of geometrical patterns, dots, and after-images (where imagery is more related to physiological stimuli) from observations of seemingly exact memory imagery, and imagery of things and situations uncharacteristic of our experience of the "day world." Nor have there been sufficient research efforts with subjects trained to observe a variety of imagery. The visual image is only one possible form of imagination. All imagery is not imagination, and imagination is not all imagery. Although the study of particular types of imagery can illuminate the field of the imagination, it can never hope to encompass it. In experimental psychology the imagination is often discarded as a romantic concept not allowed for in the laboratory, and yet one has the feeling that it is implicitly identified with imagery. As long as the forms of imagery are not separated and the imagination is somehow on the one hand not acknowledged and on the other is identified with imagery, imagination can be tacitly conceptually reduced to whatever eye the experimenter sees his data through—memory, information processing, reticular activating system, one hemisphere or another. In concentrating on visual imagery research continues to isolate the imagination from daily life. How are images already being lived? And what is the relation of these to those the subject experiences under different situations of sensory deprivation and stimulation?

Now as there exist more and more subjects who can report their experiences of imagination, let us try to "forbid" our "premature closing of accounts" in terms of how to regard them, as William James suggested in the beginning of this history. Let us use what seems to flow from the imagination not only to reflect on our conscious lives, but let us ask what it reflects about the world of the imagination. Though we may come to feel that the idea of an imagination itself is an inadequate way to describe our subject, let us not in the process of discarding the name, discard from our consciousness and our explorations the aspects of it that we experience.

Chapter 6

Movements in Imaginal Space

Image as guide

The imaginal has the quality for us of being another world about which we know practically nothing. We never go to bed knowing what dream will be shared with us in the night or what image will arise in the afternoon. We are abducted and transported to landscapes and dramas beyond our conscious ability to conjure, or to predict. We move in seeming darkness. Our usual lights of knowing cannot penetrate her. Guidebooks and guides[1] have arisen to help us learn to distinguish the moving shades and shapes that we might encounter; to help us learn means of moving in relation to this alien territory. These do their work of quickening the connection between the individual and the imaginal with metaphor and symbol. The imaginal resists being known except in its own terms. Image requires image. Image evokes image. Systems of understanding arise, themselves symbolic. It is as if one can say what the imaginal *is like*, but cannot utter what it *is*. These systems of imaginal "knowledge" can posit metaphorically where images reside, who created them, how one can meet them, be with them (see Chapter 2). Once such a system has enabled a relation to form between the imaginal and the individual, the images themselves can become the real guides.

Each image discloses its own character — the particular way it shapes and expresses the nature of the imaginal — by being itself. It tells what it is doing by doing it, by acting itself out. Whether it means to tell — that is, whether we can impute an intentionality to it — must be decided according to each phenomenon. We, however, can use the phenomenon for telling of itself. It does not seem likely that we can say all images intend to teach us, but we can say that by dwelling with all images we can learn something of them.

---

[1] For instance, *The Tibetan Book of the Dead* and alchemical texts; shamans and medicine men.

Some images, however, have themselves expressed that they intend to teach or guide the individual to whom they appear. Throughout history one encounters stories of imaginal figures in the form of angels, spiritual gurus, and human or animal companions that announce they have come to lead the individual through imaginal landscapes, to share with them their reality, their values and wisdom.[1] Abu'l Barakat (1165), a Jewish thinker who in late life became Islamic, expressed this idea as follows:

Some souls . . . have learned everything from invisible guides, known only to themselves . . . The ancient Sages . . . taught that for each individual soul, or perhaps for a number of souls with the same nature and affinity, there is a being of the spiritual world, who, throughout their existence, adopts a special solicitude and tenderness toward that soul or group of souls; it is he who initiates them into knowledge, protects, guides, defends, comforts them . . .

Quoted in Corbin, 1970:34

Images which claim to teach of their reality need not all be as comforting as the ones Abu'l Barakat mentions, as many examples of devils and witches might bring to mind.

In our culture one is more than ever dependent from the start on recognizing that the image itself can teach and guide one into a relation with the imaginal. The relationship demands what it needs if we are sensitive about it and remain true to it. In some forms of psychotherapy, however (as discussed in the last three chapters), the therapist has become a guide to the individual's waking dreams. In these "oneirotherapies" information has been reaccumulated to help the person experience the imaginal through the medium of the waking dream. A learning process is begun which seeks to develop in the individual an attitude of openness toward symbolic experience and a sensitivity towards its difficulties and dangers as perceived by the particular therapist. One is taught how to deal with the images that arise and how to begin to find relationships between the real and imaginary worlds. This learning process can be facilitated by an individual who has himself experienced such an attitude and a sensitivity. One who has learned through the particular medium

---

[1]For example: (1) The Angel in the Islamic school of Sheik al-Ishrâq's is an interior guide, an invisible master (Corbin, 1970:33). "What the Sufi prays for from the depth of his being is a messenger, a teacher of truth, a companion and spiritual guide who points out the way home" (Corbin, 1966:384); (2) Beatrice in Dante's work; (3) Philemenon, Jung's inner guide or guru (Jung, 1961:183); (4) Hermes, the Greek psychopomp who leads souls into the underworld.

(painting, dancing, visualizing, writing, etc.) the journeyer wishes to begin with, can help him develop a sensitivity toward how to use the language and technique of that particular form to enter into a relation with the imaginal.

We must acknowledge, however, that what makes the guide so needed in our culture—our ignorance of the imaginal—also makes the notions of guides and guiding particularly dangerous. *A* way of moving in imaginal space or being with a threatening image are more eagerly accepted and welcomed as *the* way. Once this process begins we can all too easily find ourselves dealing with an unknown as if it were a known. We cease to discover or allow ourselves to be open to invention and suggestion. We fall into the mistaken habit of doing the right thing in the wrong place because we treat a unique image as a stereotyped one. The subtlety of relation that we could discover with each different image is thereby lost, and the imaginal is homogenized with our good intentions and psychological technocracy.

My concerns are that the prejudices and misunderstandings we have that keep us away from the imaginal be clarified; that we have some way to begin a relation to the imaginal; and that we do not take our manner of relating for granted and, in so doing, unknowingly obscure the imaginal's reality. For just as soon as one tries to be helpful and set down "how" one might go about doing something, a mixture of good and evil is evoked. The evil lies in the fact that every way to do something may tacitly exclude other ways which might reveal other things. So keep in mind that

> . . . These are only hints and guesses,
> Hints followed by guesses . . .
> The hint half guessed, the gift half understood . . .
>
> Eliot, 1943:44

We must get in the habit of questioning and re-questioning what each of us is saying about the imagination in order to discover the assumptions which obscure by their mere presence. Once we have begun to relate to our images, we should then try other ways that occur to us, or that may arise spontaneously from our experience with a particular image. For instance, some people may not wish to emphasize the separation of the ego from its usual preoccupations for it is within these that they can most easily find the fantasies and images of their personal myths. Other individuals may not want to relax their body for the state of it at present might be how they can best get in touch with the images affecting them.

Already in the brief history of psychology's attempt to learn of the imaginal, styles of imagining have been set down in ways that do not stir one to question. There are many ways or types of imagining and many possible movements towards and away from the reality of the imaginal. By observing how we resist moving towards and into relation with an image, it is possible to discover ways of being with the image that give it the freedom to teach us. In an imaginal psychology,[1] a psychology preceding from the imaginal itself, the guide[2] — when one is felt to be necessary — would try to help the journeyer keep returning to the image. Once one can remain with the image (whether it comes from a waking dream, dream, or one's activities, thoughts, or feelings) the image itself can teach and disclose its nature and its world through its own being. Our listening to it (in the ways that its nature, *not* our theory, call for) develops a sensitivity in us towards the imaginal, so that its movements and echoes in life can be more readily and truly felt and followed.

On beginning to listen

To enter into the half-dream state the ego goes through various processes of transformation. Kinds of imagining can be discriminated through observing how the ego is transformed and used in the waking dream. We must remember, therefore, that these kinds of imagining are related not as much to the nature of the imaginal as to the possible variations of the ego, which result in different relationships. As we have seen, the confusion here has served for the experience of daydreams (where the ego is not aware but is in a state of identification), to discredit the imagination, when in truth it should have discredited the kind of ego present. In a daydream there is no attempt to transform the ego. In a waking dream there is.

The ways to go about this transforming are not all similar, nor do they lead to the same end, to the same kind of imagining. In most the ego's capacity for awareness, to attend and to remember, are first

---

[1] I am not speaking of a psychology of the imaginal but of an imaginal psychology. The former would imply the use of psychology to understand the imaginal. The latter implies that a study of psyche — that is, "psychology" — would develop from the nature and reality of its experience, which is understood here to be images.

[2] In this text when I mention "guide" it can be taken not only to stand for a concrete figure in the external world, but also for an imaginal part of oneself who might aid one in implementing the suggestions put forth here.

strained from it. What happens to the ego's worldly concerns and values differs, however, and is reflected in the varying purposes for doing waking dreams as well as the types of relationships formed with the images. Here we have been (see Chapter 2) and will be concerned with what seems to be an opus of transforming the ego from its use as an agent of the usual conscious activity and thought, to an agent of the imagination. It is hoped that in this way types of imagining can evolve that reflect more about the imaginal than about the usual way in which we use the ego.

Some medieval alchemists claimed that to begin their opus every material must be turned to water first. Water itself originates no movement but is itself infinitely movable. It is able to receive and record impressions. Its colorlessness, odorlessness, and shapelessness make it the perfect element against which one can see other things. In order for us to be more receptive to the imaginal we can pretend that a part of us must become more like water. That would first mean that it must learn to cease the movement it itself initiates.[1] We are all the time initiating movement by thinking thoughts, doing activities, being involved in daydreams. We rise and fall, flow, and swirl. All our different motions affect one another, flow into one another. It becomes impossible to tell what motion comes from which movement and thereby what the qualities of any one movement, provoked by any one particular thought, action, or feeling, are. The images that are reflected onto us from what is around us become part of us. When we are so full of our own movements though, the reflected images are bounced and stirred. Their unique shapes, light, color and movement are lost.

Think of a body of water. The nature of the movement and being of all that comes in contact with the water can be known by its effects on the water. The fish, plants, winds, creatures, all make their presence known by the currents they create, the colors they seem to shed. The water reflects what is going on within it as well as what is going on around it. When part of us tries to become as water it gains (through its own cessation of initiating movement) the ability to reflect. One does not become stiff in a type of blank stillness. Then everything would be frozen and, just as before the process of stilling, one could not discern the qualities of things because one is not moved by them.

---

[1]In Beethoven's "Moonlight Sonata" the first movement can be listened to as if it were a process of stilling, a gaining of the quality of water. Every climax and build-up of tension is avoided, is dissolved. It is as if this is a necessary background, discipline almost, to be laid for the rest of the movements that register great activity.

The images cannot change — not because they do not want to, but because one imprisons them (or perhaps one's ability to be moved by them) in a kind of unyielding iciness.

You can actually pretend you are a body of water. At first notice how your usual thoughts and preoccupations create waves and ripples — flowing, curling, whirling activity. Gradually try to become still. Your ripples become slower and steadier. Feel yourself in these ripples.

One need not abandon all one's activities and thoughts to be in touch with the imaginal. Images inhabit each thought and occupation. But part of oneself must be prepared to be sensitive and reflective enough to one's movements so that their imaginal qualities can come to be known. The Sufis explained this water-like quality by speaking of the science of imagination as also being the "science of mirrors, of all mirroring surfaces and of the forms that appear in them." Images appear in the mirror though they are not part of the mirror itself (Corbin, 1970:218).

When we attempt to transform our ego by separating its usual, active, dominating, overwhelming aspect from its capacity to register and to allow movement (to become as water or as a mirror), we may at first be hindered by our critical judgments (attempts to keep the ego in its old mode), a bodily restlessness, and difficulty in the first steps of beginning to unfix the bind, the identification, between usual ego concerns and awareness. Jung aptly described some common experiences which occur when one first sits down to contemplate an image (1968b:93).

The art of letting things happen, action through non-action, letting go of oneself, as taught by Meister Eckhart, became for me the key opening the door to the way. We must be able to let things happen in the psyche. For us, this actually is an art of which few people know anything. Consciousness is forever interfering, helping, correcting, and negating, and never leaving the simple growth of the psychic processes in peace. It would be simple enough, if only simplicity were not the most difficult of all things. To begin with, the task [might consist] in objectively observing a fragment of fantasy in its development. Nothing could be simpler, and yet right here the difficulties begin. No fantasy-fragment seems to appear — or yes, one does — but it is too stupid — hundreds of good reasons inhibit it. One cannot concentrate on it — it is too boring — what would it amount to — it is "nothing but," et cetera. The conscious mind raises prolific objections, in fact it often seems bent upon blotting out the spontaneous fantasy-activity in spite of real insight, even of firm determination on the part of the individual to allow the psychic processes to go forward without interference. Often a veritable cramp of consciousness exists.

If one is successful in overcoming the initial difficulties, criticism is still likely to start in afterwards and attempt to interpret the fantasy, to classify, to aestheticize, or to depreciate it. The temptation to do this is almost irresistible.

We continually compare what is happening to our expectations (though we seldom know exactly what it is we do expect). We condemn the images as silly, illogical, non-sensical. We open our eyes and quit. When we are trying to get in touch with an image we must refrain from trying to interpret it or to "figure out" what is going on as it is happening. Our usual ego keeps throwing up resistances — belittling our attempts, bringing other obligations to mind, feeding all manner of self-doubt. The doubt that says one is making up everything that is happening (and therefore it is all worthless) inhibits many people. Steady observation though will allow one to understand how "all the time we are dependent upon the things that literally fall into our consciousness" (Jung, 1968a:173). We credit our conscious selves with far too many of them. This habit works against us when attempting waking dreams because we think we are merely creating them with our ego and that therefore they have no unconscious significance. Observe carefully how an image may spontaneously change or reoccur without thought. Such occurrences come from other than the conscious self. Before beginning one could never predict what image will arise or how one already chosen will change. You might become afraid that nothing will come to *you* and thereby you find yourself busily fabricating. In Chinese (as well as many "primitive" languages) one would not say that "I think a thought" but rather "It thinks me." This seems quite strange unless one understands that from a certain introspective position one can actually see the thought enter consciousness and then move the individual, as he identifies with it.

Many people complain they do not really understand what it means to imagine and that they fear they never really have done it. We are imagining in a way all of the time. What we must develop is our awareness of this. A young woman complained about her complete lack of ability to fantasize, as she understood it. As she left the house she went to open a screen door. Her hand fell through space and she apologized for her wrong action. "Oh, I thought there was a screen door there." It was snowy outside and there had never, at any rate, been a screen door there. Her friend asked curiously what she had felt when she went to open the door. She did not know at first and did not understand what the friend meant. Then she confessed to herself that for a moment she had felt how she had in the summertime. It was as if she was swinging open her cabin door in a place she had once lived in the country. In that one moment a whole image was contained in a fleeting feeling (or vice versa). It took a mistaken action, an action true in the imaginal realm but not in the material, to jolt her into awareness of the fantasy.

There is a story (Ka' annahu huwa, XXVII:44) told by Ibn 'Arabi, a Spaniard who became an Arab theologian and mystic (1165-1240), about King Solomon inviting the queen to enter the palace floored with crystal. She mistook the glass floor for a pool of water and picked up her robe to avoid getting it wet. Solomon immediately used this example to try to make her understand that "every object, perceived at every instant, is a 'new creation' and that the apparent continually consists in a manifestation of likes and resemblances" (Corbin, 1970:239). These resemblances produce feelings of constancy and continuity that trick our awareness into a state of sleep. Objects are always in a sense "new creations" because there is something working on them, making them more than just material statements that never change.

One of Jung's patients complained that he was worried because he could not understand "active imagination." At the railway station one day he decided to look at a poster and pretend that he was in it. He found himself walking through the country and down a path to a chapel. When he entered the chapel he saw something with pointed ears behind the altar. "He thought, 'Well, that's all nonsense' and instantly the whole fantasy was gone. He was confused whether what he had done was really active imagination, so he entered the picture as before. Everything was the same, up to and including the pointed ears. Then he was able to trust that in fact his imagination was intent on making this scene and that he could learn further how to enter it" (Jung, 1968a:190). If he had stopped after his first fantasy he would have gone on thinking that he could not get in touch with an image, except for those he fabricated. He would not have found that the image has a real and autonomous life.

The self-critical and judgmental thoughts that say this attempt at imagining is silly, or that we are not doing it right, or that even if we were nothing would come of it, themselves have images within them that we could become sensitive to. But much of the time critical judgments spring up to keep us from using the ego differently. These are objections that the usual ego uses in an attempt to maintain its sovereignty. They keep us from "becoming water" by making us move in our usual ways. As we keep ourselves from the imaginal we fall into a hundred daydreams about what we are doing that steal our awareness from realizing the movement of images. Let your thoughts occur but try to separate yourself from them so that, for instance, instead of feeling the whole thing is impossible, you see that there is a feeling and a fantasy that the whole thing is impossible. In this way a part of you does not enter the daydream but can remain still enough itself so that this thought that "all is impossible" can produce certain ripples. It is possible for one to enter into relation with them and to observe them if one is not identified with, or is not the same as, them.

The body *may* at first assist you more if it is thoroughly relaxed. This is not always so. Later especially the state of the body itself can be seen to hold many images which relaxation would obscure. Some images can be used to relax yourself. Try to find one that works well for you.[1] Here are a few suggestions:

1) Lie down on a floor or bed. Feel your body touching the surface at all points—your head, shoulders, buttocks, thighs, heels, etc. Feel the heaviness of your body pulling you into the bed. The bed is supporting you. The heavier you feel and the more you can allow the bed to support you, the more your body will feel as if it is sinking further into the bed. You can pretend it is a cloud or a bed of leaves, or let it remain open to see whatever image may appear.

2) Pretend you are lying on a beach in the summertime and the sun is shining all over you. It is hot and relaxing. As in the last one, let your body sink into the sand.

3) Imagine that your body is full of sand and that there is a little hole out of which the sand slowly pours, easing the tension in your body as it slowly trickles out (Christopher Beck).

4) Pick an image that reminds you of tranquility—a cloud floating or a still lake—and become it. This is especially useful because it enables us to distance ourselves from having to be centered around our "I-ness."

Of course in all of these the image can be dropped after relaxation has been obtained. In some cases though one may find that they influence subsequent imagery. In that instance you should decide whether that is all right or not.

To aid in the initial separation of your awareness, it is sometimes helpful to have an element which easily combines with the awareness (thus drawing it away from its usual identifications) but which can itself easily be discarded after the awareness has been extracted. For example, this element can be a simple geometric form, the breath, an

---

[1] A modified form of the autogenic relaxation method developed by Schultz and Luthe (1969) is given in the first appendix.

external object, an image, the sound of waves, or of the wind in the trees. It is not important what the element is when the object is to separate out awareness. With time one can easily make the transition from the ego in a state of identification to an ego which is in a state of awareness. When your awareness is focused on the breath, for instance, recognize what tries to take you away from your concentration but return to the object again. Eventually one can follow what tries to take one away, without being taken away; i.e., without losing the autonomy of awareness, without losing that quality of water, of reflectiveness.[1]

Imaginings

One may begin by observing any image(s), in any form,[2] that appears.[3] For some people it might be easier to start out with an initial image. Some theorists have suggested initial images which they believe to be part of the imagination's many landscapes and themes. By placing oneself in these situations (walking in a meadow, climbing a mountain, entering a cave, descending or ascending through space, talking to a wise man, exploring underwater, etc.), one is reputedly facilitated in one's entrance into the imaginal. There is also often the hope to explore certain areas of personality through specific themes. In this instance, one is already using the image with an idea of what it means and to what ends it may serve. If you consciously choose an initial image, it is important that it is a vital one for your imagination — and not just to your conscious personality. Theoretically one can start with anything and through the process of imagining have its imaginal

---

[1]If relaxation and the separation of awareness do not appeal to you as "entry vehicles" for the voluntary seeing of visions and images, keep in mind one used by a group of Australian aborigines (Naranjo, 1971:107). Go to a lonely abyss or cave. Rub one small stone over a large one in the direction of the sun. Continue for three days. After the third day (as it is reported) a spirit you can talk to will emerge from the rock!

[2]Here I often use the example of the visual image — but only as an example. The imaginal often makes itself available to us through our senses, but not always. See the appendix for some suggestions of how to get in touch with the imaginal through painting, music, movement.

[3]Some people visualize better with their eyes open and fixed on a spot in space. It has been suggested that this is often useful when frightening imagery is occurring and also in cases when the individual is highly introverted. Experiment for yourself but remember that the image need not be visual at all.

background restored. In the beginning, however, the closer the image is to what we know is spontaneously occurring in the imagination, the easier it seems to be able to get in touch with the imaginal. One also decreases the likelihood that one is going to the imaginal with a conscious concern that one merely wants solved, in which case the imagination is not respected in and of itself — but merely as a possible adjunct to the usual ego.[1] Thus taking an image or a scene from a dream is an excellent way to begin.

If, for instance, a bird appears or we have chosen it from a dream, realize how important that bird is. Of all the possibilities it is a bird that is flying in our waking dream, or dream. We may know something about birds but we as yet know nothing about this particular bird. Our way of getting to know the bird must be derived from the bird itself and we must always remember not to assume things about it (him? her?) from other experiences with birds. It is not a "real" bird and it is not just any bird. We will not find *this particular bird* in those dictionaries of symbols. We do not know that he or she is a spirit or a dark or holy aspect, or a messenger, the holy ghost. That labelling is not our concern. It kills the bird that is in front of us right now. If we carry all of our interpretative notions with us as we imagine, the bird seems to cease being itself for us. We can no longer see it as it is.

Experience how you feel with it. Watch it carefully; trying to note its qualities and movements. When trying to learn about it you can think of the bird as a teacher. Approach it with curiosity and patience, as if it were the most important thing right now. You do not have to worry about getting it to do something. The bird invents itself and is not dependent on our conscious egos. We must give it our time and space, though, if we wish to learn from it. Allow it to move and change as it desires. You may have the wish to ask it questions, as that is our usual method of finding out about things. Sometimes images do talk, but not always. The important thing is to realize though that it already *is* what it can convey. The image is a complete statement in and of itself. Ibn 'Arabi explained, "they do not answer in articulate

---

[1]"There are even people who are willing to look at themselves, but only in order to be stronger than the other person or to master a situation; they still retain an ego-power purpose, and they even use the techniques of Jungian psychology — active imagination, for instance — but with their eyes fixed on power, on overcoming the difficulty, on being the big stag who *did* it." "Looking at oneself only in order to exercise power over others (becoming an analyst); looking within not for its own sake — not just because one has the need to be more conscious. Thus power sneaks into everything again and again, and turns that which has been a living spiritual manifestation into a trick, a technical trick in the possession of the ego" (von Franz, 1970:X, 17).

speech, because then their discourse would be other than their essence, than their person; no, their apparition, their coming (*wurùd*) is identical to their discourse; it *is* this discourse itself and the discourse is their visible presence" (quoted in Corbin, 1970:327). In some circles there is a large emphasis placed on conversing verbally with each image. Perhaps this comes not as much from an insensitivity toward the image, as from a feeling that by conversing one is able to accept more responsibility for the relationship to the image.[1] It is also perhaps a precaution against the deterioration of the waking dream into a daydream. Not to converse verbally, however, need not mean a lessening of our conscious presence in the fantasy.

If we expect the image to communicate and move in a certain way we are apt to dismiss it or miss it before long. Each image has a particular nature and we must assume that what it is doing is the way it must do. If we assume that an image should always talk (and stand still when we are talking to it), if we assume that once an image has announced a quality that it must maintain that quality and not take on another, then we are not allowing the image to teach us of its imaginal ways and reality. We can persist in seeing an image as clumsy, as stepping on its own feet, of contradicting itself, of not emphasizing the right thing, of exaggerating the meaningless, or being dumb and not at all sufficient for what it communicates. But it is more than likely that we have incorrectly assumed what it is trying to communicate — not to speak of whether it aims to communicate at all! Since we really know nothing about its reality we must sit simply with the fact that what it communicates is what it is; that it is sufficient for its own nature. By refraining from saying that it is a message but that it does not do it in the best way, we can notice just what it does do and from these observations understand the nature of the imaginal as it presents itself to us. We will notice that each image is multidimensional. It has form, color, texture, emotionality (Berry, 1974:96), ways of moving. The qualities belong to the image as it presents itself. They set up the imaginal environment in which our awareness is travelling.

Some people find it helpful in the beginning to relate the waking dream as it occurs to another person, real or imaginary, because doing so keeps alive both the experiential and the self-reflective levels of the waking dream. One should try as carefully as possible to describe and note the imaginal environment as it appears. Some people will find it easier to do this with color, sound, movement or drawings rather than

---

[1]As we shall examine later, it also results from an over identification of consciousness with one particular image, one particular "I."

with words. With time one will be able to remember how each image changed, what it was like and how one participated with it. If you are working with another person it is helpful at times to ask questions like "what color is that?" "in what sort of substance is he moving and how?" in order for him or her to become more aware of the details of each image. This is invaluable for the effect of placing oneself in imaginal space. Attention to the details of each image develops an imaginal perception, a sensitivity to the images's nature.

Sometimes no image will seem to arise. Further relaxation, patience, the suggestion of a dream image, or of an ascent or descent may be helpful. Take plenty of time and observe your worries about not having any imagery, but try not to identify with these concerns ("Why don't I have an imagination?" "I must be full of resistances," etc.). Feelings of insecurity and inadequacy are accustomed to undermining you. Notice them for the fears and fantasies they are; try to let them pass in the beginning, unless you can recognize the images they are coming in without immediately identifying with them (and thereby gaining no awareness of them). Often one does not recognize an image when it does occur. In the previous case, we can find that our feelings about ourselves are not simple results of fact, of who we are "in reality." The appearance of a thought like "I have no imagination" is parented by a whole imaginal script of what we are missing and what that means, how it happened and how it all must make us seem to others.

More simply, however, someone may report, "Oh, I was thinking of a red barn, but it isn't an image." "I felt like I wanted to swim, but that isn't anything." "I just saw . . . but . . . ." It is not important that you *see* the barn. Recognise that the image of barn appeared in thought-form. One should know beforehand that different people have different media with which they are most comfortable in terms of experiencing imagination. Some people, for instance, are more at home with images that come through the body than with visual imagery. It is sad that often people with different proclivities do not recognize them but rather persist only in the recognition of what they have difficulty doing. The freer the person is to express his experiences when relaxed, the more likely it is that the guide can encourage the person to experience waking dreams in the medium that he or she would feel best in at the moment. This changes through time and with different images. One should be careful not to get in a rut . . . afraid to use other media[1] about which one may know little. Imagination may

---

[1] See Appendix 2 for a selected bibliography concerning different media for waking dreams.

not appear as what we think of as images but can at times be recognized as a quality to experience.

Another frequent occurrence in the beginning of waking dreams is too much imagery. You may have pictures from past memories, from commercials, cartoons, people, objects, colors, all flash before your eyes. Listen and watch for a while to see which images recur. It is often the first ones that appeared. Return to the recurring image and try to exclude other ones for a while until it becomes established in your consciousness and you in its reality. In the *Odyssey* (Fourth Book, verses 330 ff), Menelaus is trying to come to some terms with the sea god Proteus. Proteus keeps changing himself — from a lion to a snake, a dragon, a large boar, running water, a high tree. Menelaus keeps holding onto Proteus until he is tired, at which point he resumes his normal shape (Hannah, 1953:57). One should develop the ability to hang onto the image. When imagery changes, however, we must be careful. The discontinuousness of images is due partly to the ephemeral nature of the image and partly to our shifting attention (Casey, 1974). When the image changes, it could be a matter of our lack of involvement with the image, or with our incapacity to concentrate steadily enough. It could also, however, be our lack of understanding of the ways of the imaginal. The figure that is always nice and kind to us faces us this evening with some form of torture and we open our eyes. Surely we must be doing something wrong, we hope. This isn't the fellow he is supposed to be. In this case there is probably not a problem with our meditation, as much as with our refusal to accept that each image has many aspects and faces.

If you know that it is difficult for you to steady your concentration on a single image, try at times to do so with a simple image or form. Concentration can be trained in this way. This skill is invaluable during waking dreams when resistances throw us a barrage of images in order to wash our awareness and concentration away. Once you are established in the image's reality, changes may occur but they more frequently have to do with the image and not with resistances. As long as you still feel connected to the imaginal scene it is probably all right.

The relationship between the Little Prince and the fox in Antoine de Saint-Exupéry's (1962:79-84) story gives an account of how one might go about forming a relation to an imaginal figure or image. The fox asks the Little Prince to "tame"[1] him and explains that this means

---

[1] In the original French version de St.-Exupéry made up a word which in the English version is inadequately translated as "to tame." He no doubt was trying to introduce a concept different from that of taming.

to establish ties, which then make the other unique in all the world. Once they have "tamed" each other different things in the world will remind them of each other. One will see the image in other things. "One only understands the things one tames," the fox teaches. In order to tame one must be "very patient."

First you will sit down at a little distance from me—like that—in the grass. I shall look at you out of the corner of my eye, and you will say nothing. Words are the source of misunderstandings. But you will sit a little closer to me every day.

The next day the fox advises that the Little Prince should observe certain rites (rites make "one day different from another, one hour from other hours"), one of which is to come at the same time every day.

The fox leaves the Little Prince with his secret that "it is only with the heart that one can see rightly; what is essential is invisible to the eye." "It is the time you have wasted for your rose [the most important image in the Little Prince's life as de Saint-Exupéry saw it] that makes your rose so important." Once one has established ties with the image one is responsible for it forever. Later the fox declares:

What moves me so deeply about this little prince who is sleeping here is his loyalty to a flower—the image of a rose that shines through his whole being like the flame of a lamp, even when he is asleep.

How one is involved in the imaginal scene constitutes different kinds of imaginings. One can observe something similar to this within nightly dreams also. The dream ego is not always even apparently similar to the dreamer. Within the dream one may feel oneself and yet be in a different body. One may be a woman and not a man, a dog not a person, a child not an adult. One may be two people at once. Sometimes one is in the scene but is invisible. One can see oneself moving in the dream but feels oneself not to be the "I" moving but the "I" watching. One can be other images as well as oneself. The dream ego may react more or less like we do usually or it may vary greatly to a point where we can hardly recognize ourselves upon waking. In waking dreams these differences are important to recognize because we are in some ways in control of how (and as who) we let the dream ego move. If we think the only way we can move in imaginal space is as we are in daily life, our ignorance and conscious preference limit our movement severely. We leave little room for the imaginal to create us within the waking dream.

Some different kinds of imagining[1] are the following:

1) You are watching the images but are not yourself among the images. You, as you know yourself, are the one watching.

2) You see yourself watching the images from within the imaginal scene. For example, you see yourself looking down from a tree.

3) You see yourself interacting with images within the landscape of the imagination.

4) You are within the scene watching the images (you yourself are in the tree).

5) You are interacting with images within the landscape of the imagination as yourself.

6) You are interacting with other images in an imaginal body not your own. You are still willing your actions.

7) You are interacting within the imaginal landscape but not as you usually would. Your actions are not initiated from your conscious ego. *You* are moved, as well as the rest of the images.

8) You are interacting within the imaginal landscape not as yourself but as a peripheral image to the scene. For example, you are a tree and being the tree are in touch with the other images around the tree. Here also you do not think what the tree is going to do. You are whatever the tree does.

9) You are an image. You are not in your imaginary ego or body. You feel and move and are the ground or the bird. You are not your normal ego in the bird's body. You are the bird.

10) You are watching the images from within the imaginal scene but the you that is watching them is a different kind of ego with different ways of perceiving and movement than we would notice at first.

In the first example the ego is completely separate from the imaginal scene. In the second and third though there exist two egos. One is still separate from the imaginal. The imaginer is not in either

---

[1]The words "imaginer" and "imagining" are misleading. They often leave one with the feeling that the "imaginer" is the one who creates images. It is our viewpoint here that the "imaginer" is not responsible for the images that arise, but for how he allows himself to be involved with them. These different ways of involvement constitute different kinds of "imagining."

ego within the imaginal scene himself. These three kinds of imagining might be called "spectatorial imagining." The imaginal is watched by the usual ego which remains outside.

In the fourth and fifth kinds of imagining there is a major qualitative change. The imaginer is *in* the imaginal scene. The ego enters an imaginal body and can move itself in imaginary space. One can learn how to enter the imaginary body. Often times one begins by seeing oneself in a scene, being a spectator (the first type of imagining). The task can be envisioned as putting yourself within the body of the you observed in the scene. Try to look out of the eyes of the you within the scene. Turn your imaginary head so that you can look around. Smell the place that you are in. Feel the dampness or the sunlight. Touch the things that are around you by moving your imaginary arms.

Feel the clothes on you and the muscles in your body as you move. Notice your shoulders, your neck, your legs, etc. How do they feel? How long are they? Are there any differences between your real and your imaginary body? Notice them. There is no reason they should be the same. Later you may want to draw a picture to represent these differences. If you have a lot of trouble getting into your imaginary body try the following exercise with closed eyes (Frétigny and Virel, 1968). Stretch out your imaginary hand and pretend that you see it before you as you would in reality. Raise your imaginary head and imagine that you see the front of your body, your clothing, and shoes. Describe the landscape you see in front of you in your waking dream and then turn your imaginary body around and describe the one in back of you.

Inserting yourself in your imaginary body enables you to become directly involved with the images, qualities and affects of the imaginal environment. One's experience is fundamentally different than when one sees images as if they were a filmstrip or flashing slides in front of them (regardless of whether or not the individual is one of the characters that he observes). A picture of an avalanche may not be very scary but being near one moves us. We then become involved in the imaginal scape. To see an ocean being explored is different than doing it ourself.

A woman whom Jung was analyzing reported the following active imagination: "I am by the edge of the sea and I see a lion coming, but it turns into a boat." He replied: "That is not true. If you are by the edge of the sea and you see a lion coming you feel afraid, you tremble, you wonder what to do. There is no question of it turning immediately into a boat."

Humbert, 1971:104

Imagining in the style of the fourth and fifth categories can quickly turn into the first until one has learned how to move within the imaginal body. Continual reassertion may be necessary in the beginning—i.e., stopping and trying step by step to feel and move within the you that you began to observe.

The depth of participation in the imaginal often can be assessed by several factors. A primary indication is affect. Does the imaginary environment effect the participant? When a swordfish swims right towards one, does one become anxious (recognizable by an increase in muscle tension, quickened breath and pulse, coldness)? Also, is one able to maintain vivid images? Can he hold onto a theme or image for a period of time? Is one moving around in an imaginary body? Can one approach the elements of the scene? Has awareness of the reality surroundings been lessened or is one still easily interrupted by street noises and the like. The guide can ask and suggest things like the following: "Try to get nearer to the (image)," "Try to let yourself feel the emotions that the small body evokes in you," "What exactly does the man look like?" Until the subject does it naturally the guide can continue to help the journeyer become grounded in the imaginal scene through asking him to describe unmentioned features of the environment, his feelings, and his imaginary body. In the sixth form of imagining one may assume the imaginary body of another image but one is still identified with the usual ego. One moves or speaks because one thinks and wills oneself to do so.

It is possible to understand different types of imagining as belonging to different archetypal modes. The fifth reminds one of the hero who leaves his home and travels to the underworld and the heavens as himself. The ego that travels to the imaginal is the same as the ego in the "real" world, with the same characteristics and ways of going about things. It is wilfully controlled, desiring to overcome obstacles and to triumph in order to remain in rule. This kind of heroic ego enters the imaginal but often for its own gain and in order to return to its usual kingdom richer and wiser than ever.

It may digress, meet obstacles, even descend to the underworld, but its course of upward progress places a negative sign upon digressions and descents.

The immersion is to be endured for the sake of a later advantage on the path of linear development.

Hillman, 1972a:284

In the seventh form of imagining one is inserted in the imaginal scene but not as the imaginer knows himself to be. The imaginal ego is different from the heroic ego. This difference may take many forms, as the seventh, eighth and ninth types of imagining suggest. Most of these variations have yet to be set down. The imaginal body may look different from our "real" body. The sex, the age, the characteristics — even the species — may be different. More importantly though this kind of imaginal ego does not move only when you, your heroic ego, tells it to. You move but not only (or even) at your own request. You find yourself wandering and doing things, watching, etc. but it is not a result of your thinking, "Now I am going to approach the tree and ask it a question." These imaginal egos are a great source of insight. By moving in them we see the imagination from different standpoints than we ever have before — for now we are part of it. We are not only moving within the imaginal, we are being moved *by* it. We are not limited by the ways of our heroic ego which are often quite clumsy and insensitive when it is not in its own realm. One may sometimes find that personified images just do not want to talk to us when we are going around in our "heroic" egos. Everything we say or do just annoys them as if they were having to put up with the kitchen help eating at their table. Their response, if we are sensitive enough, trains us in a sense to give up our habits and to begin to move in an ego that is more attuned to the imaginal. Remember the warning of Artemidorus. One may never ask a god one question too many. One must not bumble into the imaginal, failing to feel its qualities and customs.

To see how this is essentially different from the more heroically active imagining of number five, imagine the situation of being in a waking dream and a scary creature comes up to you. You decide that it would be best to kill it. In some psychotherapeutic uses of fantasy this is in fact urged (when the therapist thinks that the patient is capable of succeeding). It is believed that it strengthens the ego if you can conquer the creature, as the hero would. So you set out to plan your strategy and perpetrate the deed. In the seventh type of imagining, however, the creature comes towards you and your usual consciousness does not reflect on what you are doing. You feel an extreme emotion of fear and simultaneously you find you begin to stab him. Now this is not the heroic ego overcoming anything. It is an action of an imaginal ego and therefore belongs to the imagination and not to the strengthening of the conscious personality.

It may be easier to understand this type of imagining in forms other than the visual. When one does free-form dance, for instance, one is active and yet can be moved by the image. The image comes into one, so to speak, and expresses itself using the dancer. When the dancer is aware they discover because the image invents using them. One does not move simply as one is accustomed to. Nor does the dancer move simply because his ego gives commands. When one allows oneself to be moved, other ways of moving, inherent in different images, present themselves and become embodied in the evolving dance they are creating by their presence.

In the seventh type of imagining where the ego is an imaginal one the archetypal mode of Dionysus can be seen. Dionysus has a home in the sea, in water, as well as one on land.

The libido descends for refuge when driven by the excessive demands of Lycurgus, the blind tyranny of the ruling will which that mythic king in the *Iliad* exemplifies. Dionysus is a god of moisture, and the descent is for the sake of moistening. Depression into these depths is experienced not as defeat (since Dionysus is not a hero), but as downwardness, darkening, and becoming water.

Hillman, 1972a:284

One comes to a place where one is no longer out of one's element when one is with an image. Though one is not synonymous totally with the imaginal one has a home there as well as elsewhere. One does not continue as an Englishman in Africa but, rather, is changed by the imaginal. Going into the imaginal then becomes not a matter of preserving oneself in a foreign land but rather of a returning home.

Psychotherapeutically the aims of the ego psychologist would never be met with the seventh or eighth types of imagining; nor would the aims of a psychology based on imagination be satisfied with the fifth. The fifth relates everything to the heroic ego. The imagination is considered important only in so far as it touches this ego. We see from our usual set of eyes. Just as a person is different with you than he is with me or his brother, or a tree, or a brook, so too is the imagination revealed differently depending on who, which kind of ego, it is with.

Imagine, for instance, that you are watching an opera, say *The Magic Flute*. You identify with Papageno or the hero or heroine and move through the scenes with one of them. But what of the hand-maidens or the priests of knowledge? What is their day like? We experience them in terms of their relation to the character we have identified with, but where do they go when they are not in our view? What are they thinking and eating and dreaming? Who do they spend long night meals with?

If you are in a drama it is completely different depending on whose part you have become, who is moving you. Bernard Shaw said that once he created the characters of his plays, they took over and made their own lives. In so doing these images created Shaw as surely as they did the actors who later played them. The Sufi Sheik al-Ishrâq was "able to create marvellous ones because he was endowed with the interior vision of the figures with which he symbolized (Corbin, 1973:32). He could become his figures and see as they did.

This leads us to the eighth and ninth types of imagining, where we are present in the imaginal scene but not as a personified form. We are ourselves (not just in our imaginary bodies) an image other than a humanly embodied image. This may at first sound quite strange. But allow yourself to think back to childhood. You become your doll and cry and speak and move as the doll. You are on the floor moving the car with your hand but in actuality you are the car. You are making its sounds and as you raise it in the air with great speed you feel that swoosh of wind. Then you pull up in front of the gas pump and you are the gas pump. People pretending they were something else could easily scare us when we were children. We would beg them to stop being a gorilla or a burglar because to us they surely became that through their pretendings. Remember a version of a song and dance done by little girls, "I'm a little teapot short and stout; tip me over and pour me out"? One dances like a teapot but when it comes time to "pour," the teapot-child tumbles on the floor because she has become tea water being poured. In these examples one can see not only that it is an ability we have to become an image other than a person, but that once this has happened we follow not the rules of logic and linear space and time but rules of the imaginal. *There* it is not inconsistent for a cloud to turn into a blanket. In these kinds of imagining, as in the seventh, we, whatever image we are, are moved by the imaginal, not by the heroic ego.

Through examining literature one can discover the different types of imagining discussed here (and probably many more!). When Virginia Woolf in *Flush* dreams herself into Elizabeth Browning's cocker spaniel and sees all in the scenes from that perspective, she is imagining differently than the writer who houses himself within the stage manager's body (he who sees and comments on all the action but who stays in the wings). When Joyce in *Ulysses* keeps trying to enter each character's inner soliloquies and perceptions, he is imagining differently from the author who enters the main character of his drama and sees everything from those eyes. Does the poet observe things from the outside or the outside from within a thing—an image? Does the poet become tree and wind? Or does he recount their action upon himself? Or upon his lover?

The tenth kind of imagining is bound to appear inescapably abstract unless it is confused with the first or the seventh. Unlike the first there is no split between the imaginer and the images, and yet one is not involved with them in a dramatic way. This ego is involved and yet in ways that are so foreign to us that we would easily mistake it for detachment. One can perhaps compare it to a dream where we surely are and yet do not appear in one form in the drama. We could not even rightly call ourselves spectators. We are more surely, at least from the experience of it, part of all the elements of the image simultaneously.

Hopefully it is now more evident that different kinds of movement in imaginal space depend at least partly on different kinds of egos. Some may argue, perhaps correctly, that these egos not only appear to be essentially different but indeed have no kinship to each other. I think they can, however, be understood as resulting from various processes of transforming awareness. In this way we can understand the heroic ego we are accustomed to as one of the possible transformations, not as the *prima materia*. This seems a bit foreign because we are accustomed to taking our usual mode of ego-consciousness for granted as *the* mode. The imaginal is peripheral and foreign when we are in this frame of reference. Here however the first step has been defined as a separation of awareness from the heroic style and its many identifications. That awareness is then the *prima materia*. What happens is in reference to that. In this way of approaching the subject the imaginal egos are not transformations of the "I" that goes to the grocery store, daydreams and strives for the bigger and better, but are more clearly styles of awareness that are related to the imaginal — and, as we shall hope to see, are created by the imagination itself.

Wrathful images (the raping of the heroic ego)

If the sword of your anger puts me to death,
My soul will find comfort in it.
If you impose the cup of poison upon me,
My spirit will drink the cup.
When on the day of resurrection
I rise from the dust of my tomb,
The perfume of your love
Will still impregnate the garment of my soul.
For even though you have refused me your love,
You have given me a *vision of You*
Which has been the confidant of my hidden secrets.
                                        Sa 'di, Persian poet and mystic
                                        (quoted in Corbin, 1970:283)

We have not yet done with describing how the heroic ego resists the processes of transformation which could create a more imaginal awareness. Its resistances are not at all easy for us to see because most of the time it is their eyes we are seeing through. When a strong heroic ego is the aim of psychology, resistances are seen (when seen) not only as purposive in terms of preserving the nature of the ego, but also often as positive. We shall not doubt their purposiveness in maintaining the personality as we know it but we shall inquire into the valuation of this by attempting to understand what the imaginal's point of view is.

Just as the nature of consciousness becomes transformed by the activity of the heroic ego, so too does it change during involvement in imaginal activity—the activity of images. We have mistaken and failed to recognize what opus(es) of transformation the imaginal could create because we have persevered in looking at her images from the standpoint of the heroic ego. From this viewpoint one resists her because the heroic ego in charge does not choose to suffer, to allow itself to be diminished—as it would be if the imaginal was allowed to do her work. She would, through her images, change the allegiance of some of our awareness, drawing energy away from the heroic ego. So the heroic ego has resisted, preferring to see the image (if at all) as something that has to do with its world. We translate the image into advice concerning our activities and thoughts and forget the meta-phorical nature of the image. We forget that the image draws one elsewhere, by its nature.

When we think back to our dreams, fantasies, and thoughts, what are the images that discourage and frighten us most—making us want to draw away from their world? It is usually images of maggots and decay, of death and self-annihilation, of sexual torture and perversion, of madness, hysteria, possession by devils and despicable people. We fear letting go to these images for they seem to want to devour us—to make us crazy, to drive us to death, or into unspeakable actions and thoughts. We fear the depression we feel as we contemplate them. Images of closed wards and phenothiazines, of uncontainable rage, unmoving lives of speechlessness containing the visions of lunacy.

We resist. If we are doing active imagination we try to develop our relationship to the kindlier figures or give in to the shadier sorts, only to finally have done with their disturbance of our lives. We will approach these fellows if we must but not in and for themselves but for our "growth"—which will hopefully take us away from them. Once we are cured we won't have to worry about going crazy.

We sit down to do a waking dream and a figure approaches us and stabs us. We open up our eyes, stand up and wonder why we can't get in touch with what is really happening . . . or hope to God that that was somehow a mistake. Our nightmares may serve to be more convincing. They are not mistakes. They seem more like intricate plays of the imagination allowed to continue through the beneficence of sleep. Yet if we cannot say they are mistaken we approach them as if *we* were mistaken. We "must be doing something wrong in our conscious life to have a dream like that." As long as there is a mistake we can do something to rectify it. "We feel impelled to correct, straighten, repair" (Hillman, 1973:124). If there is some mistake there is some hope of fixing the situation and thereby getting rid of the image, or exchanging it for a better one (to reflect how well we are dealing with our life; how well the heroic ego is doing after all).

Here our resistance is subtler than the opening of eyes on a bloody occasion. We deal with the image and think we are giving it its dues. The image asks for our attention and we assume that it is asking us to change our life and so we turn from the image and take a different job, play tennis an extra two hours a week, get more related, take up watercoloring on the beach, let our anger out at more dinner tables.

Now it may be true that the image is asking us for our attention and that it wants us to change our. life, but when we turn from the image and change our life in the world in terms simply of activity, the image becomes incredibly frustrated because that is not her only world. She lives within all activities but doing more (or less) of them does not in itself make us any more aware of her life within them. She did not raise her voice to have us turn further from her. Nor does it seem as if she would work so hard at night to create us a drama of madness to so deeply affect us in order for us to retreat to a psychotherapy that tries to deaden her presence for us. In our thinking so we have raised supreme resistance—for we have convinced ourselves that we are doing the opposite of what we are. We change our life and feel we have complied with the unconscious. But is it not likely that she tries to change our relation to her? That this is what she cares about? She is telling us of her own world in a way that could make us reflect on it, acknowledge its reality. She gives us an image of insanity and we react with fright. The image threatens us because of our wish to maintain a certain kind of "I"[1] and because we confuse the image with the literal,

---

[1] In the Tibetan Book of the Dead the initiate is taught to recognize various kinds of images and ego reactions to them. Physical symptoms such as nausea and trembling were not attributed to the wrathful deities of the Second Bardo Visions but rather to the ego's attempt to regain control.

with the "matter" that is part of it. We reduce it to that. We leave our relation to the specific image when we turn to obsession about how not to go crazy. We confuse "something sick with something wrong" (Hillman, 1973:124). In the material daily world this is so. But it need not be so in the imagination—indeed, it does not seem to be so when we allow ourselves further access to these visions.

We forget that the image occurs in dream speech, and that even the affliction we feel as a necessary part of that speech is too fantasy: the affliction refers to movement, a *pathos*, taking place in the psyche and its images which is not wrong because it is not literal and medical.

To stand for the imaginal we must

refuse the assumption that something is wrong. Not for a moment may we entertain the notion that these images of sickness should not be there or that they are diagnostic or prognostic of literal or natural danger.

Hillman, 1973:124, 125

If we can refuse this assumption when we look at the image, her loud voice no longer sets us running to the doctor or the movies but captures our attention. It is as if she wants us to turn our awareness towards her and so she strikes us where we will be stunned in a direction that faces us towards her. Her images frighten us because they remind us of the mortality of our stance in the world. We are no longer certain. The heroic ego becomes relativized as the imaginal becomes more apparent. The ego's whole castle built of cards falls with the breath of certain images. The imagination scoops them up and away from the hero and continues to build her own structures and designs.

What process do these horrifying, wrathful aspects start if we dwell with them? We, our "heroic" egos, become less sure. The heroic ego is put at the mercy of the imaginal. It is being murdered, driven insane—or if it is not the object of these images it is none the less touched by them. The hero is made humble which makes him no longer a hero. At this point the awareness is loosened from his grasp. At the same instance the images grab our attention. They arrest us in our activities and usual thoughts. They stick by us during the day, demanding us. They say "no" to our usual paths, forcing us off into lanes we have never before wandered into. To what purpose? What happens? It seems that the imaginal itself, when we lend it our awareness, works a process of transformation. On the one hand, it draws the attention, the awareness, towards the imaginal, and on the other it weakens the heroic will, the notions of supremacy and of that "only" reality that our daily ego has. In doing this it gradually creates a more imaginal ego; an ego that is able to be moved by the imaginal and to answer to her. They turn us, in part, into water.

There is apt to be a fury of criticism if it is not made clear once again that, in this talk of "turning to water," we have not been speaking of the actual dissolution of the ego. To talk derogatorily about the ego threatens at every breath. One fears being abducted forever by the ghost of the unconscious. Here, however, we have not been speaking of weakening or murdering the ego. We have been considering possible transformations and styles of ego and, in so doing, our usual type of ego has been made relative. In all kinds of imagining, described here as waking dreams, one is aware, conscious, able to remember what has gone on. One is not tossed helplessly in a sea of daydreams and hallucinations. While engaging in the latter types of imagining described here (types seven through ten) one does create for oneself a home (as Dionysus had) in the imaginal. This home, the various imaginal egos, is created from the very material of the imaginal—images. With its creation the non-material side of metaphor becomes more apparent, more inhabited, more clearly a part of our wanderings. We are not only living with the image but are aware that we are doing so. One is not just involved in fantasy (daydream) and identified with it, but is aware of the fantasy as fantasy, of the image as image. Otherwise we would be as identified with the image, as absorbed by it, as we ever were with our heroic intentions and perceptions. The self-reflection that frees us from complete identification with the material reference[1] of the image can transport us into the multidimensional layers and scapes of the imaginal. Once we lose our self-reflection, however, we immediately become lost from the imaginal and grab back onto the literal ground of the image. Our consciousness falls back asleep. At that point the image may be taken as real—but not real within its own imaginal sense and ground.

Our hysterical rationalism is forever attempting to pull the unknown onto its land. There, the subtle is made to seem concrete, the metaphorical literal. This is so not because they are, but because the transposition from their own realm, their own way of knowing, destroys their nature. The way of rationalism pulls the image into matter and action, into the realm of events, history, decisions,

---

[1]For example, one could confuse the image of being chased with the concrete experience of that or the advice of a dream figure as something which should be actually carried out.

theories, prognoses. The rationalist translates into his terms what he can of the image. The rest, the symbolic side of metaphor, is lost and not grieved for. The way of imagination, as Paracelsus described it, is to "transmute gross matter into subtle, immaterial bodies." The makings of the rationalist's world are taken not at face value, but metaphorically. The imagination translates also, but the directionality of its movements reverse those of the literalist, the materialist. The image and the fact lead to different ends though they share a common ground.

As psychologists we have dealt with images in a rationalistic way. We have too frequently denied them their own directionality. How would we deal with the image in an *imaginal* way? What would that mean? First of all, we would have to watch carefully as we relate to an image for the points at which we try to bring it up on land, where we translate it to the concrete surfaces of our living. Each time we found ourselves once again on familiar ground — thinking we finally know what the image is all about — we would have to surrender and swim back to it, realizing we had left its depth far behind (as we unknowingly had used our own means of translation upon it). To remain dwelling with it, to perseveringly return to it — these we would have to promise. For only then would we give it an occasion to teach us its currents and ways of moving, its ways of transforming and of relating.

Chapter 7

Movements From and Towards the Imaginal

The psyche reveals herself in the form of images, for that is her experience. If we wish to befriend her, to love her, we must take great care in how we react to her, as her life speaks of itself to us. Our relation to the image, therefore, becomes all important.

When a friend tells us of an experience, how do we move in relation to it? How do we hope *others* will respond to *our* revealing of experiences? We do not want to be interrupted in our story; nor do we wish to be rushed. When our experience has moved us we are connected with it through the telling. It lives as we tell it, especially if the other person is receptive. If the other is not, we begin to say words but are no longer connected to them. The telling has become dead. We wish we had not begun.

Every detail has a place. We seldom find someone who allows us to tell it all out. The other feels a need to break in—to label, to judge, to advise. They wish to be helpful. But we want them to help us spin it all out. We desire them to question every point—not to bring it into question, but to make us elaborate on each element.

We want to repeat our important stories. We do so daily from within, dwelling with them; surrounding them with special spaces of time and emotion. We want to recapture them with another but sometimes the other person rushes to tell us what we might do about them. Then, at that moment, we are torn from our story and thrown into future time. We lose our connection to the experience. They may tell their own experiences which ours reminds them of. If the experiences are equated, the uniqueness of ours is lost. If they are drawn into their telling, we are either left alone with ours or pulled into theirs, out of ours. Sometimes the experiences seem to be echoes of a common theme. But this is rarer than is hoped for. There is a tendency for people to think they understand what the other is talking about.

They easily simplify it and can thereby equate it with their own or with concepts they have acquired. Comparisons fly. The subtle differences are lost. One loses the chance to see the other's experience more in terms of itself than in terms of oneself. This makes us keep seeing whatever it is we are already seeing, over and over. We hear something unknown in terms of something known and, in so doing, we learn nothing. Now, you may argue, we can only know in terms of the known. That is not as true as it sounds. An experience provides its own terms for its understanding. The more our friend elaborates on his or her story the more a structure becomes evident. If we have refrained from being absorbed in our means of structuring and interpreting, his or her structure strikes us. It has itself a context, a frame. It lends its own hints as to weight and significance.

If it is a difficult experience they are trying to tell us, we are often driven by our own anxieties to do something about it: to relieve them (i.e. to sever their connection with it and thereby ours) or to draw from the complexity a moral or conclusion, to become pragmatic—even if those were not the terms in which the other is speaking. We may take their experience from their hands, and put it to the light of day to examine just how it can be changed for the better. Where would they have to go? What could we do? We try to see how such a thing developed historically (even if that was not their concern) in order, perhaps, to see how it can be avoided in the future, and where the blame lies in the past. Perhaps we are the essence of friendliness and kindly deeds. But though the treatment is outlined, the progress assessed, the history completed and the goals insighted, that possibility (always lingering, always fragile) between two people is mercilessly killed, unknowingly, quietly.

What is it that our story wants? It keeps coming to the tip of our tongue. It rushes into empty spaces and flees from unhearing ears. It repeats itself, filling out each detail, trying to become real to us. It wants the other to dwell with it, to question, to ask for repetitions, to be made still by it. We rush in with some insignificant fact to relieve the silence, as we secretly wish the other to bring us back—to say that the silence was not empty, that it was filled with our experience, that it was given a place, and that the span of time marked its reality. We want to "get it across" from this space, to that between, to the other. It seeks to move one, to be known, to establish itself. When the other ceases to offer hope or advice, when they listen to our tale for no ulterior motive of their own, when they are still and can yet be moved. . . then something happens. The experience we are recounting connects us. It lives with us. It is what at that one moment makes us live. It thereby becomes real in a new sense.

So it is between the image and myself. I can do a thousand things wrong in trying to listen to it. I run off into interpretations, amplifications, ramifications, ways to change, to compare, to cure, to care. And with each of these I risk losing the possibility between us. The imaginal's experience itself is lost to me. I cannot sit still with it: refraining from gaining control over the situation, ceasing to impress it with my understanding and knowledge, becoming willing to stay with it even when it may begin to stink to my civilized nose.

The longer one sits with the other and lets him or her spin their experience, the deeper it becomes — the more profound. The more we hinder the other's connection to their story, the shallower it all becomes. Our feet finally touch bottom, as they did in the beginning. We scoop only a cup or two of water from their story and although we may come to know that, that was not the experience. Its dimensionality of depth, and its qualities of body are lost. We keep ourselves out of it. We take spoonfuls and carefully subject them to our own tests, supposing all the time that a relationship is developing.

With the image we create currents that keep drawing us back to shore, to what we already know. We think the image leads us there and thereby confirms our world. But this is not so. The currents that return us to the shallows of our familiar experience are of our own making. Keeping us from the depths, they kill the possibility of our relationship to the imaginal's experience — images.

The image dwells in depth, in depths created by shadows and reflections, depths that can be dived into and treaded amongst. Depths cannot be made shallow without losing themselves. The ocean is poured into the pool. It is safer that way. One can stand up in it. One can see bottom all the time. Everything that moves here is within our control, within our view. Here the image, like a fish, can always be caught. One can use it as food for the continuation of the usual life. But if one wanted to know the natural life of the fish, one has lost all by just such a move. The shallows destroy the usual life of the fish in the ocean. Is the fish really even "fish" anymore?

When we experience an image in a dream or waking dream, we usually want to know what it means — how it is connected to our lives. It seems apparent that there is some relationship. We want to seize it and place it on a shelf easily viewed in our daily lives. Then we would be able to say, "This here, this one, is the same as that over there."

When our friend tells us his story and we feel related to it, what we do with that sense of relation is important. Sometimes it is a case of empathy and his or her experience resonates somewhere within us and we feel a kinship. Sometimes it suggests to us one of our experiences. We may see theirs in a new light or we may then think of their experience in terms of ours. If we do not equate them they may serve to highlight parts of each other, drawing us closer to what they mean.

Often with the image we are reminded of experiences we have had. But what makes us think this is the image's purpose? Would we be presumptuous enough with our friend to think he had an experience he wishes to tell us about in order to remind us of our experiences? When we set to think about the experiences the image brings to mind, we may lose the image. We are pulled away from her. (Our friend is left in the dark while we go about our reminiscing.)

Now there is a way to let those experiences we remember, that we associate with the image, help us hear her better. But they must be used to keep us coming back to the image. A student dreams that his mother goes to the chairman of his academic department to apologize for the young man's work. He is then on a high mountain and begins to lose control of his car, speeding downward. After the dream he begins to think about his mother's critical attitude toward him; how she sides with the forces he is having a hard time contending with. He begins on the objective-material level where images are equated with their concrete reality. The image of the mother, for example, is taken to be the actual biological mother. Jung understood that images also have a subjective level of significance (see Chapter 3). This means that the mother in the dream is not just the biological mother but is representing a part of the dreamer's personality. The image is not the same as the concrete embodied form. It is always more than and different from. If the dreamer realized this he would see that the image of the mother represents a psychic reality, perhaps an attitude, in him. He remembers when he saw his teacher the day before the dream and how he had belittled his plans. He thinks about this because he understands that the image is composed of day residue. But if the dreamer had thought that the day is likely to be composed of dream residue (i.e. that the real and the imaginal worlds are at least equal, that the imaginal does not only serve the day-world), then not only would he be free to see the image as being related to his self-deprecating attitude but he would see also that his self-deprecating attitude is a reflection of an imaginal movement, an imaginal reality. When he sees this he is less likely to only take part of the total dream image and get involved in thoughts of school, of his inability to succeed because of his own "inner" mother always turning him in. If the concrete events are as likely to reflect the imaginal movement as the other way around, then the dreamer would not leave the image as soon as he had found a material likeness to it within the day residue. He would realize he is not done with the image and would return to it and try to see more of what is happening there.

It then strikes him that there is not only a critical, betraying mother but that as this mother speaks the dream ego loses control and falls downward. As he goes through the day the dreamer could note the "residue of the dream" in his dayworld. Where does he feel this out-of-control feeling, this downwardness? If he kept this in mind he would feel close to the image as he felt himself filled with anxiety when he lapsed into his self-deprecating thoughts. He would learn to observe the fantasy beneath the emotion and the thought. Instead of only discovering the daily history reflected in the dream, one looks for the reflections of the imaginal within the day. In this way the relating of the day and the dream world does not lead always in the direction of the dayworld, but circles back and forth, never getting far from the experience of the imaginal. When he feels the "downwardness," he could look around also for the apologetic mother. Where has she been lurking in his daydreams and thoughts? If he identifies with the dream ego then he experiences this mother as a victim would. Her energy is always pushed up against his. His car swerves. If he could loosen his identification with the dream ego, he could draw nearer to observing this "mother." If he could accept that in an imaginal sense he is her as well as the car, the student son as well as the professor, he would gain new means of seeing how the image creates his daily world. He tells a friend whom he respects and wants to be respected by that another friend is not trustworthy. He works all day and yet a part of him thinks it is not enough. He becomes easily convinced and apologizes within. When he is not as identified with the role of the son he can see that the image of mother is related not only to the son but to the image of the car. By becoming the mother in fantasy, by assuming her nature, he can explore her interconnections with the other images, which are probably even further from his conscious view than those relations formed by the dream ego. When the image is seen metaphorically it has many sides and allusions. It cannot be reduced to one type of experience. It can never be equated, or dealt with sufficiently. One type of experience, however, can be used to get closer to an aspect of it, to an echo or a shadow of it. The mother's relation to his talk with the professor, the image of mother related to the biological mother, the car and his emotion, the inner car crashing tomorrow afternoon as he stands speaking, the anxiety of downwardness even as he tries to relax, the mother and the car, the apologies, the criticisms, the regrets, the disguised badgering: all are aspects. The drawing of lines of cause and effect can oversimplify the network of simultaneity, of directionalities and interconnections. Each experience, each relation, can deepen us into the reality of the image, its world. The metaphor becomes filled out. Always requiring more. No poem ever completed. No image quite reached. Always a little further out. Keep swimming. But each new depth sets up its own likenesses and its own shadows, its own revelations and obscurities.

When a friend tells us of a situation and we draw from it conclusions as to what step should be taken — or even if we feel that an action or a conclusion should be drawn at all — we depart from the context given to us. Images describe. They do not say to get a divorce, or go into analysis, or quit school. The total image states a situation. It *may* include cause and effect,[1] but it does not usually include dictums as to what one should do. Even if it does give a dictum one must realize first of all that the image's landscape is not the same as that of the "real" world. An obvious example is the following dream:

In the dream I am an analyst and a voice says to me that when analysis is not going right with a patient, I should take their bones and bury them deep within the earth.

Now, one does not think that one should actually do this in a concrete sense. And yet, if someone dreams that their analyst tells them they have to have a divorce in order to succeed in their analysis, the person is likely to begin thinking about divorce and analytical progress in a very concrete sense. The image in itself does not necessarily mean that you should divorce because your inner or outer analyst said to, any more than one should set out to capture an analysand's bones because of a dream. In this example, as soon as one gets lost in contemplating actual divorce one falls out of relation to the image. One simplifies the image to a single event in the "real" world and forgets that in the imaginal there is a figure suggesting divorce. All the many dimensions of the image are lost as the movement in the imaginal is reduced to one actual divorce. Now this does not mean that one cannot contemplate one's divorce in a way that would help them understand the image, or the image in a way that would deepen their understanding of some of

---

[1] I say "may" because one can look at the dream as a complete image in which no one part can be singled out as causing another. The end is just as necessary for the beginning, as the middle is for the end (Berry).

the dynamics of the divorce. The person who dreams of the burial of
the analysand's bones as a way to deepen the connection to the
analytical process can contemplate this act in great detail. He has the
help, however, of realizing that he is engaging in a fantasy. If the
woman realized the metaphorical side of her contemplations about
divorce, they too could help her feel the imaginal reality from which
the image sprang. When she loses this sense and deals with it simply as
concrete decision and further questions whether her analyst really
thinks that, the image's world is taken as simply another expression of
our usual world. However, when she wonders about what her analyst
thinks and also has an ear to this inner conversation as fantasy, the
concrete and the imaginal are connected and reflected in each other
through her wondering. She starts to discover how the imaginal is
interweaved with the daily.

Our friend tells us that her analyst suggests divorce. Do we decide it
is right or wrong and tell her to go get the papers or talk to her
husband? Or do we try to help her express how it feels to have this
analyst say this thing in this setting? Although we may turn to
contemplating divorce for ourselves, we realize that this is not what our
friend is talking about. It may be that something in our friend's talk
sparks us to think about it and we may even get really involved in the
whole issue. But that, in and of itself, has nothing to do with our
understanding what our friend is trying to say.

The image may move us to think about decisions and judgments,
but in itself it is neither advising nor moralizing. It may say, given this
situation, that happens. That may suggest to us a situation in our daily
world. We may apply the dream to it saying "If I do this, that will
happen." But at that point we have left the image. We have forgotten
it for the daily world and forgotten to hear if it spoke of something
else. We may wish to use it in this way—a kind of learning from
likenesses, from similar experiences. But let us not forget the friend in
the corner and the fact that his or her experience is unique. No matter
how similar the image is to a concrete happening, it is different from
it.

We may come to know the image through specific daily instances.
This appears fine because we respect the implication (the material,
active extrapolation) more than the imaginal. But if we looked more
closely we would see that when we are

regarding the dream from its implications, we realize the narrower selectivity within
which we are operating. And this seems paradoxical for it feels (because of our greater
conceptual development? because of our iconoclastic tradition?) as if the image were

the more limited mode. The dream only says this or gives these particular images, while implications seem to extend in many directions. But by moving away from the image and into implication we forego the depth of the image — its limitless ambiguities, which can only partly be grasped as implications. So to expand upon the dream is also to narrow it — a further reason we wish never to stray too far from the source.

Berry, 1974:98

The image states a fact — but that fact is a psychological one. When compared to concrete facts it may appear foolish, nonsensical, or extraordinarily wise. Yet, even in the latter case, to reduce the metaphor to the material, the psychological to the pragmatic, denies the imaginal its ontology.

Often when we consider a dream or waking dream we pick out one or two elements that strike us. There is a valuation process going on that we should be aware of. We should ask ourselves why we are considering this part and not that. We should watch quite carefully the direction our answers are indicating we are flowing to. What do we want out of those elements? What are we hoping for? Do they take us into thinking about a situation that happened, a relationship or a plan? Which image of ourselves that we wish to retain, do they fulfill? Do we want them to tell us what to do or not ? How do we really feel? Are they the dream images that struck the dream ego as much as the "I" (the waking ego) now studying them? How did the other dream figures respond to them? Were they pulled by them? Did they value them in the same ways as the waking ego does?

Now if these striking elements serve to pull us into the dream, into a relation with it, we are probably on the right track. But if we neglect the feeling tones and subtle interplay of all the images, we are taking a piece of the dream (as we might of anything else) in order to feed our usual self with it; wandering off from the imaginal (with more self-created justification) into our usual frame of consciousness and pursuits. When we take one element *out* (not when we get pulled *into* the dream by one element) we use the dream. We single out something that interests us and let the rest go down the drain to forgetfulness. We think we are "giving a lot of attention to our dreams," but we are not. We are giving a lot of attention to the part of ourselves who sucks the image for its own gain. The imaginal scene has an integrity. Each element is *absolutely* necessary for the total image. Each detail must be understood as the best possible way of conveying whatever the experience (imaginal experience) is that the image deals with. When we neglect elements and details of the image we forsake its experience and the structure it gives to it. We avoid learning how different the imaginal is from our usual world. When we single out one aspect we do not face the weave of ambiguity and elaboration that exists in the total imaginal scene. We make something that is straightforward and commonsensical (to fit our desire for easy opinions and solutions) from something that is thick, full of pockets, curves and tunnels into itself.

You know times when a friend will single something out of your story because it fascinates him. He is absorbed into it and exaggerates it out of proportion to the way it feels for you. You want to move on and feel his attention not on what you are trying to convey but on something of his own. The slant and feeling of your story is lost. Sometimes, however, the person can be fascinated by your particular story in a way that makes them want to know everything around it that became important to you. They are drawn closer to your experience through their fascination with the particular. They do not want to impose values on it because they are so fascinated by the thing-in-itself that they want to know how it values.

One must try to keep the image in its context. One can try to see what emotion the image conveys, not just the emotion evoked in one afterwards. We should give the image freedom to pick among our emotions the one(s) it most naturally evokes. Some people consciously try to be the same with each image, as if bowing to some rule of objectivity. Others think too much about how they should or consciously want to react to an imaginal experience. Each misses the opportunity to learn about the image by the way it evokes in one to be with it. One can be politely curious and find out only one side of an image, over and over. If the image is malicious, one can continue to be a smiling (but frightened) victim. At some point an impulse to rage or to ignore may arise from deep within—not as a conscious strategy—but as a reaction that is related to the quality of the image, not just the ego notions of how one should be.

It is important that we do not subject the image to a judge's hearing. "Should this character have done that?" "If I [that is the dream ego to which he is falsely equating himself] had reacted in this other way it would have turned out better." Such inquisitions, self-recriminations and value judgments are imposed on the image by the ego. The image's reality, however, is that each part did as it must do. Each was necessary to express the situation of the psyche. Try to take the image as a given and as completed, rather than a play which you, as ego, must rework and finish. The dream may be dreamed onwards, but hopefully it is the imagination which is given the freedom to elaborate on its own expression. In this way the imaginal context of the dream or waking dream is more closely preserved.

One must also take care that the telling of the image (to oneself or to another) does not alter it. One can try to keep from translating the image into words (when it did not express itself verbally) by attempting to re-enter the image in the medium it used (seeing, moving, feeling). In telling about the image one often "gives an irreversible direction and forces the dream into a definite pattern" (Berry, 1974:99) that was not present as the image first appeared. What was in experience beautifully ambiguous becomes "one thing rather than another" (*ibid*). The idea of progression that we superimpose onto the image encourages both us and the analyst to say that each portion is the result of what came before. This lends itself to the assumptions of those who wish to take the image as a prescription, or as a key to the causation of symptoms. The ego's tendency to see in terms of cause and effect too often loses the non-progressive and simultaneous aspects of many images. The necessity of the end for the nature of the beginning is overlooked.

Unfortunately part of what we use to remove the image from its own earth are the very tools and methods that were created for and guaranteed to protect it. Those of us who are students of psychology have become heirs to a potential arsenal of ways to kill the image. We allow our psychological language to mislead us in direction. Instead of the language we use drawing us closer to the experiences it attempts to describe, we too often use it to lead us the other way — away from direct experience of an image, towards a concept. Often a concept is created when an individual is struck by what seems like many variations or repetitions of a single theme. The concept serves to draw attention to this and to propose something of the nature of the phenomenon that stands out to that particular observer. The concept is a symbolic way of encompassing a collection of experiences. In itself it is not identical to any single experience within the group. It is more stereotypic in nature. If we have an experience and compare it to a concept, several things can happen. We can say, "Oh that was my anima talking" and we then think not of the experience but of whatever constructs the word "anima" symbolizes for us. Once we compare, we often too easily equate, and the "anima" (which was Jung's word), the concept, becomes what we are left with.

Our images become standardized according to the common code, and we enter into "processes of individuation," "strengthening the ego," "getting in touch with the shadow," "integrating" our thises and our thats. But none of these may be true to the process happening in the psyche — our psyche. It is true that each of these words has experience behind it, but for us they hold none unless we use them in relation to our experience and in order to keep referring us deeper into it. The concept can help us recognize certain movements within the imaginal, but then it is the movements themselves which should become important —not which psychological word they are. We can go to analysis, be students and teachers of psychology, researchers of the psyche, and by manipulating the symbols of our chosen systems we can somehow escape the direct experience of psyche or whatever "that" was which gave rise to psychology. There is a great danger in this—for it happens to us slowly as we grow up and learn. It attacks us quite subtly, but from all sides. It is more deadly to those who would seemingly be most exempt. Sadly we end up using psychology to gain distance from the experience of psyche, but it is not at all obvious to us. We continue defending our good intentions, but only with our bad practice.

Our ways to deal with images, themselves symbolic, have been denied their own metaphorical aspects, their own ability and necessity to point beyond. That which promised connection to soul betrays it. The common metaphors end up leading to entrapment, monotony, sterility. The hours of analysis may pass and one fights the realization that one is unmoved; that when the light goes out one feels the same things and the same about them. One has gained no further access to inner life.

What makes us get involved in, get thinking and talking about, our "animuses" our "inferiority complexes," our "tricksters," our "trans-ferences," and our "libidinal flows?" When you hear a person speaking this language do you not try to find out *what* they are talking about, i.e. what experience moved them? One often finds that a very complex image, full of shades and depth, has struck them. They then dilute it through the language of psychology. It becomes an "anima experience" and every man has an anima. So one can talk about it as if it were a cup of coffee in the morning (after all, everyone has one, right?). If, however, it strikes the individual that this commonality of imagery points to the fact that his experience is one that is central to the psyche he may take more care with it.

If the word takes one away from the image and allows what appears to be the image to be grasped and controlled and talked about, then what has been grasped is not the image but the concept. It is the usual ego who is grasping so frantically. Not being able to dwell with the image, it climbs up and over the edge into its own terrain. Now if we took the word or concept and with it hunted for the images, and having once found some, dwelled with them, then the concept would be used by the ego to get us into touch with the imaginal. It would help us swim out, and once we were there we would be moved by the depths' own current.

Magicians have the trick of dropping the rabbit in the hat and then pulling it out again (von Franz, 1970:XII-17). We do not see them drop it in and so we are amazed what wonders come from the hat. At least magicians know that they are pulling out what they are dropping in. We drop in our psychological language and theory and come up with what confirms it because we often come up with what we put in but do not know it. We decide the dream image tells us about yesterday or tomorrow and we relate the images to yesterday and they tell us something about it. But we may as well take that same image and compare it to anything whatsoever and, with some skill, we can get it to tell us something about it. In this way we keep finding out what we already know.

We also reduce the imaginal to the conceptual, and in so doing keep out of relation to what we do not yet fully know. One must be so careful. Most of the time those of us adept in psychology kill the image before we have hardly awakened. We think we are remembering our dream and keeping in touch with it as the dawn light comes. But before dawn the image is already on the operating table and we are performing a hundred tasks of labeling, sorting, equating, trimming, transplanting. We have removed the seemingly unnecessary and tossed it aside in the empty lot of forgetfulness (only to have it multiply and reappear more vigorously). We have rearranged what seemed only like disorder, hoping that now the image will work better, will be clearer to our view. (We are too sleepy to know what notion of order we compared it to.) We begin to transplant amplifications and interpretations, concepts and conclusions for what is naturally given. What creatures are still alive run from the surgeon's light and knife back beneath the rocks, hidden from our view — safe in their moist darkness.

People neglect images so much that when we seemingly remember ours and put an interpretation to them, we feel proud. However, we must at many points refrain from interpreting. I do not mean that we should let the dream and the waking dream entirely alone; that we should wilfully be the ones to chase them under the rocks. We should, however, refrain from a finalistic and reductionistic type of interpretation in order to remain in connection with them. There is a saying "traddure e tradire," "to translate is to betray." How many times do we think we know by the time breakfast is finished what a dream image meant? Or, as we begin a waking dream, how frequently are we continuously classifying what occurs in our catalogues of psychological experience? We tell the dream figures we know what they are saying—that they needn't go on. We betray them with our sweet understandings. We pocket the theory which we applied to the image and leave for work thinking we have done justice to the image. We come to understand, for instance, that we are dealing with our shadow, but the specificity of exactly what our psyche is imagining may be lost. In order to learn about the imaginal we must not allow ourselves to rest with what little theory we have. If we can keep returning to the image and experiencing it anew, we will be able to see for ourselves just where a concept aptly describes or sadly misleads. We will not end up resting for years with a concept like "animus," that does little to describe the actual experience of the masculine in the female psyche. Nor will we trim our imaginal experience to fit the concept, discarding the contradictory and the unique as superfluous and irrelevant.

Our concepts of the imaginal and our attempts to amplify images with myth and folklore can be creatively used as education about the imaginal, as long as we do not discard our own direct experiences of images. Amplification can teach us how to imagine from the specific to the general and back again. By leading us among the members of a family of images we can gain familiarity with their ways and importance. Amplification, by using images to learn about images, allows us to draw closer to the imaginal without leaving it. Interpretations, on the other hand, can transplant us to an intellectual system or to a judgmental code, or cause a reduction to the non-psychological. Often when we begin to make an interpretation, we do so in order to draw ourselves away from the imaginal and onto commoner shores. If we could be aware of the point at which we begin to interpret, we could see whether, at that point, we did not have a choice. Sometimes it is just as the image begins to move us towards it that we turn to other terms. Just as we are aware of the image, as in a waking dream, we must also be aware of our reactions towards it. If we could keep an ear to the images within the interpretations, within the systems we are using, we could use the interpretation almost like amplificatory material, helping us maintain the imaginal's own directionality (from material to immaterial). The specific image should not be forgotten in favor of any amplificatory or interpretative material. That a figure is like Demeter must help us to understand the figure first of all—not mislead us to thinking only of Demeter.

We should be careful that our notion of "psychic integration" does not justify our ego's attempts to consume the image as the bird would the spider. "Psychic integration" can be used as a process of pulling everything into the area of the ego and having once converted it into words and interpretations, the ego then swallows it all and becomes seemingly larger. Integration between the ego and the image may be seen more as a system of fine silk threads that pull both into connection and relation without destruction, without losing the nature of the image. In this sense interpretation is not a reductive process, but more an attempt to pull into relation gently and through the dimension of time. Our associations to the image then do not lead us away but rather form the threads that bind our consciousness of the imaginal more closely to the real, the real to the imaginal. Interpretation in this way does not destroy and betray the image. It tries to aid the metaphor in continually placing the material and the imaginal side-by-side, with their own natures retained. By keeping both elements of the metaphor together, the interpretation allows for the material to be seen in relation to the imaginal background that couples it.

Some dreams in and of themselves make a statement with one group of images and then with another, and yet another. Series of dreams or fantasies (those that deal with a common element) do this also. Each set of images brings us into connection with different aspects. When we allow the dream to be imagined on—as in the case of a waking dream or a meditation upon a dream—we allow the images to multiply and develop further within our view. Each one can add to our empathy with the original and with the piece of the imaginal from which they arise.

Think of a poem or a piece of music that you read or hear over and over again. As the poem moves to be the tawny cat, the room behind the store, that feeling as dusk draws the shade down, as it changes location and emotion, you travel with it. Its images transform you as they pile one upon the other. You exist in the present moment with the experience of all that has come before. Layer upon layer, the larger image comes into being within you. It comes not just on its own—as a single set of words on paper—but rather as the poem streams through you, it collects likenesses among the other images of your soul. It draws to it cast out memoria, landscapes (actual and imaginal), emotions. It ferrets out your hopes and your fears. All this it pulls through you separating out some as the image becomes more specific, drawing more along as it widens. The poem pulls you into its world through your own world. Each image amplifies itself naturally so as to be closer to your sensitivities. You may interpret as a way of hearing the poem.

Your associations may lead you into your realm of knowledge and theory. Yet even here you can be aware of the images within the specific knowings you desire to draw the poetic image to.

Each time you hear it a bit differently. You see it from images within yourself. You not only hear *it* differently, but it causes you to hear other things differently. The poetic image creates perceptions, modalities of perceiving. You see not only different things, but things differently (Raines, 1967:113). It is not really, as one usually thinks of it, solely a matter of your creating sense out of the poem. For as you set out on such a fantastic endeavor, it is steadily creating the you who is endeavoring. It is drawing you into its landscapes and adding not only to your experiences but to your ways of experiencing.

The poem can be used to teach one to be a poet (Bachelard, 1963:16) in the same way that the dream can be used to enable one to dream (not just to passively receive a dream but to voluntarily enter into imagining). In both, the giving of oneself to an image teaches the art of imagining. The poem and the dream lead us into the sites of revery. If we develop our observing consciousness we can follow the revery as closely as the written poem.

Images demand that we develop the facility to inhabit new sites, in new terms all the time. Each image in itself and in the variety of amplifications that it evokes in us continuously changes, showing ever greater depth and variety. It teaches one to lose the ego fantasy of permanence and continuity. Within the dream, the poem, one can be all figures, all landscapes, all emotions. Indeed to grow closer to them, one must assume their universe.

As we move within images foreign to our ego we experience reverberations within ourselves. The "otherness" we had perceived in the image becomes familiar—not only in the moment that we entertain it, but arising from the past. It pulls things from us that show our participation, though often largely unconscious, in it. As we imagine, we learn to recognize not only the possibility, but also the actuality, of a consciousness with a polymorphous nature. The fact that the past has been created by just such an assumption and possession of us by various images becomes more undeniable.

As we move from encountering each image with our usual "I-ness," to entering each image and allowing it to structure our perception and movement, a new realm is opened. For now we are able to encounter the relation between images—not merely from the viewpoint of one observer (one ego, one "I"), but from within the perspective of other images as well.

We have spoken about remaining in the context of the imaginal either by using associations and interpretations in a circular direction (not only out of the image to the interpretation, but from the interpretation back to the image) or by taking interpretations and other associations in an imaginal way also (searching for the images they enclose). To assume different images, however, we must learn more specifically to deepen ourselves into the context of the individual image. By spending time with it, trying to feel it, to slip into it, we can try to note where and how it lives. How does it spend a day? What is its sense of time? (Some people say that the imagination is "timeless." It would be more accurate to say that it contains many different senses of time.) When one imagines oneself into a cow, one discovers a sense of time quite unlike that of a bird or a Princeton professor. By attuning oneself, to that alone, one feels viscerally a quality of energy that possesses one periodically. Each image and system of images has its own sense(s) of time, its own emphasis or ignorance of past, present and future. It accomplishes actions or moves through duration "in its own time." The ego identifies with clock time and ignores its experience that does not verify this as real time (experienced time). Images are free to move to their own sense of time and timing. The Little Prince learned that to draw closer to his rose he must "waste" time. He must surrender time as he knows it to be.

We do not always have only to sit with closed eyes, moving around in our heads, to draw closer to an image. We can put it in our pocket and carry it with us throughout days and nights. We can assume, for instance, its "timing" (Lopez-Pedrazo) as we move in the world. With it in our pocket we are more apt to recognize when the way we are moving corresponds to the image. By holding the image near we can do the same with its ways of perceiving other things, its thinking and feeling.

Entering into the context of an image is easier, the more developed the image has been allowed to become. Recurring dreams and images with the same theme, or encompassing the same figure or emotion, can be compiled.[1] By watching the development of and the elaborations on this part of the imaginal, by listening to the multiple ways it describes itself, the things it includes and touches, we can more easily

---

[1] For the purpose of compiling descriptions of the imaginal from images themselves, a journal of waking dream and dream experiences is invaluable. An image journal true to the nature of the images would most likely not be straight prose. The image demands shape, color and poetry to approximate it. Pictures, for instance, can place all the parts of the image together in a way unlike usual words.

enter its mood and landscape, imagining ourselves (in one form or another) amongst it all. Psychological facts and experiences (those of the psyche) can be more clearly seen. Repeating the images over and over again, allowing them to expand (visually, mentally, in painting, writing, movement), to set in our consciousness their non-linear history, enables us to begin to grasp and feel them. The emergence of figures, where they go, with whom and in what way they deal, unravels. The different places of the imaginal begin to stand out. The possibility of an archetypal topography begins to emerge. One comes to have an idea of where archetypes can be located in relation to each other (Casey, 1974). We give the imagination a chance to reveal to our consciousness the arrangement in depth of its interior space. The autonomy of the imaginal, the fact that it has an independent order and a continuousness, become evident when series of images are examined. The seemingly random nature of images, that strikes the beginning rememberer of dreams as he initially begins the practice, dissolves with time.

Waking dreams make us familiar with the imaginal. This familiarity allows us to recognize the activity of the psyche in our daily lives. We learn to feel when we are inhabiting a certain image and reacting to another. The unspoken metaphors of our living are revealed in just this way—not for just their material aspect, nor just their symbolic, but rather as the co-creation of the physical and imaginal qualities of our lives.

Chapter 8

On Imagining about Imagining

It is ironic that those psychologies which seem to give the greatest respect to the imaginal have not inquired into the subject of what *they* have imagined about imagining. If, in fact, the imaginal is as integral a part of our activites as the modern oneirotherapies claim, then there is little doubt that one is imagining not just while participating in waking dreams, but also within the acts of theorizing about and doing therapy with waking dreams. Perhaps part of why the fantasies beneath the activities of imagining about the imagination, images, the imaginer, and imagining itself have been left untouched has to do with the nature of these modern imaginings about imagining.

The imagination is treated as if it were an internal place. One closes the eyes to the outside and gradually one begins to enter a sleeplike state of relaxation, as if one is travelling or falling into this interior space. Images begin to appear. At first they are fleeting and fuzzy as if one is on the outskirts of a town at dawn. Then clearer, more continuous. One believes that one sees the imaginal landscapes and figures as they really are. Amongst these images (primarily visual) are favorable and unfavorable ones. There seem to be unspoken criteria for judging some imaginations as sick and others as healthy. Therapy becomes viable because it supposes not only that it can evoke the imagination but that it can alter images and, thereby, the imagination itself. Through suggestion and restructuring (see Chapters 3 and 4) images can be influenced to change from the "outside." This assumes a dialectic between an imaginer (outside of the imagination) and the imagination. The former does things to the latter. The doctor and the patient experience themselves as continuous "I's." The "I," although connected to the imagination, is none the less outside of it. One enters into a relation with images with this "I." The "I" not only observes but decides how to act with images: how and what to say, what tactics of approach to use, how to relate the images to the concrete details of daily life. In the same way that it seems natural for the dreamer to

identify with the dream ego, it appears natural that the imaginer
should travel through the imagination in the figure that appears to be
him.

Part of the ambiguity that remains in views on imagination is its
status vis-à-vis "reality." In one way its reality has been clearly
substantiated by some psychologies, and yet even within these its realm
of reality seems to be limited—not in a wholly rational way either, but
rather as if by prejudice. The imaginal is real and present . . . but not
all of the time. There are invisible fences (themselves ghostly images?)
that attempt to keep certain provinces clear of the imaginal (to keep
our awareness of images out?), as if to allow that if there are images
within these boundaries they would decrease the sanctity, the reality,
of the terrain. So images are real . . . but when we really want
something to be real it should not have any images in it. This is
especially present in that which we would like to regard as "true."

Our ability to imagine such fences has allowed us to see distinctions
between our daily reality and that of a waking dream, our ego and the
images in the waking dream. These are the distinctions that give rise in
part to the idea of an "I" outside of the imagination, going into it and
exploring it. If such fences were not imagined, it would seem that even
before we start to imagine we are already held within an image(s),
acting out images, and responding to images (in this case the images of
"going into" the "imagination," of "doing a waking dream," or an
"active imagination").

To begin to ground ourselves in the earth of the imaginal real we
must work against the boundaries and habits that formerly were
created to pull out and separate the notions of our identity from this
ground. The activity of waking dreams can be used to perpetuate and
to strengthen our attempts at separation, or it can serve to break
through the fences already built. In the conceptualization presented
here, attention has been given to the relationships among the ego,
awareness, and images. Our usual ways of thinking have equated ego
with awareness, and in doing so they have created a blind spot.
Whenever awareness is subsumed by one set of images, it is unable to
observe that set. It is possible, however, for awareness to be strained
from the ego and by doing so to create a vantage point separate from
the ego.

When awareness is identified with the ego, it is the ego's eyes
through which awareness perceives. In this state the ego acts as if it is
at the center of all that is to be perceived. It appears distinct from the
circle of images around it, because it itself is unable to be perceived by

awareness. All relating done in view of awareness is that of ego to other, of ego to image, of ego to object. However, when the ego is seen as an image(s) among images it takes its place on the circumference of the circle, and it is awareness that is able to reside in moments in the middle. This enables a type of imagining to arise that perceives inter-relationships among images other than those between ego and object. Once our awareness has succeeded in establishing itself independently from our egos, its later identification with any set of images would not remove them from the circles of the imaginal into a center of reality, but awareness would travel among images and would recognize them as such. The change in perspective could be likened to the one which occurred when people realized the earth was not the center of the universe, or that humans were not the first, and thereby most important creation.

If waking dreams perpetuate a type of imagining in which awareness is always dependent on the eyes of the ego (where earth is always in the center) and is unaware of this, one can observe a tendency to see all other images only as they relate to ego (all planets exist because of earth or are important only because of their relation to earth). That this is a perspective which exaggerates some qualities of images and negates others would not be apparent. The ego seems to try and subsume not only awareness, but imagination as well. The particular qualities of these is lost as the ego tries to make them mere satellites. It is inevitable that the non-ego in this case is reduced to those terms in which the ego can perceive and understand.

To ground ourselves in the imaginal real we must have a means of uniting in our awareness sense data with the symbolic transformations it undergoes and of uniting symbols with the "reality" they create. These require not a fence, but a bridge by which the process of making metaphorical symbols can be followed. This is dependent on an awareness that can serve as an intermediary from the matter of metaphor to its other base in the immaterial, in the imaginal. Awareness allows one to travel from what is perceived to how it is perceived and back again. One knows not only the content of perception, but the imaginal context of perception—*who* (which image) is perceiving.

Here (Chapter 6) it was suggested that different kinds of egos resulting from various processes of transformation could enter into relation with the imaginal. Each of these transformations is based on the shift of awareness from identification with one group of images to another. These identifications determine not only our imaginings about imagining, but also how we act with other images, what we look for, shy away from, how we interpret, how we connect the experience of waking dreams to the daily.

By observing images we can determine how a single image acts differently according to which other images it is amongst. Through assuming the identity of various images that appear we can explore the interactions not only between ourselves as "I" and another image, but between any image (or group of images) and any other single image or image group. If we can experience that images have relationships together in the imaginal that are unique for each coupling, then we cannot fail to suppose that each image we encounter is different according to which image we ourselves approach it as. Just as one person evokes reactions of a certain kind in another person, so too do we (formed out of our identifications with certain images) evoke certain qualities in the images we encounter. We cannot suppose that the images we observe are simply the way they are by nature. We must take into account in our descriptions of them that they appear as they do in a situation of being in relation to certain images, i.e. the ones we are at that moment identified with.[1]

If we take responsibility for our creating part of the nature of each image we encounter in a dream or waking dream, then we must also re-evaluate our tendencies to censor images as unhealthy, bad, or crazy, and to subsequently deprecate solely the imagination for these qualities. If they are "unhealthy," part of the responsibility for that must lie on our shoulders. We cannot so simply agree that that is the way the image or the imagination is. Some oneirotherapies, as discussed in Chapter 4, attempt to "strengthen the ego" (to change the images it is identified with in a specific way) by suggesting ways to encounter various threatening images. In this instance, it is seemingly acknowledged that the particular face of the ego creates and per-petuates the faces of the imaginal. If the ego can be changed—to learn new ways of movement—then the imaginal will change.

There is, however, a loophole here. The above theory assumes that the reason images are frightening is because the ego is not strong

---

[1]We must take into account that the relationships among images are not apparent to rational assumptions. The multi-faceted nature of each image makes possible a variety of extremely different couplings. In one instance a figure that appeared as a nun to a young man in a series of waking dreams was married (he found in a nightly dream) to a haggard but wise caretaker in his dreams. The nun's rather nursing-supportive attitude to the young man was quite different from her independent airs with her husband.

enough. This however is the way it would be imagined by the archetype of a strong heroic ego. It makes as much sense to say that the images are frightening because the ego is so strong . . . that they must be frightening in order to make their values known, to impress them upon the imaginer.

What is the image's wrath that so threatens us? Often one persists in taking these images as evidence of literal harm. One identifies with the dream ego to such an extent that one can only feel identity as a victim, not as the other images that victimize. One equates ego with the "real" identity, and sees from this perspective the threatening images as imaginal purveyors of evil, attempting to destroy the "real" self. But what if the threatening images are granted as much reality as the ego? If both are understood to be aspects of the personality with the same quality of realness? The struggle could then be understood as one between different ways of perceiving and valuing, embodied within the various images. To try and remove the individual from the struggle by strengthening one side must be seen and accepted as a decision based on the preferences and prejudices of particular images. If it is not, one becomes involved unconsciously in negating some aspects of the imaginal by calling them imaginal and supporting others because they are more "real." Let it serve as a warning that when a therapist or an individual sides with some images against others, their victory must signal a defeat in some other corner.

Each image has its own set of values. It need not appear as an appendage of morality but rather as its preferred style of going about things or perceiving things. When an image is especially wrathful to us we can inquire into what its values are and how in particular our present way of valuing may interfere with it. By not giving all of our attention to kindly figures (those that seem to be at peace in relating to us) we can allow ourselves to be made aware of imaginal styles further in our consciousness from the ones we are presently identified with. It is possible not only to become familiar with them as distinct entities from ourselves, but also by imagining ourselves into them. The latter enables us not only to learn of the existence of the particular image, but also to view from its perspective the images we have been previously identified with. The distinction between them and us is simplistic because when seen from a position outside of theirs or ours, both parties seem to reside in the same house. As long as our awareness is identified with the images that create our particular ego however (so that it can see other things but not what it is identified with) it is bound to experience a dichotomy between those images recognized as images and those not (those having to do with the ego). The notions that occur around the relation between an image and the perceiver of the image (for instance, image as object or subject to perceiver, image as encompassing perceiver, or perceiver encompassing image) point to fantasies of space and place which determine part of the nature of certain kinds of imagining.

By disidentifying awareness with "ourselves" and allowing it to inhabit other images from dreams and waking dreams, we allow it the opportunity to look at "us" from a position where the imaginal role of "ourselves" can be more apparent. The more we find out about this, the more evident it will appear that our imaginings about imagination precede from the archetypal mode we are usually most identified with. If we could relate our thoughts on imagination to this mode we could use the nature of these thoughts or imaginings to describe this archetypal mode.

Each set of images we are identified with has us move in respect to other things, including the imaginal, in certain ways. The realm of action and decision making is one possibility (see Chapter 7). The ego sees itself as lying between the realm of images and the realm of action. To connect the two the ego envisons a horizontal movement from the image to the material.

From the point of view of the imaginal it would appear that the ego is not independent of images. It is not seen to lie in between action and image. Indeed the imaginal and the material seem to be laid upon each other in layers, and movement between them is not horizontal at all, but rather vertical. One is involved in moving in depths. Perhaps from an imaginal point of view the image is at the base of these vertical constructions. This would set in motion a downwardness, a movement always from the concrete to the image. It would be as Paracelsus has described it—from material to immaterial. From a dual perspective (that of metaphor) its motion might seem more circular—returning intangible to tangible and vice versa. The reduction of images to the concrete is abusive to the imaginal mainly because we have failed to see the fantasy in the concrete—in our facts and actions. If we did grant imaginal aspects to these things the association of image to behavior would not be a flat reduction.

Our attempts at exploring our imaginings about imagining are not designed to argue the validity of one way of imagining over another (although at points that has proved to be enjoyable, as I am rather fond of my particular fantasies about the subject). They are, however, persistent in urging that we see our views about imagination as real imaginings. That we ask at each moment *who* is doing the imagining. In this way we automatically widen the boundaries that we have initially set to the imagination. It is no longer a distinct place to which we go to receive visual images. It is present now (*who* is reading this book?) and we can be aware of it through our modes of thinking and acting. To be imagining and not to know it, to continually ascribe what is the work of images to the faculty of reason and the person of ego, keeps us away from the imagination not in terms of participation, but in those of awareness. If we continue to see from within a certain set of images and fail to hear what it is saying as metaphorical and from a particular viewpoint, our dealings with the imaginal will more firmly entrench us in our present unconscious position, will provoke inconsistency with regard to our dealings with images, and theoretical debates as to which findings about the imagination should prevail. The question is not which is better, but what each is imagining and what effects (in actions, thoughts, feelings, perceptions) that has.

The presence of images causes imagining, just as the activity of imagining would seem to create images. If we apprehend images around us and not the ones within us, we are aware of imagining in one sphere of existence and not in another. A waking dream or an active imagination seen from the perspective of one who is *not* usually aware of images can be envisioned as a momentary change in consciousness or awareness. For a few minutes we grab a handful of images which we can ponder and further mythologize. For those moments we are aware of image as image, but in an object sense. Image is image but only as object. This decreases our ability to see ourselves as image, our lives as being imagined—that even the most concrete and truthful aspects are in relation to the imaginal.

With our awareness that we are imagining (and are imagined), our intentions toward psyche themselves become of more interest. Which images do we wish to starve and which do we wish to support? Which image—of integration, of wholeness, communication, ego strengthening, politicization, of consciousness, self-awareness, alteration of behaviour patterns—do we wish to make the imagination serve? How do we wish the imaginal to be related to the daily? What ontology will we grant images? What section of our experience?

When we are aware of the action of images that imagine us into the specific shapes of our identities, we can see that the waking dream is but one instance of imagining. It serves as a training ground for our awareness of images. It is as if the dream and the waking dream take the elements of our lives and imagine (do "dream work") on them. In this process they become other than themselves. They are made symbolic and their actions and nature serve to clarify the world of the imaginal that the activity of imagining creates. The fact and the thought, the plan and the decision, the child and the father, are returned through imagining to their places in imaginal space, in psychological space.

Returning there also, allowing oneself to observe and to follow the possible paths of imagining, does not change the imaginal as much as it changes he who comes to imagine as well as to be imagined. If one does not try to use the imagination as a tool for the extension and strengthening of the images one is already identified with, while remaining unaware of this intention, the activity of imagining can put consciousness into a different relationship to experience, both of self and not-self.

Historically it is the content of images that has caused people to judge the imagination as a god, demon, or muse. The content has given rise to ambiguous philosophies of how to deal with imagery. One can take some images as real, others as symbolic, still others as nonsensical; some as demons, others as wise companions, bringers of confusion or despair. The snare seems to be in the relative neglect of one's relation to images. Being still boggled about allowing things into the notion of reality (which seemed as if it must, against all else, be preserved) we have perhaps not allowed ourselves enough time with the image. We have not trusted ourselves to its depths and to its different ways of being. If we did our worries of content would eventually fade or at least take on a different significance. There would be no question that the image is real, nor would there be doubt that it is wholly different from our technical ideas of reality and yet synonymous with our experience of it.

Although any attempts to define the nature of an imaginal psychology must remain tentative at this point, it would appear that the idea of therapy would not have to do with changing images, but rather with changing our means of relating to them. Awareness would be a tool not of the ego but of the imaginal—in the sense that its primary purpose would be to apprehend images. Dwelling solely with the material aspects of external reality would be seen as a flight from reality (imaginal reality), in the same way as the ego sometimes perceives involvement with images as flight from its reality (Corbin, 1966:408). The ability to amplify images would rely less on knowledge of comparative symbolism and more on the training of the individual to be able to imagine in such a way that the connections between images can be perceived and understood experientially. One would become aware when imagining that the imaginal mode one is identified with is not only responsible for creating images but for limiting them; not simply for allowing them to describe themselves but for dictating the terms of description it will perceive and value. This process of allowing and limiting cannot be overcome for it is a result of the necessarily dialectical nature of relationship.

In order to perceive more aspects of an image it is necessary at a certain point not simply to perceive more, but to perceive differently. It is necessary not only to be aware of the images one is perceiving from and moving within, but also to be able to shift one's ability for perception and movement into other images. By assuming the identity of a different image, the image which is the object of perception appears to change. This change, however, is not inherent in the object. It is more aptly described as the yielding of aspects unrevealed in the previous relationship, but able to become apparent on the occasion of a new coupling.

In dreams one notices that a character can at first be a sister, then a lover, then both, then a garden. The dream ego itself similarly changes identity. In the imaginal there is both a fluidity and a simultaneity of identity. When we attempt waking dreams within an ego model we freeze the possibility of our directly experiencing these characteristics. As soon as we believe our identity to be attached to one group of images, we limit the number and the nature of our relationships, as well as our experience of imaginal existence as a whole.

An imaginal psychology would proceed from the nature of the imaginal. The substance of this would be grounded in a phenomenology of images. This phenomenology would rely on the ability to be aware of which imagistic mode one is in, so that statements about images and imaginal movements are not understood as simply facts but as descriptions of imaginal relationships. Another way to describe this is to speak of ways or types of imagining. Each specific type of imagining is grounded in the identification of consciousness with an image. This image makes us imagine in a certain way and to thereby see all images from a certain perspective. A phenomenology of the imaginal is dependent on the endless discovery of ways of imagining— each yielding both a new vantage point to other images as well as a new experience of "oneself." To extend the descriptions yielded' by the perceptions and interactions of one imagistic mode, an imaginal psychologist would of neccessity have to learn how to switch modes. To be able to shift with awareness between ways of imagining not only generates knowledge about the imaginal, but allows the imaginer to inhabit countless ways of perceiving, moving, feeling, thinking, being. By shifting amongst them, the lines of power between them change. Each way of imagining sets up a whole structure of relationships among images and experiences in general. The hierarchy and weaving of lines change their patterns as a different kind of imagining is assumed. Therapy based on an imaginal psychology would first of all encompass an awareness of the images a person is presently identified with and their modes of being. The person would learn to know the images presently constellated in dreams, interactions, thoughts and feelings. He would learn to know them through various kinds of imagining — not just be imagining in such a way that each image is an object of the ego's attention. Therapy would not be concerned with introducing foreign images to the individual or with fixing the imaginer into one mode of imagining or acting. The object would not be to integrate images, but rather to become aware of how one is in image-specific ways integrated into them To do this one must become aware of which images one is already in at different times.

The activities of recognizing and sorting the various images at the base of theories about and approaches to the imagination and waking dreams is a crucial first step, because although each image discloses experience it also limits and determines how we can go about imagining. Even further, however, our ways of studying and theorizing about the imaginal must proceed from an awareness of their own imagining. If they do not the imagination is literalized before we begin and despite our agility at seeing visions, talking with figures, and exploring under imaginal seas, we will have come no closer to being aware of the activity of images in the rest of our lives, and of the rest of our lives in the activity of images. The awareness that is needed — a metaphorical awareness — keeps action and image together. It allows the substance of images and the fantasy of thought and behavior to become apparent. The waking dream becomes envisioned less as an excursion to and from an imagination, and more as a means of growing closer to the imaginal reality of our daily lives.

Appendix 1

Autogenic Relaxation

The following is a basic relaxation exercise adapted by Henry Reed from Schultz and Luthe's system of autogenic therapy (1969). It can be used as an entry vehicle for waking dreams. Through concentration on the various formulas, which are repeated to oneself, the actual physiological conditions the formulas refer to are created. A deep relaxation results. In the beginning it is often difficult for people to ascertain the line between relaxed awareness and sleep. If you have trouble staying awake, try sitting down, rather than lying down. Acquaint yourself with the instructions. Repeat each one to yourself until you feel its effect. Eventually it will take a much shorter time each session to achieve the "autogenic state" of relaxation. Unpleasant sensations of numbness, coldness, muscle twitch or tremor which occasionally occur should disappear with time. Lie or sit down with your back straight and eyes closed.

1) Be conscious of where your back touches the bed, floor, or chair. Feel the pressure of the floor pushing up and your back pushing down.
2) Lift your right arm six to eight inches and let it be pulled back to the floor by its own weight. Do the same with the left arm, right leg, left leg, head.
3) Repeat to yourself "My right arm is heavy and I have let go."
4) Repeat "My left arm is heavy and I have let go."
5) Repeat "My arms are heavy and I have let go."
6) "My right leg is heavy and I have let go."
7) "My left leg is heavy and I have let go."
8) "My legs are heavy and I have let go."
9) "My arms and legs are heavy and I have let go."
10) "My right arm is warm and I am at peace."
11) "My left arm is warm and I am at peace."
12) "My arms are warm and I am at peace."
13) "My right leg is warm and I am at peace."
14) "My left leg is warm and I am at peace."
15) "My legs are warm and I am at peace."
16) "My arms and legs are warm an I am at peace."
17) "It breathes me."

Optional additions (de Ropp, 1968:238)

18) "My solar plexus is warm."
19) "My forehead is cool."[1]

---

[1] These instructions may also be used by people who have difficulty falling asleep.

Media for Waking Dreams

"A man of knowledge has his own predilections; mine is just to *see* and to know; others do other things."

"What other things, for example?"

"Take Sacateca. He's a man of knowledge and his predilection is dancing. So he dances and knows."

"Is the predilection of a man of knowledge something he does in order to see?"

"Yes, that is correct."

"But how could dancing help Sacateca to know?"

"One could say that Sacateca dances with all he has."

"Does he dance like I dance? I mean like dancing?"

"Let's say that he dances like I *see* and not like you may dance."

"Does he also *see* the way you *see*?"

"Yes, but he also dances."

"How does Sacateca dance?"

"It's hard to explain that. It is a peculiar way of dancing he does when he wants to know. But all I can say about it is that, unless you understand the ways of a man who knows, it is impossible to talk abour dancing or *seeing*."

"Have you ever *seen* him doing his dancing?"

"Yes. However, it is not possible for everyone who looks at his dancing to *see* that it is his peculiar way of knowing."

Castaneda, 1971:20-1

Living in any of its elements or as a whole presents us with a theatre where our myths can work their ways. Different individuals can avail themselves of various ways to realize and to aid this process. The following is a selected bibliography of works which might help the reader explore imaginal dimensions through the use of a particular medium.

Movement and dance: (1) Saunder, *Mudra;* (2) La Meri, *The Gesture Language of the Hindu Dance;* (3) Giu-Fu Feng and Kirk, *Tai Chi . . . A Way of Centering and the I Ching;* (4) Taylor, *A Time to Dance, Symbolic Movement in Worship;* (5) Duncan, *The Art of the Dance;* (6) Martin, *Introduction to the Dance;* (7) Pesso, *Movement in Psychotherapy: Psychomotor Techniques and Training;* (8) Wigman, *The Language of Dance;* (9) the schools of Gurdjieff and Rudolf Steiner contain systems of movement (see writings on eurythmy).

Painting and drawing: (1) Lyddiatt, *Spontaneous Painting and Modelling;* (2) Milner, *On Not Being Able to Paint;* (3) Gordon, *A Step Ladder to Painting;* (4) Cane, *The Artist In Each Of Us;* (5) Read, *Icon and Idea—The Function of Art in the Development of Human Consciousness;* (6) Malraux, *The Psychology of Art—The Twilight of the Absolute;* (7) Jung, "The aims of psychotherapy," 1938, 175-84; (8) Tucci, *The Theory and Practice of the Mandala;* (9) writings of Josef Garai.

Clay: (1) Berensohn, *Finding One's Way with Clay;* (2) Richards, *Centering: In Pottery, Poetry and the Person;* (3) Rix-Weaver, *The Wise Old Woman.*

Music: (1) Bonny and Savary, *Music and Your Mind, Creative Listening* records; (2) Ehrenzweig, *The Psychoanalysis of Artistic Vision and Hearing;* (3) Zuckerkandl, *Sound and Symbol—Music and the External Word;* (4) Hesse, *The Glass Bead Game.*

Drama: (1) Grotowski, *Towards a Poor Theatre;* (2) work of J. L. Moreno; (3) Japanese *Noh* dramas.

Poetry: (1) Maritain, *Creative Intuition in Art and Poetry;* (2) Leed, *Poetry Therapy;* (3) Hourd, *The Education of the Poetic Spirit;* (4) Muhl, *Automatic Writing.*

Revery in general: See the works of Bachelard.

Fantasy exercises: (1) Laura Huxley, *You Are Not the Target,* "Your Favorite Flower and Rainbow Walk" (record); (2) Masters and Houston, *Mind Games;* (3) Stevens, *Awareness;* (4) Crampton (see bibliography for full list); (5) Assagioli, *Psychosynthesis.*

Bibliography

Adler, Gerhard. (1961) *Living Symbol:* A Case Study in the Process of Individuation. N.Y.: Pantheon.

———.(1969) *Studies in Analytical Psychology.* N.Y.: Capricorn.

Andersen, Harold (ed.). (1959) *Creativity and Its Cultivation.* N.Y.: Harper and Brothers.

Antrobus, J. S., Antrobus, Judith S. and Singer, J. L. (1964) "Eye movement accompanying daydreaming, visual imagery, and thought suppression." *J. Abn. & Soc. Psychol.,* **69,** 224-252.

Ardis. (1956) "Hypnagogic imagery and mescalin." *J. Ment. Sci.,* **102,** 22-29.

Arguelles, José and Miriam. (1972) *Mandala.* Berkeley: Shambhala.

Assagioli, R. (1965) *Psychosynthesis: A Manual of Principles and Techniques.* N.Y.: Viking.

Bachelard, Gaston. (1958) *La Poétique de l'espace.* Paris: Presses Universitaires de France.

———.(1960) *La Poétique de la rêverie.* Paris: Presses Universitaires de France.

Barber, T. (1971) "Imagery and hallucinations under L.S.D. and with hypnotic suggestion." In S. Siegal (ed.). *The Adaptive Function of Imagery.* N.Y.: Academic Press.

Barratt, P. E. (1956) "Use of EEG in the study of imagery." *Brit. J. Psychol.,* **47,** 101-114.

Barron, Frank. (1958) "The psychology of imagination." *Sci. Amer.,* **199,** 50, 150-156.

———.(1968) *Creativity and Personal Freedom.* Princeton: Van Nostrand.

Baynes, C. (1954) *Mythology of the Soul.* London: Routledge and Kegan Paul.

Beck, A. T. (1970) "Role of fantasies in psychotherapy and psychopathology." *J. Ment. & Nerv. Dis.,* **150,** 1, 3-17.

Béguin, Albert. (1939) *L'âme romantique et le rêve.* Paris.

Beirnaert, Louis. (1951) "Le symbolisme ascensionnel dans la liturgie et la mystique chretiennes." *Eranos Jahrbuch,* **19,** 41-63.

Berdach, E. and Bakan, P. (1967) "Body position and free recall of early memories." *Psychotherapy,* **4.**

Berdyaev, N. A. (1955) *The Meaning of the Creative Act.* N.Y.: Harper.

Berensohn, Paulus, (1968) *Finding One's Way With Clay.* N.Y.: Simon and Schuster.

Beres, D. (1960a) "Perception, imagination, and reality." *Int. J. Psychoanal.,* **61,** 4-5.

———. (1960b) "The psychoanalytic psychology of imagination." *J. Amer. Psychoanal. Assoc.,* **8.**

Berry, Patricia. (1973) "On reduction." *Spring 1973.* N.Y. and Zurich: Spring Publ.

———. (1974) "An approach to the dream." *Spring 1974.* N.Y. and Zurich: Spring Publ.

Bertini, M., Lewis, Helen and Witkin, Herman. (1969) "Some preliminary observations with an experimental procedure for the study of hypnagogic and related phenomena." In C. Tart (ed.), *Altered States of Consciousness.* N.Y.: John Wiley.

Betts, G. H. (1904) *The Distribution and Function of Mental Imagery.* N.Y.: Teachers College, Columbia University.

Biddle, W. E. (1963) "Images." *Arch. Gen'l Psychiat.*, **9**, 464-470.

———. (1969) "Image therapy." *Amer. J. Psychiat.*, **126**, 408-411.

Binet, Alfred. (1922) *L'Etude expérimentale de l'intelligence.* Paris: Alfred Costes.

Blofeld, John. (1970) *The Tantric Mysticism of Tibet.* N.Y.: E. P. Dutton.

Bois, Samuel. (1966) *The Art of Awareness: A Textbook on General Semantics.* Dubuque Iowa: Wm. C. Brown.

Bonime, W. (1962) *The Clinical Use of Dreams.* N.Y.: Basic Books.

Bonny, Helen and Savary, Louis, M. (1973) *Music and Your Mind,* N.Y.: Harper & Row.

Brittain, W. L. (1907) "A study of imagination." *Pedagogical Seminary,* **14**, 137-207.

Brown, George. (1968) "The creative sub-self." In Herbert Otto (ed.), *Ways of Growth,* N.Y.: Viking.

Brown, Joseph Epes. (1971) *The Sacred Pipe.* Balt.: Penguin Books.

Buber, Martin. (1958) *I and Thou.* N.Y.: Scribners.

Buhler, Charlotte. (1971) "Basic theoretical concepts of humanistic psychology." *Amer. Psychologist.* **26**, 4, 378-386.

Campbell, Joseph. (1949) *The Hero with a Thousand Faces.* Cleveland: World.

———. (1968) *The Masks of God: Creative Mythology.* N.Y.: Viking.

———. (1970) *Myths, Dreams and Religions.* N.Y.: E. P. Dutton.

Cane, Florence, (1951) *The Artist in Each of Us.* N.Y.: Pantheon.

Carroll, Richard. (1973) Unpublished senior thesis on dream incubation research. Princeton University.

Caslant, E. (1921) *Méthode de développement des faculté supranormales.* Paris: Edition Rhea.

Cassirer, Ernst. (1952) *Philosophy of Symbolic Form: Mythical Thought* (Vol. II). New Haven: Yale University Press.

Castaneda, Carlos. (1971) *A Separate Reality.* N.Y.: Scribner's .

———. (1973) *Journey to Ixtlan.* N.Y.: Simon and Schuster.

Chapell, M. N. and Stevenson, T. I. (1936) "Group psychological training in some organic conditions." *Ment. Hygiene,* **20**, 588-597.

Clark, B. and Hawkes, A. (1963) "Let's enjoy sitting-standing-walking: body re-education through self-therapy." N.Y.: Barbara Clark. (mimeographed manuscript).

Coomaraswamy, Ananda. (1934)*The Transformation of Nature in Art.* N.Y.:Dover.

Corbin, Henry. (1966) "Visionary dream in islamic spirituality." In G. E. Grunebaum and Roger Caillois (eds.), *The Dream and Human Societies.* Calif.: Univ. of Calif. Press.

———. (1970) *Creative Imagination in the Sufism of Ibn 'Arabi.* R. Manheim (trans.), London: Routledge & Kegan Paul.

———. (1972) "Mundus imaginalis or the imaginary and the real." *Spring 1972.* N.Y. and Zurich: Spring Publ.

———. (1973) "Humcur." *Spring 1973.* N.Y. and Zurich: Spring Publ.

Costello, C. G. and McGregor, P. (1957) "The relationship between some aspects of visual imagery and the alpha rhythm." *J. Ment. Sci.,* **103**, 786-795.

Coutu, Walter. (1949) *Emergent Human Nature: A Symbolic Field Interpretation.* N.Y.: A. A. Knopf.

Crampton, M. (1965) "Answers from the unconscious: a technique of symbolic visualization." N.Y.: Psychosynthesis Research Foundation.

————. (1968) "The 'who am I?' techniques in psychotherapy." N.Y.: Psychosynthesis Research Foundation.

————. (1969) "The use of mental imagery in psychosynthesis." *J. of Humanistic Psychology*, **9**, 2, 139-153.

Crocket, R., Sandison, R. A. and Walk, A. (eds.). (1963) "Hallucinogenic drugs and their psychotherapeutic use." *Proceedings of the Royal Medico-Psychological Association.* London: H. K. Lewis.

Daudet, Léon. (1927) "La plante merveilleuse: le Peyotl." *L'Action Francaise,* May.

Davidson, Dorothy. (1966) "Transference as a form of active imagination." *Society of Analyt. Psych. Limited.* **2**, 135-146.

de Becker, Raymond. (1968) "Incubation and induced dreams." In *The Understanding of Dreams.* N.Y.: George Allen and Unwin.

de Castillejo, Irene. (1973) *Knowing Woman, A Feminine Psychology.* N.Y.: Harper Colophon.

de la Mare, Walter. (1939) *Imagination.* N.Y.: Knopf.

Delay, J. and Benda, Ph. (1958) "L'expérience lysergique (L.S.D. 25), A propos de 75 observations clinique." *L'Encéphale,* **48**, 3, 169-209; 4, 309-344.

de Ropp, Robert, S. (1968) *The Master Game, Pathways to Higher Consciousness Beyond the Drug Experience.* N.Y.: Dell.

de Saint- Denis, Hervey. (1867) *Les Rêves et les moyens de las diriger.* Paris.

de Saint-Exupéry, Antoine. (1945) *The Little Prince.* Katherine Woods (transl.), London: William Heinemann.

Desoille, Robert. (1938) *Exploration de l'affectivité subconsciente par la méthode du Rêve Éveillé.* Paris. Ed. D'Autrey.

————. (1945) *Le Rêve Éveillé en psychothérapie.* Paris: Presses Universitaires de France.

————. (1961) *Théorie et practique du rêve éveillé dirigé.* Geneva: Mont Blanc.

————. (1966) "The directed daydream." N.Y.: Psychosynthesis Research Foundation.

Dessauer, P. (1965) *Natural Meditation.* N.Y.: P. J. Kennedy.

Digby, George W. (1957) *Symbol and Image in William Blake.* Oxford: Clarendon Press.

Duncan, Isadora. (1968) *The Art of the Dance.* N.Y.: Theatre Arts.

Dunn, I. J. (1961) "Analysis of patients who meet the problems of the first half of life in the second." *J. Analyt. Psychol.,* **6**, I.

Durand, Gilbert. (1963) *Les Structures anthropologiques de l'imaginaire: Introduction à l'archetypologie générale.* Paris: Presses Universitaires de France.

————. (1971) "Exploration of the imaginal." *Spring 1971.* N.Y. and Zurich: Spring Publ.

Ehrenzweig, Anton. (1953) *The Psychoanalysis of Artistic Vision and Hearing.* London: Routledge and Kegan Paul.

————. (1967) *The Hidden Order of Art.* L. A.: Univ. of California Press.

Eliade, Mircea. (1949) *The Myth of the Eternal Return.* N.Y.: Pantheon Books.

————. (1952) *Rites and Symbols.* N.Y.: Sheed and Ward.

————. (1957) *Myths, Dreams and Mysteries: The Encounter Between Contemporary Faiths and Archaic Realities.* N.Y.: Harper and Row.

————. (1962) *The Forge and the Crucible: The Origins and Structures of Alchemy.* N.Y.: Harper and Row.

Eliot, T. S. (1930) *The Complete Poems and Plays.* N.Y.: Harcourt Brace and World.

————. (1943) *Four Quartets.* N.Y.: Harcourt Brace and World.

Ellenberger, Henri. (1970) *The Discovery of the Unconscious.* N.Y.: Basic Books.

Evans-Wentz, W. Y. (1960) *Tibetan Book of the Dead.* N.Y.: Oxford Univ. Press.

———. (1967) *Tibetan Yoga and Its Secret Doctines.* N.Y.: Oxford Univ. Press.

Fabricius, Johannes. (1967) *The Unconscious and Mr. Eliot.* Copenhagen: Nyt Nordisck Forlag Arnold Busck.

Feng, Gia-Fu and Kirk, Jerome. (1970) *Tai-Chi . . . A Way of Centering and the I Ching.* London: Collier Books Ltd.

Ferenczi, S. (1950) *Further Contributions to the Theory and Technique of Psychoanalysis.* London: Hogarth Press.

Feshbach, S. (1955) "The drive reducing function of fantasy behavior." *J. of Abn. and Soc. Psychology,* **50,** 3-11.

Fingarette, Herbert. (1963) *The Self in Transformation: Philosophy and the Life of the Spirit.* N.Y.: Harper and Row.

Fisher, Seymour. (1970) *Body Experience in Fantasy and Behaviour.* N.Y.: Appleton-Century-Crofts.

Follett, Barbara, (1966) *Barbara: The Unconscious Autobiography of a Child Genius.* Harold Grier (ed.), Chapel Hill: Univ. N. Carolina Press.

Follett, M. P. (1930) *Creative Experience.* N.Y.: Longmans, Green and Co.

Fordham, Michael. (1955) "Active imagination and imaginative activity," *J. of Analyt. Psychol.,* **I,** 1-2.

———. (1957) *New Developments in Analytical Psychology.* London: Routledge and Kegan Paul.

———. (1958) *Objective Psychology.* London: Routledge and Kegan Paul.

———. (1967) "Active imagination—deintegration or disintegration?" *J. of Analyt. Psychol,* **12,** 51-66.

Foulkes, D. and Vogel, G. (1965) "Mental activity at sleep onset." *J. Abn. Psychol.,* **70,** 231-243.

Foulkes, D., Spear, P. S. and Symunds, J. D. (1966) "Individual differences in mental activity at sleep onset." *J. Abn. Psychol.,* **71,** 280-286.

Frank, Ludwig. (1910) *Die Psychoanalyse.* Munich: E. Reinhardt.

Frederking, W. (1948) "Deep relaxation and symbolism." *Psyche,* **2.**

Freedman, S. J. and Marks, P. A. (1965) "Visual imagery produced by rhythmic photic stimulation: personality correlates and phenomenology." *Brit. J. Psychol.,* **56,** 95-112.

Frétigny, R. and Virel, André. (1968) *L'Imagerie Mentale: Introduction à l'onirothérapie.* Geneva: Mont Blanc.

Freud, Sigmund. (1943) *A General Introduction to Psychoanalysis.* Garden City: Garden City Publ.

———. (1952)"Dostoyevskei and parri cide." *Collected Papers,* V, London: Hogarth Press.

———. (1965) *Interpretation of Dreams.* N.Y.: Avon Books

Freud, Sigmund and Breuer, J. (1953) *Studies on Hysteria.* Standard Ed., Vol. 2.

Friedman, Maurice. (1967) *To Deny Our Nothingness—Contemporary Images of Man.* N.Y.: Delta Books.

Fromm, Erich. (1951) *The Forgotten Language.* N.Y.: Grove Press.

Galton, Francis. (1919) "Antechamber of consciousness." *Inquiries into the Human Faculty.* N.Y.: E. P. Dutton.

Garai, Josef E. (1972) "The humanistic approach to art therapy and creativity development." (Mimeograph available from author, c/o Pratt Institute, N.Y., N.Y.)

Gendlin, E. T. (1962) *Experience and the Creation of Meaning.* N.Y.: Free Press.

——. (1969) "Focusing." *Psychotherapy,* **6,** 4-15.

Gendlin, E. T. and Olsen, Linda. (1970) "The use of imagery in experiential focusing." *Psychotherapy: Theory, Research & Practice,* **7,** 4, 221-3.

Gerard, R. (1964) "Psychosynthesis: a psychotherapy for the whole man." Psychosynthesis Research Foundation.

——. (1967) "Symbolic identification—a technique of psychosynthesis." Paper presented at the Seventh International Congress on Psychotherapy, Wiesbaden.

Ghiselin, B. (1952) *The Creative Process.* Berkeley: Univ. of Calif. Press.

Giorgi, Amedeo. (1970) *Psychology as a Human Science.* N.Y.: Harper and Row.

Goldberger, E. (1957) "Simple method of producing dreamlike visual images in the waking state—a preliminary report." *J. Psychosom. Med.,* **19,** 127-33.

Goodenough, D. R., Shapiro, A., Holden, M. and Steinschriber, L. (1959) "A comparison of 'dreamers' and 'non-dreamers'." *J. Abn. Soc. Psychol.,* **59,** 295-302.

Gordon, J. J. (1961) *Synectics.* N.Y.: Harper and Row.

Gordon, R. (1966) "The concept of projective identification." *J. Analyt. Psychol.,* **11,** 1.

Graeter, Karl. (1933) *Le Traitement des troubles afféctifs et l'art de vivre.* Strausburg.

Groch, Judith. (1969) *The Right to Create.* Toronto: Little, Brown and Co.

Grof, Stanislav. (tbp) *The Agony and Ecstacy of Psychiatric Treatment.*

Grotowski, Jerzy. (1968) *Towards a Poor Theatre.* Polish Lab Theatre, Institut Badan Metody Aktorskig, Denmark.

Grunholz, Gerhard. (1971) "Visualisierung psychodynamischer Prozesse durch die autogene Imagination." *Praxis der Psychotherapie,* **16,** 2, 75-88.

Hammer, M. (1967) "The directed daydream technique." *Psychotherapy: Theory, Research, Practice,* **4,** 173-181.

Hannah, Barabara, (1952) "Course on active imagination." (Typescript).

——. (1953) "Some remarks on active imagination," *Spring 1953.* N.Y.: Analyt. Psychol. Club.

——. (1954) "Hugh de St. Victor's conversations with his anima," *Harvest.* London.

——. (1967) "Active imagination." (Record of a talk given in Zurich, Sept. 25, typescript).

Happich, Carl. (1932) "Das Bildbewusstsein als Ansatzstelle psychischer Behandlung." *Zbl. Psychother.,* **5.**

Harding, Esther. (1953) "Our search for mental health," *Spring 1953.* N.Y.: Analyt. Psychol. Club.

——. (1963) *Psychic Energy: Its Source and Transformation.* N.Y.: Pantheon.

Haronian, Frank. (1970) "Psychosynthesis—A psychotherapist's personal overview." N.Y.: Psychosynthesis Research Foundation.

——. (1971) "The ethical relevance of a psychotherapeutic technique." N.Y.: Psychosynthesis Research Foundation.

Hebb, D. O. (1954) "The problem of consciousness and introspection." In J. F. Delafresnaye (ed.), *Brain Mechanisms and Consciousness.* Blackwell.

——. (1960) "The American revolution." *Amer. Psychologist,* **15.**

——. (1974) "What psychology is about." *Amer. Psychologist,* **29,** 2, 71-79.

Hesse, Hermann. (1969) *The Glass Bead Game.* N.Y.: Holt, Rinehart and Winston.

Hillman, James. (1964) *Suicide and the Soul.* London: Hodder and Stoughton.

——. (1967) "Senex and puer: an aspect of the psychological and historical present." *Eranos Jahrbuch,* **36.**

————. (1972a) *The Myth of Analysis*. Evanston: Northwestern Univ. Press.

————. (1972b) *Pan and the Nightmare*. Zurich: Spring Publications.

————. (1973) "Pathologizing (or falling apart)." *Art International*, Sept., 120-129.

————. (1974) "Dreams and the underworld." Lectures at C. G. Jung Institute, Zurich, winter semester.

Hinkle, Beatrice. (1939) *The Re-creating of the Individual. A Study of Psychological Types and their Relation to Psychoanalysis.* N.Y.: Dodd, Mead and Co.

Hobson, Robert. (1971) "Imagination and amplification." *J. of Analyt. Psychol.*, 16, 1, 79-105.

Holt, R. R. (1964) "The return of the ostracized—imagery." *Amer. Psychologist*, 19.

Holt, R. R. and Goldberger, L. (1959) "Personological correlates of reactions of perceptual isolation," WADC Tech. Rep. 59-753, Wright-Patterson A.F.B., Ohio.

Hora, Thomas. (1962) "Existential psychiatry and group therapy." In H. Ruitenbeek (ed.), *Psychoanalysis and Existential Philosophy.* N.Y.: E. P. Dutton.

Horowitz, Mardi J. (1964) "The imagery of visual hallucination." *J. Ment. & Nerv. Dis.*, 138, 513-523.

————. (1970) *Image Formation and Cognition*. N.Y.: Meredith Corp.

Hourd, M. L. (1949) *The Education of the Poetic Spirit*. Heinemann.

Houston, Jean. (1973) "New ways of being: consciousness and its transformations." Lecture presented at annual meeting of Assoc. for Humanistic Psychology, Montreal.

Hudson, Liam. (1972) *The Cult of the Fact*. London: Jonathan Cape Ltd.

Hull, R. F. C. (1971) "Bibliographic notes on active imagination in the work of C. G. Jung." *Spring 1971*. N.Y. and Zurich: Spring Publ.

Humbert, Elie. (1971) "Active imagination: theory and practice." *Spring 1971*. N.Y. and Zurich: Spring Publ.

Humphrey, Robert. (1954) *Stream of Consciousness in the Modern Novel.* Berkeley: Univ. of California Press.

Humphreys, Christmas. (1959) *Concentration and Meditation.* London: Watkins.

Huxley, Aldous. (1962a) "Education on the non-verbal level." *Daedalus*, 91, 279-293.

————. (1962b) "Visionary Experience." Copenhagen: Munksguard.

Huxley, Laura. (1963) *You Are Not the Target*. Hollywood: Wilshire Book Co.

Isakower, Otto. (1938) "A contribution to the patho-psychology of phenomena associated with falling asleep." *Int'l. J. of Psychoanalysis*, 19, 331-345.

Jackson, C. W. and Pollard, J. C. (1962) "Sensory deprivation and suggestion: a theoretical approach." *Behav. Sci.*, 7, 332-342.

Jacobson, E. (1938) *Progressive Relaxation*. Chicago: Chicago Univ. Press.

————. (1951) *You Must Relax*. N.Y.: McGraw Hill.

Jaensch, E. R. (1930) *Eidectic Imagery*. London: Kegan Paul.

Jaffe, Aniela. (1971) *The Myth of Meaning*. N.Y.: G. P. Putnam's Sons.

James, William. (1885-1889) "Automatic writing." *Proc. of the Amer. Soc. for Psychical Research*, I, 548-564.

————. (1890) "Imagination." *The Principles of Psychology*, 2. N.Y.: Dover.

————. (1912) "Does consciousness exist?" *Essays in Radical Empiricism.* N.Y.

————. (1953) *The Varieties of Religious Experience: A Study in Human Nature.* N.Y.: The New American Library.

Janet, Pierre, (1888) "Les actes inconscients et la mémoire pendant le somnabulisme." *Revue Philosophique*, 25, 1, 238-279.

————. (1889) *L'Automatisme psychologique.* Paris: Alcan.

————. (1892) "Etude sur un cas d'amnésie ánterograde dans la maladie de la désagrégation psychologique." *Int'l Cong. of Experimental Psych.* London: Williams and Norgate.

————. (1897) "Sur la divination par les miroires et les hallucinations subconscientes." *Bulletin de l'Université de Lyon,* 11, 261-274.

Jaynes, Julian. (To be published). *The Origin of Consciousness and the Breakdown of the Bicameral Mind.*

Jellinek, A. (1949) "Spontaneous imagery—a new therapeutic approach." *Amer. J. Psychotherapy,* 3, 372-391.

Jones, Richard M. (1968) *Fantasy and Feeling in Education.* N.Y.: Harper.

Jones, Ernest. (1963) *Life and Work of Sigmund Freud.* Lionel Trilling (ed.). N.Y.: Anchor.

Jourard, Sidney. (1968) *Disclosing Man to Himself.* N.Y.: Litton Educ.

Jung, C. G.[1] (1933) *Modern Man in Search of His Soul.* N.Y.: Harcourt, Brace and World, 66-73, 175-84.

————. (1936) "Fundamental psychological conceptions, a report of five lectures by Jung." London Lectures, London Multigraph Typescripts, 214-235.

————. (1937) "Psychological analysis of Nietzsche's *Zarathustra.*" (Privately mimeographed seminar notes of Mary Foote).

————. (1939) *Integration of the Personality.* N.Y.: Farrar and Rinehart, 30-51.

————. (1944) *Psychology and Alchemy.* Collected Works, 12.

————. (1953) *Two Essays on Analytical Psychology.* Collected Works, 7.

————. (1954a) *The Development of the Personality.* Collected Works, 17.

————. (1954b) *The Practice of Psychotherapy.* Collected Works, 16.

————. (1957) "On the psychology and pathology of the so-called occult phenomenon." Collected Works, 1.

————. (1958) *Psychology and Religion East and West.* Collected Works, 11. (see especially "Psychological commentaries on *Tibetan Book of the Dead*").

————. (1959a) *Archetypes and the Collective Unconscious.* Princeton: Bollingen, Collected Works, 9, 290-354.

————. (1959b) "Concerning mandala symbolism." *The Archetypes and the Collective Unconscious.* Collected Works, 9.

————. (1960) "The transcendent function." *The Structure and Dynamics of the Psyche.* Collected Works, 8.

————. (1961) *Memories, Dreams, and Reflections.* Aniela Jaffe (ed.), N.Y.: Random House.

————. (1963) *Mysterium Coniunctionis.* Collected Works, 14.

————. (1961-3) "The interpretation of visions." *Spring 1961,2,3,* N.Y.: Analyt. Psychol. Club.

————. (1968a) *Analytical Psychology: Its Theory and Practice.* N.Y.: Vintage Books, 190-204.

————. (1968b) "Commentary on the 'Secret of the Golden Flower.'" *Alchemical Studies.* Collected Works, 9.

————. (1971) *Psychological Types.* Collected Works, 6.

————. (1973) *Selected Letters of C. G. Jung.* Gerhard Adler and Aniela Jaffe, (eds.), Princeton: Princeton Univ. Press.

---

[1]The edition of the collected works referred to are the Bollingen Series XX, published by Princeton Univ. Press, R.F.C. Hull (transl.).

Kagan, Jerome. (1967) *Creativity and Learning.* Boston: Beacon Press.

Kamiya, J. and Zeitland, D. (1963) "Learned EEG alpha wave control by humans." Report No. 183, Dept. of Ment. Hygiene, Research Div., Calif.

Keup, Wolfram, (ed.). (1970) *Origin and Mechanism of Hallucinations.* N.Y.: Plenum Press.

Klein, Melanie. (1948) "The importance of symbol formation and the development of the ego." *Contributions to Psychoanalysis (1921-45).* London.

Klinger, Eric. (1971) *The Structure and Functions of Fantasy.* N.Y.: John Wiley and Sons.

Koch, Sigmund. (1964) "Psychology and emerging conceptions of knowledge as unitary. In Trenton Wann (ed.). *Behaviorism and Phenomenology* Chicago: Univ. of Chicago.

Koch, W. (1968) "Expériénce catathyme des symboles." *Informations de la Société Internationale des Techniques d'Imagerie Mentale.* Proceedings of the 1st annual congress. Paris: S.I.T.I.M.

Koestler, A. (1964) *The Act of Creation: A Study of the Conscious and Unconscious in Science and Art.* N.Y.: Dell.

Kretschmer, Wolfgang. (1969) "Meditative techniques in psychotherapy." In C. Tart, (ed.), *Altered States of Consciousness.* N.Y.: John Wiley.

Krippner, Stanley. (1968) "The ten commandments that block creativity," *Education Digest,* **23**, 23-26.

Kris, E. (1962) "On preconscious mental processes." *Psychoanalytic Explorations in Art.* N.Y.: Int'l. Univ. Press.

Krojanker, R. J. (1966) "Leuner's symbolic drama." *Amer. J. Hypnosis: Clinical, Experimental, Theoretical,* July **9**, (1).

Kubie, L. S. (1943) "The use of induced hypnagogic reveries in the recovery of repressed amnesic data." *Bull. Menninger Clinic,* **7**, 172-82.

La Meri, R. M. (1964) *The Gesture Language of the Hindu Dance.* N.Y.: Columbia Univ. Press.

Langer, Suzanne, (1942) *Philosophy in a New Key.* N.Y.: Mentor Books.

———. (1953) *Feeling and Form.* London: Routledge and Kegan Paul.

Lazurus, A. (1968) "Learning theory and treatment of depression." *Beh. Research & Ther.,* **6**, 83-89.

Leary, T., Metzner, R. and Alpert, R. (1964) *The Psychedelic Experience — A Manual Based on the Tibetan Book of the Dead.* New Hyde Park: University Books.

Leed, J. J. (1969) *Poetry Therapy.* Phila.: Lippincott.

Leuner, Hanscarl. (1969) "Guided affective therapy (GAI): a method of intensive therapy." *Amer. J. Psychotherapy,* **23**, 1, 4-22.

———. (1970) "Das Katathyme Bilderleben in der Psychotherapie von Kindern und Jungendlichen." *Praxis der Kinderpsychologie und Kinderpsychiatrie,* **19**, 6, 212-223.

Levak, Milena. (1969) "Eidetic images among the Bororo in Brazil." *J. Soc. Psychology,* **17**, 1, 135-7.

Levitsky, A. (1966) "The constructive realistic fantasy." *Amer. J. Hypnosis: Clinical, Experimental, Theoretical,* July, **9**, 1.

Lewin, Bertram D. (1969) "Remarks on creativity, imagery, and the dream." *J. Nerv. & Ment. Diseases.* **149**, 2, 115-121.

Long, Constance. (1920) *Collected Papers on the Psychology of Phantasy.* Bailliere: Tindall.

Lyddiatt, E. M. (1972) *Spontaneous Painting and Modelling: A Practical Approach in Therapy.* N.Y.: St. Martin's.

Maitland, Edward. (1896) *Anna Kingsford, Her Life, Letters, Diary and Work.* London. (See 129ff).

Malraux, André, (1950) *The Psychology of Art. The Twilight of the Absolute.* N.Y.: Pantheon Books.

———. (1961) *Man's Fate.* N.Y.: Random House.

Maritain, Jacques. (1953) *Creative Intuition in Art and Poetry.* N.Y.: Bollingen Fdnt.

Marjula, Anna. (1963) *The Healing Influence of Active Imagination in a Specific Case of Neurosis.* Zurich: Schippert.

Martin, John. (1965) *Introduction to the Dance.* Brooklyn: Dance Horizons.

Martin, P. W. (1955) *Experiment in Depth.* London: Routledge and Kegan Paul.

Maslow, Abraham. (1959) "Creativity in self-actualizing people." In H. H. Anderson (ed.). *Creativity and Its Cultivation.* N.Y.: Harper.

———. (1962) "Lessons from the peak experience." *J. of Humanistic Psych.*, 2, 9-18.

———. (1962) "The need to know and the fear of knowing." *Toward a Psychology of Being.* Princeton: D. Van Nostrand.

———. (1971) "Creativeness." *The Farther Reaches of Human Nature.* N.Y.: Viking.

Masters, R. E. L. and Houston, Jean. (1966) *The Varieties of Psychedelic Experience.* N.Y.: Dell.

———. (1973) *Mind Games.* N.Y.: Dell.

Maupin, Edward W. (1969) "Individual differences in response to a zen meditation exercise." In C. Tart (ed.), *Altered States of Consciousness.* N.Y.: John Wiley.

Mauz, F. (1948) "Der psychotische Mensch in der Psychotherapie." *Arch. Psychiat. Neurol.*, 181, 337-341.

Mearns, Hughes. (1959) *Creative Power.* Garden City: Doubleday.

Meerlo, Joost. (1968) *Creativity and Eternalization: Essays on the Creative Intellect.* N.Y.: Humanities Press.

Meier, C. A. (1954) "Ancient incubation and modern psychotherapy." *Spring.* Analyt. Psychol. Club of N.Y., 59-74.

———. (1966) "The dream in ancient Greece and its use in temple cures." In G. Grunebaum and R. Caillois (eds.), *The Dream and Human Societies.* Evanston: Northwestern Univ. Press.

———. (1967) *Ancient Incubation and Modern Psychotherapy.* Evanston: Northwestern Univ. Press.

Miller, Henry. (1960) *To Paint is to Love Again.* Alhambra: Cambria Books.

Milner, Joanna. (1957) *On Not Being Able to Paint.* N.Y.: Internat. Universities Press.

Montaigne. (1940) *Essais.* Paris: Ed. Pléiade.

Muhl, Anita. (1964) *Automatic Writing.* N.Y.: Garrett Press.

Muratorio, Lodovico. (1745) *Della Forza della Fantasia Umana.* Venice: Presso Giambatista Pasquali.

Murray, Henry (ed.). (1960) *Myth and Mythmaking.* Boston: Beacon Press.

Myers, Frederic. (1885-7) "Automatic writing." *Proc. Soc. for Psychical Research*, 3, 1-63: 4, 209-261.

Nachmansohn, M. (1957) "Concerning experimentally produced dreams." In D. Rapaport (ed.), *The Organization and Pathology of Thought.* N.Y.: Columbia Univ. Press.

Naranjo, C. and Ornstein, R. (1971) *Psychology of Meditation.* N.Y.: Viking Press.

Needleman, Jacob. (1972) "Subud." *The New Religions.* N.Y.: Pocket Books.

Neihardt, John. (1960) *Black Elk Speaks.* Lincoln: Univ. of Nebraska Press.

Neumann, Erich. (1954) *The Origins and History of Consciousness*. Princeton: Princeton Univ. Press.

―――. (1959) *Art and the Creative Unconscious*. Princeton: Princeton Univ. Press.

Nietzsche, F. (1954) "Thus Spake Zarathustra." In W. Kaufmann (ed. and transl.) *Portable Nietzsche*. N.Y.: Viking Press.

Osborn, A. F. (1953) *Applied Imagination: Principles and Procedures of Creative Thinking*. N.Y.: Charles Scribner's Sons.

Ostrowski-Sachs, Margaret. (1952) "Painting for growth and understanding." *Inward Light*. Fall, Wash. D.C., No. 42, 10-15.

Ouspensky, P. D. (1949) *In Search of the Miraculous*. N.Y.: Harcourt, Brace, and World.

―――. (1968) *The Psychology of Man's Future Evolution*. N.Y.: Bantam Books.

Pahnke, W. (1969) "LSD assisted psychotherapy with terminal cancer patients." *Current Psych. Ther.*, **9**, 114-152.

Paivio, A. (1969) "Mental imagery in associative learning and memory." *Psychol. Review*, **76**, 241-263.

Pálószi-Horváth, G. (1959) *The Undefeated*. Boston: Little Brown.

Partridge, G. E. (1898) "Reveries." *Pedagogical Sem.*, **5**, 445-474.

Penfield, W. and Jaspers, H. (1954) *Epilepsy and the Functional Anatomy of the Human Brain*. Boston: Little Brown.

Perls, F. (1969) "Dreamwork seminar." *Gestalt Therapy*. Lafayette: Real People Press.

Perls, F., Goodman, P. and Hefferline, R. (1951) *Gestalt Therapy*. N.Y.: Delta Books.

Pesso, Albert. (1969) *Movement in Psychotherapy: Psychomotor Techniques and Training*. N.Y.: N.Y. Univ. Press.

Peterson Severin. (1971) *A Catalogue of Ways People Grow*. N.Y.: Ballentine Books.

Phillips, D. P., Howes, E. B. and Nixon, L. H. (eds.). (1948) *The Choice Is Always Ours: An Anthology on the Religious Way*. N.Y.: Richard R. Smith.

Pinard, W.J. (1957) "Spontaneous imagery: its nature, therapeutic value, and effect on personality structure." *Boston Univ. Grad. J.*, **5**, 250-153.

Plaut, A. (1966) "Reflections about not being able to imagine." *J. Analyt. Psychol.*, **11**, 113-133.

Progoff, Ira. (1959) *Depth Psychology and the Modern Man: a new view of the magnitude of human personality, its dimensions and resources*. N.Y.: Julian Press.

―――. (1963) *The Symbolic and the Real*. N.Y.: Julian Press.

―――. (1970) "Waking dream and living myth." In Joseph Campbell (ed.), *Myths, Dreams, and Religion*. N.Y.: E. P. Dutton.

Raines, Kathleen. (1967) *Defending Ancient Springs*. London: Oxford Univ. Press.

Rapaport, D. (1941) *Organization and Pathology of Thought*. N.Y.: Columbia Univ. Press.

Read, Sir Herbert. (1955) *Icon and Idea: The Function of Art in the Development of Human Consciousness*. Cambridge: Harvard Univ. Press.

Reed, Henry. (1973) "Learning to remember dreams." *J. Humanistic Psych.*, **13**, 3.

―――. (1974) "Dream incubation: a reconstruction of a ritual in contemporary form." *J. Humanistic Psych.*, **14**.

Reyher, J. (1963) "Free imagery: an uncovering procedure." *J. Clin. Psych.*, **19**, 454-459.

Reyher, J. and Smeltzer, W. (1968) "Uncovering properties of visual imagery and verbal association." *J. Abn. Psychol.*, **73**, 218-222.

Richards, Mary C. (1962) *Centering in Pottery, Poetry, and the Person.* Conn.: Wesleyan Univ. Press.

Richardson, Alan (1969) *Mental Imagery.* N.Y.: Springer.

Rigo, L. L. (1970) "L'Imagerie di gruppo negli adulti." *Proc. 3rd Int'l. Cong. Société Internationale des Techniques d'Imagerie Mentale.* Cortina, Italy.

Rigo-Uberto, S. (1970) "Un caso di sintomatologia nevrolica grave fobico-ossessiva in un s. preadolescente trattato con un tecnica psicoterapia includente anch l'imagerie mentale." *Proc. 3rd Int'l Cong. Société Internationale des Techniques d'Imagerie Mentale.* Cortina, Italy.

Robertson, Mary. (1969) "Shadow therapy with children." *Amer. J. Psychotherapy,* **23,** 3, 505-509.

Roheim, Geza, (1952) *The Gates of the Dream.* N.Y.: Int'l. Universities Press.

Rohwer, W. D. (1970) "Images and pictures in children's learning." *Psychol. Bulletin,* **73,** 393-403.

Rose, G. J. (1964) "Creative imagination in terms of ego 'core' and boundaries." *Int. J. Psychoanalysis,* **45,** 1.

Rosen, V. H. (1960) "Some aspects of the role of imagination in psychoanalysis." *J. Amer. Psychoanalyt. Assoc.,* **8,** 229-251.

Roszak, Theodore. (1969) *The Making of the Counterculture.* N.Y.: Doubleday.

Sacerdote, P. (1968) "Induced dreams." *Amer. J. Clin. Hypn.,* **10,** 167-173.

Sanford, Catherine. "A personal experience of archetypal images in the individuation process." (typescript).

Saint John. (1953) "The dark night of the soul." E. A. Peers, (trans.), *Complete Works of St. John of the Cross,* London.

Sartre, Jean-Paul (1966) *The Psychology of Imagination.* N.Y.: Washington Square Press.

Saunders, Dale. (1960) *Mudra.* N.Y.: Pantheon Books.

Schachtel, Ernest. (1959) *Metamorphosis: On the Development of Affect, Perception Attention and Memory.* N.Y.: Basic Books.

Schonbar, R. (1959) "Some manifest characteristics of recallers and non-recallers of dreams." *J. Consult. Psychol.,* **23,** 414-418.

Schorer, Mark. (1960) "The necessity of myth." In Henry Murray (ed.), *Myth and Mythmaking.* Boston: Beacon Press.

Schultz, J. H. and Luthe. W. (1969) *Autogenic Methods.* N.Y.: Grune and Stratton.

Secret of the Golden Flower. (1962). Richard Wilhelm (trans.). N.Y.: Harvest Books.

Segal, S. J. and Glickman, M. (1967) "Relaxation and the perky effect: the influence of body position and judgments of imagery." *Amer. J. Psychol.,* **60,** 257-262.

Seitz, P. D. and Molholm, H. B. (1947) "Relation of mental imagery to hallucinations." *A.M.A. Arch. Neurol. Psychiat.,* **57,** 469-80.

Shapiro, David L. (1970) "The significance of the visual image in psychotherapy." *Psychotherapy: Theory, Research, & Practice,* **7,** 4, 209-212.

Shapiro, Stewart. (1966) "Explorations in positive experience: an existential approach to psychotherapy." *Explorations,* July, **8,** 25-40.

Sheehan, P. W. (1967) "A shortened from of Betts questionnaire upon mental imagery." *J. Clin. Psychol.,* **23,** 385-389.

Short, P. L. (1953) "The objective study of mental imagery." *Brit. J. Psychol.,* **44,** 38-51.

Silberer, Herbert. (1909) "Bericht über eine Methode gewisse symbolische Halluzinations-Erscheinungen hervorzurufen und zu beobachten." *Jahrbuch für Psychoanalytische und Psychopathologische Forschungen,* **6,** 513-525.

———. (1912) "Zur Symbolbildung." *Jahrbuch für Psychoanalytische und Psychopathologische Forschungungen*, 4.

———. (1951) "Report on a method of eliciting and observing certain symbolic hallucination-phenomenon." In David Rapaport (ed.), *The Organization and Pathology of Thought.* N.Y.: Columbia Univ. Press.

Singer, Jerome. (1966) *Daydreaming.* N.Y.: Random House.

———. (1971a) "The vicissitudes of imagery in research and clinical use." *Contemporary Psychoanalysis,* **7,** 163-180.

———. (1971b) "Theoretical implications of imagery and fantasy techniques." *Contemporary Psychoanalysis,* **8,** 82-96.

Singer, June. (1970) *The Unholy Bible: A Psychological Interpretation of William Blake.* N.Y.: Putnam.

Sirhindi, Shaikh Ahmad. (1625) Maktubat (Lucknow), III, 57.

Sontag, Susan. (1961) *Against Interpretation.* N.Y.: Dell.

Stein, Calvert. (1972) "Hypnotic projection in brief psychotherapy." *Amer. J. Clinical Hypnosis,* **14,** 3, 143-155.

Stevens, John O. (1971) "Fantasy journeys." In *Awareness: Exploring, Experimenting and Experiencing.* Lafayette (Calif.): Real People Press.

Storm, Hyemeyohst. (1972) *Seven Arrows.* N.Y.: Harper and Row.

Swartley, W. M. (1965) "Initiated symbol projection." In Assagioli, R., *Psychosynthesis.* N.Y.: Viking Press. (Based on unpublished manuscripts by Hanscarl Leuner and H. J. Kornadt).

Tart, Charles. (1969) *Altered States of Consciousness.* N.Y.: John Wiley.

Tauber, E. S. and Green, M. (1959) *Prelogical Experience.* N.Y.: Basic Books.

Taylor, Graham. (1968) "Approaches to the self: the 'who am I?' techniques in psychotherapy (verbal)." Psychosynthesis Research Foundation.

Tompkins, S. (1962) *Affect, Imagery and Consciousness* (Vol. 1). N.Y.: Springer.

Toynbee, Arnold. (1947) *A Study of History.* N.Y.: Oxford Univ. Press.

Tucci, Guiseppe. (1969) *The Theory and Practice of the Mandala: with special reference to the modern psychology of the subconscious.* N.Y.: Samuel Weiser.

Tyler, Leona. (1973) Presidential address to the annual mtg. of the Amer. Psychol. Assoc., Montreal.

Underhill, E. (1970) "The dark night of the soul." *Mysticism.* N.Y.: World Publ.

Van de Castle, R. (1971) *The Psychology of Dreaming.* N.Y.: General Learning Press.

Van den Berg, J. H. (1952) "The human body and the significance of human movement." *Phil. Phenomenol. Res.,* **2,** 1, 159-182.

———. (1955) *The Phenomenological Approach to Psychiatry.* Springfield, Illinois: Charles C. Thomas.

———. (1962) "An existential explanation of the guided daydream." *Rev. Exist. Psychol. and Psychiat.,* **2,** 1, 5-35.

———. (   ) "The Rêve éveillé of Robert Desoille." (An investigation of the character and the possibilities of a phenomenological psychotherapy), in Van den Berg, J. H., Linschoten (eds). *Person and World* (Dutch text). Utrecht: Erven J. Bijleveld, 212-243.

van Kaam, A. (1960) "The third force in European psychology: its expression in a theory of psychotherapy." N.Y.: Psychosynthesis Research Foundation.

Varendonck, J. (1921) *The Psychology of Daydreams.* N.Y.: Macmillan.

Virel, André. (1968a) "Les psychothérapies par l'imagerie mentale." Société Moreau de Tours, *Annales Medico-Psychologiques,* **2,** 4.

———. (1968b) *Histoire de Notre Image.* Geneva: Mont Blanc.

von Franz, Marie-Louise. (1949) "The passio perpetuae." *Spring 1949*. N.Y.: Analyt. Psychol. Club.

———. (1970) *The Problem of the Puer Aeternus*. Zurich: Spring.

———. (1972) *Problems of the Feminine in Fairy Tales*. Zurich: Spring.

———. (1973) "Projection." Lectures delivered at the C. G. Jung Institute, Zurich.

Watts, Alan. (1951) *The Wisdom of Insecurity*. N.Y.: Vintage Books.

Weaver, M. Rix. (1964) *The Old Wise Woman: A Study of Active Imagination*. London: Vincent Stuart.

Weil, Simone. (1956) *The Notebooks of Simone Weil*. London: Oxford Univ. Press.

Weitzmann, B. (1967) "Behavior therapy and psychotherapy." *Psychol. Review*, 74, 300-317.

West, L. J. (ed.) (1962) *Hallucinations*. N.Y.: Grune and Stratton.

Westman, H. (1961) *The Springs of Creativity*. London: Routledge and Kegan Paul.

White, M. (1969) "Extended perception through photograph and suggestion." In H. Otto and J. Mann (eds.), *Ways of Growth*. N.Y.: Viking Press.

Whitmont, Edward. (1969) *The Symbolic Quest*. N.Y.: G. P. Putnam's Sons.

———. (1971) "Nature, symbol and imaginal reality." *Spring 1971*. N.Y. and Zurich: Spring Publ.

Wickes, Frances. (1938) *The Inner World of Man*. N.Y.: Farrar and Rinehart, 248-313.

Wigman, Mary. (1966) *The Language of Dance*. Conn: Wesleyan Univ. Press.

Wilhelm, Richard (trans.). (1962) *The Secret of the Golden Flower*. N.Y.: Harvest Books.

Wilson, R. N. (1954) "Poetic creativity, process, and personality." *Psychiatry*, 17, 163-176.

Winston, Shirley. (1965) "Demonstration of a technique of group exploration of consciousness." N.Y.: Psychosynthesis Research Fdtn.

Witkin, Herman. (1965) "Pathological differentiation and forms of pathology." *J. Abn. Psychol.*, 17, 659-662.

Zangwill, O. L. and Pryce-Jones, A. (1956) *The New Outline of Modern Knowledge*. London: Gollancz.

Zuckerkandl, Victor, (1956) *Sound and Symbol—Music and the External World*. Princeton: Bollingen Series XLIV.

Zuckerman, M., Albright, R. J., Marks, C. S. and Miller, G. L. (1962) "Stress and hallucinatory effects of perceptual isolation and confinement." *Psychol. Monograph*, 549.

Author and Proper Name Index

Subject Index

Action through non-action 104
Active imagination 42-51
Alchemists 13, 14, 18, 125, 148
Amnesic blocks 58
Amplification 138
  through imagining 150
Ascension in imaginal space 58-60
Australian aborigines 108
Automatic talking 35
Automatic writing 32, 35
Autosymbolic phenomenon 42
Awareness 46, 107-8, 145
  disidentified from the ego 148
  identified with ego 144-5, 147
  imaginal 120, 150
  see Ego, transformation of

Bicameral consciousness 80

Cathartic method 56
Childhood, imagination of 1-4, 119
Conceptualizations, psychological 135-7
Concentration technique 38
Contemplation 20

Daydream, -s, -ing 18
  deterioration of waking dreams into 110
  difference between waking dreams and 102
Depression, fear of 121-2
Descension in imaginal space 58-60
Dialogue method 55
Directed revery 56
Directing waking dream experiences 34-7, 50-1, 63
  questioning the practice of 52-72
  see Image as guides
Dreaming, disciplined 19-24
  see Vision incubation and Imagining

Dream, -s 46, 80, 88, 109, 133-4, 139-40
  difference between waking dreams and 46-7
  latent content of 82
  manifest content of 82
  objective method of analysis 129
  recurring 141
  residue 129
  subjective method of analysis 43-5, 129
  see also Jung, Images, Imagining, Waking dreams

Ego
  as an image 148
  heroic 67, 116, 120, 121, 123
  imaginal 116-20
  making into water 106-7, 124
  position in relation to other images 144-6
  relationship to the imaginal 4-13
  separation from usual activities 101
  transformation of 102-7, 124, 145-6
Ego psychology
  and the imaginal 8-11, 70-2, 118, 121-5
  see also Imaginal psychology
Emergent images 55
Existential therapy, use of imagery in 94
Experiential focusing 96
Experimental dreaming 55

Fantasy
  re-structuration of 36-7
  see also Daydreaming, Imagining, and Waking dreams
Free association 38-41

171